DISCARDED

```
KF          Computers and law / edited by Indira
242           Carr and Katherine Williams. --
.A1           Oxford, England : Intellect, 1994.
C65           252     ; 24 cm.
1994
      Includes bibliographical references and
   index.
      ISBN 1871516358



      1. Information storage and retrieval
   systems--Law. 2. Legal research--Data
   processing. I. Carr, Indira. II. Williams,
   Katherine S.


          WaOE                    wln95-110652
```

COMPUTERS AND LAW

Edited by
Indira Carr and Katherine Williams

intellect

OXFORD, ENGLAND

First Published in 1994 by
Intellect Books
Suite 2, 108/110 London Road, Oxford OX3 9AW

Copyright ©1994 Intellect Ltd.

All rights reserved. No part of this publication may be reproduced, stored in a retrieval system, or transmitted, in any form or by any means, electronic, mechanical, photocopying, recording, or otherwise, without written permission.

Consulting editor: Masoud Yazdani
Cover illustration: Stuart Mealing
Copy editors: Rebecca Norris and Martin Roe

Acknowledgements
The editors and the publisher of this book would like to acknowledge with thanks Triangle Journals and Kluwer Academic Publishers for permission to reproduce copyright material from their journals *Law, Computers and Artificial Intelligence* (Triangle) and *Artificial Intelligence Review* (Kluwer).

   The editors would also like to thank Mair Williams, Catherine Bean, Christine Davies and Anne Watkyn-Jones for their help and support in preparing the manuscript.

British Library Cataloguing in Publication Data

Carr, Indira
   Computers and the Law
   I. Title II. Williams, Katherine S.
   344.103999

ISBN 1-871516-35-8

Printed and bound in Great Britain by Cromwell Press, Wiltshire

Contents

1   BYTES INTO COMPUTER LAW   1
      Indira Mahalingam Carr and Katherine S Williams

PART I: LEGAL ASPECTS of Electronic Data Interchange

2   THREE TYPES OF EDI CONTRACTS   29
      Sergej H Katus

3   THE NEED TO STANDARDISE IN AN EDI ENVIRONMENT: BALANCING THE LEGAL CONDITIONS AND IMPLICATIONS   43
      Corien Prins

PART II: ISSUES IN COMMERCIAL LAW

4   LIABILITY FOR FRAUD AND MISTAKE IN ELECTRONIC TRANSFERS OF FUNDS   63
      Maria Chiara Malaguti

5   SHIPPING DOCUMENTS AND EDI   83
      Diana Faber

PART III: ISSUES RELATING TO INTELLECTUAL PROPERTY

6   SOFTWARE PROTECTION UNDER EUROPEAN COMMUNITY LAW   99
      Andreas Wehlau

7   PROTECTING COMPUTER DATABASES UNDER THE UNITED STATES COPYRIGHT LAWS: IMPLICATION OF THE FEIST DECISION   113
      John T Cross

8   ELECTRONIC DATA INTERCHANGE: THE PERSPECTIVES OF PRIVATE INTERNATIONAL LAW AND DATA PROTECTION   128
      Thomas Hoeren

PART IV: EVIDENTIAL MATTERS

9 A FORENSIC METHODOLOGY FOR COUNTERING COMPUTER CRIME   145
P A Collier and B J Spaul

10 COMPUTERS, HEARSAY AND THE ENGLISH LAW OF EVIDENCE   159
Michael Hirst

11 EVIDENTIAL ISSUES IN AN ELECTRONIC DATA INTERCHANGE CONTEXT ACCORDING TO NORWEGIAN LAW   175
Andreas Galtung

PART V: ARTIFICIAL INTELLIGENCE APPLICATIONS TO LAW

12 THE USE OF AN EXPERT SYSTEM SHELL TO PRESENT THE MENTAL HEALTH ACT TO SOCIAL WORKERS   197
R J Hartley, S Morris and John Williams

13 THE MAINTANANCE OF LEGAL KNOWLEDGE BASED SYSTEMS   209
Trevor Bench-Capon and Frans Coenen

14 THE PROBLEM WITH LAW IN BOOKS AND LAW IN COMPUTERS: THE ORAL NATURE OF LAW   225
Philip Leith

15 COMPETENCE AND LEGAL LIABILITY IN THE DEVELOPMENT OF SOFTWARE FOR SAFETY RELATED APPLICATIONS   237
Diane Rowland and Jem J Rowland

INDEX   251

1

Indira Mahalingam Carr and
Katherine S Williams

Bytes into Computer Law

1. Introduction

In the course of this book many significant legal questions are raised. These include such problems as the relationship between electronic data interchange and the law of banking, the law of intellectual property rights, and program protection. However, this introduction will be used, not for a comprehensive survey of all the contents, but to offer a more extended commentary on just a few of the areas which are raised by the collected papers. The object is to indicate some of the practical and conceptual problems which have to be confronted by legislation directed at protecting the use and controlling the misuse of the new methods of conducting private and public business which the introduction of computers has engendered. Three broad areas have been selected for critical examination: (1) electronic data interchange and data protection, (2) electronic data interchange and computer crime, and (3) the implications of applying artificial intelligence aimed at improving and facilitating legal processes.

2. Electronic Data Interchange (EDI) and Data Protection

The general assumption in relation to EDI is that it will largely be used in the commercial sector for transferring information such as product specifications and prices at a national and international level. However, EDI is also expected to play a central role in the insurance and banking sectors[1] as well as in public administration areas such as health services, social security, customs, immigration, and the police. This means that besides information relating to commercial products and services, details about individuals and government bodies will also be transferred through the electronic network. As can be expected, some of the information transmitted in all these spheres may be of a highly confidential nature. This raises a number of interesting questions some of

---

[1] See Chapter Four (*infra*) on the liability issues in electronic banking.

which are listed below; the answers to these however are largely dependent on the principles underlying the right to privacy.[2]

(1) Should collation of information on individuals, private organisations and government bodies for non-private use be allowed without any system of control?

(2) Even if collation of information is allowed for non-private use in principle, should there be control on the contents collated?

(3) Should certain sectors of society be given special protection? For instance, should information about individuals be treated specially? Should sensitive data on individuals, like race, religion, political affiliation, be subject to special protection provisions?

(4) Should collated data be circulated nationally and internationally, without any system of control? For instance, should State A ensure that the level of data protection in State B is adequate before allowing data export even though by so doing State A stands to lose economically due to the legal controls?

In order to establish perspective, it is necessary to preface discussion of these questions with an acknowledgement of some of the advantages of EDI for data transference in all contexts. There are strong reasons for believing that, in general, the use of EDI will enhance the quality of life all round and is therefore worth promoting. To illustrate, in the commercial arena it will speed transactions thereby contributing to economic growth; and in the area of public administration it will facilitate quick decisions and actions by public bodies such as customs and police thereby improving the general security and well-being of the populace at large.[3] Both these observations are pertinent and exude good sense. The advantages are even more striking when seen in the context of the EC whose aim is to establish economic unity among the member states with the general welfare of its citizens in mind. Persuasive though these may be, one should not lose sight of the imbalance that would be caused by the promotion of

---

[2] The word 'privacy' seems to be variously interpreted in different countries. For instance, ID cards, carried by individuals in countries like Malaysia and France would be regarded as an invasion of privacy in England. In Canada, the concept is interpreted widely to encompass freedom of information, i.e. the freedom of access to information held by the government and government bodies.

[3] According to an item in the business news section of *The Independent on Sunday*, 30 May 1993, BUPA has introduced EDI for its billing service which reduces claims processing time from more than a week to two days. The information is transmitted from the hospitals in the UK to the clearing house in the US where it is formatted and subsequently deposited in the hospital's mailbox. This system is said to have a number of advantages: reduced administration cost, improved data quality and accuracy, faster payment claims and reduced bad debt.

only the economic and commercial benefits of this technology without taking due account of other factors such as the right to privacy.[4] Of course, the weighting that is to be given to each of these values will largely depend on the objectives that a given society has.

The right to privacy as a concept has been acknowledged by some states, through legislation which provides specific protection for such data, especially when held on computer, by restricting its use both within that state and its transfer to third countries. However, there is no common ideological thread connecting the actions of various nations. As a result there are disparate legislations on the kinds and the nature of information that are protected and the means through which any protection is to be achieved. This is the case even among member states of the EC despite their stated desire for harmonisation.[5] For instance, some of the EC states with data protection legislation are limited to covering personal details held on computers about living humans; others extend the protection to other legal entities such as companies and trade unions;[6] whilst still others cover manual records as well as computerised data.[7] Beyond the confines of the EC the diversity is even more bewildering. In some states data protection is limited to public sector processing of data[8] whilst a number of Third World countries, especially in Latin America and Africa, have proposed that information affecting national sovereignty, economic well-being and socio-cultural interests should also be protected.[9] Presumably, the reason for proposing protection of these types of information is a perceived need to promote political stability which in turn would enhance the economic welfare of the country.

The disparate views in relation to the kinds of information that qualify for protection and the ways these controls should be exercised mean that states may view cross border flow of information through electronic means with some suspicion. States may regulate the transborder flow of data by requiring that the recipient state offers the level of protection that is available in the originating

---

[4] See Parent, W A (1983), 'Recent Works on the Concept of Privacy' *American Philosophical Review* p,343; Rubenfeld, J (1988), 'The Rights of Privacy' *Harvard Law Journal* 102:737; *Report of the Committee on Privacy* Cmnd. 5012, 1972: HMSO; *Report of the Committee on Data Protection* Cmnd. 7341, 1978:HMSO

[5] Belgium, Greece, Italy and Spain do not have any data protection regulations. It is particularly interesting to note the lack of any protection in Spain as it was one of the first states to ratify the Council of Europe Convention which was passed in 1981 and came into force in 1985.

[6] Denmark and Austria

[7] France, Germany and the Netherlands

[8] United States and New Zealand

[9] For further details see *Intergovernmental Bureau for Informatics*, TDF 270 at p,55.

state. This, in real terms, would pose difficulties for those wishing to carry out business through EDI either at the international level or EC level. And it would not be an exaggeration to suggest that the disparities might threaten the successful implementation of the single market in the EC and the increase of trade at the international level which GATT is promoting as a tonic for global economic recovery.

Thomas Hoeren's paper[10] pin-points the disparities in legislation between Britain and Germany and arrives at the conclusion that since British law offers less protection it is less useful than German law. However, it needs to be noted that there are serious obstacles facing any judgements on the relative effectiveness of different national systems: a particular difficulty is that the methods of control adopted by the two states are different. In Britain, data protection is controlled by means of a register controlled by the Registrar. Users are simply registered and not licensed. This approach is not an uncommon one; most European systems of data protection except the one existing in Germany involve some form of registration of users. Registration is meant to identify systems and to promote compliance with standards, and the British system is wholly based on this idea. The registration is automatic on the provision of the required information to the Registrar and does not involve, as a licensing system would, the inspection of users before registration. The only control exercised on the data user is the threat of de-registration if one of the eight data protection principles is breached. This assumes that there is some form of regular inspection procedure in place. In reality, however, since the Registrar is so under-staffed it is unlikely that any such breach will be discovered unless a data subject makes a specific complaint. The control is therefore obviously minimal.

Despite these practical qualifications to the efficiency of the British registration system, it has some obvious advantages over the German approach which has rejected the establishment of a register of any sort. In the absence of such registration it is difficult for individuals to establish whether a personal file exists on them since they are unable to discover the types of files which any company holds and the uses to which such information is put. Such considerations may ban or impede the transference of information from Britain to Germany, despite the fact that the level of German protection is generally formally higher than that which exists in Britain.

As already indicated, the current British registration system is not without its shortcomings. The main issues arise in the context of human rights since the registration of data users merely records the range of records they hold. There is no system for informing a data subject when a file has been created which has information concerning that person. For example, debt agencies only have to

---

[10] See Chapter Eight *infra*.

inform the Registrar of the sort of files they keep and the uses to which they put such files. Individuals may be aware of the existence of such files but may be unaware of the existence of such files in relation to themselves. If they had such knowledge, individuals would have a real and early opportunity to examine the files and rectify information as required. The most direct way of ensuring that data subjects are aware of their inclusion on files would be to require the user to inform each individual when a file is created, but this may prove too cumbersome an administrative task. Although there is a stronger argument in terms of objectivity for saying that the Registrar as the uninterested party and the archive holder is better equipped to communicate the existence of such files to the person concerned, administrative problems would still remain.

It also seems that the present British system is unable to cope with the difficulties that may be hidden in the mass of registered information in that there is no systematised control on the users of sensitive data. The Data Protection Registrar is aware of this and two suggestions have been put forward as possible solutions[11]:

- removing small, non-sensitive users from the register to free resources for investigation of individual cases of processing of sensitive data;
- a universal registration system requiring very little information unless the user wishes to hold sensitive data.

Undoubtedly, either of these moves might increase the effectiveness of the system, but such solutions would be attractive (whatever the concept of sensitive may mean) only where the following fundamental philosophical tenets in relation to data are recognised:

- data may be sensitive because of its content;
- data may acquire sensitivity because of the use to which it is put.[12]

To illustrate, credit card companies carry information about transactions carried out by their customers. No single transaction may be considered sensitive but they may be used to indicate the spending trends of particular customers. The aggregated result may be very sensitive and could also have a high commercial

---

[11] *What are your Views? Monitoring and Assessment of the Data Protection Act 1984 - A Consultation Document from the Data Protection Registrar*, May 1988

[12] The recent news item in *The Times* of 20August 1993 reports that at least two British clearing banks have computerised information about their customers' politics and religion. This raises some very important human rights issues. It is possible that the banks might use this information to discriminate against some customers or may pass this information to others who might. The editorial suggests that the embarrassment of having to inform individuals, on request, of the contents of the information relating to them, and the likely consequence of losing custom might force the institutions to respect privacy. The economic forces argument however is not a long term solution.

utility. Such use of personal data, often referred to as 'electronic tracing' suggests that neither of the Registrar's proposals would offer sufficient protection. Both these suggestions would, in any event, probably go hand in hand with some form of self regulation for the users of less sensitive data, leaving them to be controlled only by civil action in the event of abuse. This is a trend which can be seen in Ireland and the Netherlands and is a response to the wider use of computerised systems.

The consequences that the disparities in legislation would have for businesses engaged in cross border data flow could be countered by entering into contractual agreements which guarantee the protection of personal data. The Council of Europe has recommended six clauses for inclusion in any contract to ensure equivalent protection in the context of transborder data flow.[13] Another way of ensuring protection would be to incorporate a choice of law clause in the contract. So, one could incorporate the national laws of the country from which the information is exported. The problem with contractual incorporation of suitable terms for protecting data is that the parties entering into the contractual obligations may not suffer financially for breaches thereby reducing the incentive to obey the clauses. Also, in most legal regimes the data subject (the third party) would not be able to invoke the clauses in a contract between two parties due to lack of privity. It may however be politically beneficial for the companies to ensure that the contractual obligations are followed since otherwise they would risk the introduction of more wide-ranging protective legislation.

A way out of this conundrum would be to harmonise the laws in relation to privacy and data protection.[14] The European Community has moved in this direction, and in 1990 put forward a draft directive which was subsequently amended by the European Parliament. The Council has now put forward a revised proposal that takes into account Parliament's opinion.[15]

The revised draft directive, if accepted, will mean that the Data Protection Act 1984 will have to be amended substantially to take account of the changes, some of which are discussed below. On the whole, it will have the result of placing extra burdens on businesses which process personal data, something which the 1984 Act tried to keep to a minimum. One of the motivating features behind the directive was to prevent 'data havens' being exploited by companies

---

[13] Council of Europe, *Revised Version of Proposed Clauses for Inclusion in a Model Contract Designed to Ensure Equivalent Data Protection in the Context of Transborder Data Flows,* T-PD (91)8.

[14] This is easier said than done. It took the EC over fifteen years of discussion to put forward a draft directive which was published in 1990. See *Official Journal (OJ)* No C.100 3 May 1976; No C 140 5 June 1979; No L 246 29 August 1979; No C 87 5 April 1982.

[15] *OJ* No L 123, 8 May 1992

that wanted to avoid the processing restrictions and protection which exist in certain member states. The draft directive is drawn widely to cover both manual and computerised personal data files,[16] and public and private sectors,[17] but does not extend to include legal persons.[18]

A major change introduced by the draft directive is that it lists the situations in which the processing of personal data will be lawful. These are where:
- the data subject has consented (Article 7(a));
- processing is necessary for the performance of a contract with the data subject, or in order to take steps at the request of the data subject preliminary to entering into a contract (Article 7(b));
- processing is necessary in order to comply with an obligation imposed by national law or Community law (article 7(c));
- processing is necessary to protect the vital interests of the data subject (Article 7(d));

---

[16] Under Article 2(b) 'processing of personal data' means any operations or set of operations which is performed upon personal data, whether or not by automatic means, such as collection, recording, organisation storage, adaptation or alteration, retrieval, consultation, use, disclosure by transmission, dissemination or otherwise making available, alignment or combination, blocking, erasure or destruction.

[17] The revised draft directive has dropped the distinction between the private sector and the public sector. An interesting feature of the original draft directive was the extreme tolerance with which it treated public sectors collecting information. Under Article 5 the creation of a file and any other processing of personal data would be lawful insofar as they were necessary for the performance of the tasks of the public authority in control of the file. Article 6 allowed for transfer between public sector bodies as long as they were necessary for the performance of the tasks. The data subject's consent was not required. As to what exactly 'necessary for the performance of the tasks' encapsulated was unclear. It was felt that public bodies like the police, and immigration authorities construe this phrase very widely. The individual was given the right to consult the register kept by a supervisory authority of public sector files with personal data that might be communicated under Article 7(1); however Article 7(3) in conjunction with Article 15(1) provided that consultation would be restricted for reasons of national security, defence, criminal proceedings, public safety monitoring and inspection purposes of public authorities. It was felt that these provisions were wide ranging and had a great potential for misuse. The European Parliament deleted the whole of Chapter Two on special provisions relating to the public sector.

[18] Since legal persons, like companies, are excluded from the requirements of data protection, Denmark and Austria might consider protection offered as falling below the standards required by their national laws and might restrict the flow of information to states with lower levels of protection.

- processing is necessary for the performance of a task in the public interest or carried in the exercise of public authority vested in the controller or in a third party to whom the data are disclosed (Article 7(e)); or
- processing is necessary in pursuit of the general interest or of the legitimate interests of the controller of a third party to whom the data are disclosed, except where such interests are overridden by the interests of the data subject (Article 7(f)).

Data subjects will be regarded as having consented where express indication of their wishes signifying their agreement to personal data relating to themselves being processed is present and this is freely given and specific. The following information however must be available to them:
- the purposes of the processing;
- the recipient of the personal data; and
- the name and address of the controller and of his or her representative, if any (Article 2(g)).

Article 11 further sets out minimum lists of information that must be provided to the data subject. These are:
- the purposes of the processing for which the data are intended;
- the obligatory or voluntary nature of any reply to the questions to which answers are sought;
- the consequences of any failure to reply;
- the recipients or categories of recipients of the data;
- the existence of a right of access to and rectification of relevant; and
- the name and address of the controller and of his or her representative, if any.

Where data is transferred to a third party in cases referred to in Article 7(b), (e) and (f) the data subject must be informed of this by the controller at the appropriate time, which should be not later than the time of first disclosure to the third party (Article 12).

Article 2(g) states that consent must be expressly indicated; obviously a written expression or a verbal expression will be sufficient to fulfil this. Problems can arise however in the following situations:

(1) Business forms may require the data subject to place an 'X' indicating lack of consent. If the data subject fails to place the 'X' in the required box would this be deemed as an express indication of consent?

(2) During the course of negotiations the data subject may be asked to consent to the processing of information. Would silence or a nod of assent from the data subject be sufficient to fulfil the requirement for an express indication of consent? In other words, is express indication limited to linguistic expressions or could it include non-verbal behaviour?

Under Article 2(g) the data subject is given the right to revoke consent at any time without it having any retrospective effect. But the form this revocation should take remains unstated. Could the revocation be implied or must it be express? For instance, could an individual's expression of doubts/unhappiness about the processing constitute an implied revocation? Furthermore, it is not clear whether the form of revocation should match the form of consent? That is, could an oral revocation be effective to cancel a written expression of consent?

Article 7(e) is another provision for potential concern. It appears to give free rein to public authorities like the police and customs to collect and exchange information with third parties on the basis that it is necessary for the performance of their task in the public interest. It is unclear what 'necessary for the performance of a task in the public interest' is envisaged to cover. Presumably, it will depend on the nature of the perception of the relevant public authorities. However, because of the open ended nature of the phrase there is ample scope for misuse. Likewise, Article 7(f) allows processing for the purposes of pursuing the general interest or legitimate interests of the controller and third party unless such interests are overridden by the interests of the data subject. What exactly does general interest cover? Does it mean public interest used in Article 7(e)? If so, it is indeed very difficult to think of situations where the individual's rights can be said to override the general interests, given the utilitarian thrust behind this provision.

The directive makes the welcome move of making specific reference to sensitive data.[19] Article 8(1) prohibits the processing of data revealing racial or ethnic origins, political opinions, religious beliefs, philosophical or ethical persuasion and membership of trade union and of data referring to the health or sexual orientation of the subject. This general prohibition is subject to a number of exceptions:

- where the data subject has given written consent to the processing provided the law of the Member State does not prohibit by law such a waiver by the data subject (Article 8(2)(a));
- where the processing is carried out by a foundation or non-profit making association of a political, philosophical, religious or trade union character in the course of the legitimate activities, provided that the processing

---

[19] s.2(3) of the Data Protection Act 1984 states that the Secretary of State may by order modify or supplement the seven principles for the purposes of providing additional safeguards in relation to personal data consisting of information as to the racial origin of the data subject, his political opinions or religious or other beliefs, his physical or mental health or his sexual life or his criminal convictions. This power however has not been exercised to date. The reason for this could be due to the fact that 'sensitive data' is a fuzzy concept and seems to depend very much on the circumstances to acquire its content.

relates solely to its members or persons who have regular contact with it in relation to its purposes and that the data are not disclosed to third parties without the data subject's consent (Article 8(2)(b));
- where the processing is performed in circumstances where there is manifestly no infringement of privacy or fundamental freedoms (Article 8(2)(c)); and
- where there are important grounds of public interest as laid down by the law (Article 8(3)).[20]

As far as criminal convictions are concerned data concerning these can be held only by judicial and law enforcement authorities, and by the persons directly concerned with these convictions, or by their representatives under Article 8(4).

Article 8(1), since it is widely cast, could be a source of potential problems. For instance, a person's name could reveal a lot about the person's ethnic origins and religious beliefs. In these circumstances, does Article 8(1) envisage that written consent is needed from the data subject whenever the data subject's name needs to be entered for ordinary commercial transactions such as requests for hotel and flight bookings? To illustrate, the name Inderjit Singh connotes that the individual is of Indian origin and perhaps a follower of Sikhism. So will the travel agent require a written consent from Mr Singh before he enters his name on the form? If this is the intention behind this provision then it will jeopardise business efficiency since customer service oriented acts offered by businesses like telephone bookings will no longer be feasible. Of course, it is possible to argue that the enigmatic Article 8(2)(c) exception could be used to cover such situations, since there is 'manifestly no infringement of privacy or fundamental freedoms'. However, it is not clear from Article 8 or the explanatory memorandum whether these are the kinds of situations that Article 8(2)(c) is meant to cover; some guidance on this provision could help avoid legal uncertainties.

In relation to criminal convictions there is a strong argument for saying that such data should be allowed to be at the very least accessed, if not held, by employers and service sectors like insurers and bankers since they would find such information necessary in their decision making process. For instance, a bank may seriously consider its offer of employment to a person previously convicted for fraud. Under Article 8(4) member states can lay down exemptions through legislation specifying suitable safeguards (Article 8(4)). It is highly

---

[20] Sensitive data in the 1990 draft directive was dealt with under s.17 and made specific reference to automatic processing of data which referred to racial or ethnic origins, political, religious or philosophical beliefs and membership of trade union and of data referring to the health and sexual orientation of the subject. Under Article 17 manual records of such information could be stored and freely circulated which was perceived as a wild move in an otherwise privacy driven legislation.

likely that most states will have exemptions to Article 8(4) to suit the needs of their industries, which means that there is the possibility of disparate legislations emerging from Article 8(4). In these circumstances, it would perhaps be wiser for the directive to address this issue and list the exemptions to Article 8(4).

As far as export of data to non-EC countries is concerned Article 26 generally prohibits such transfer, with some exceptions,[21] unless the receiving country provides an adequate level of protection thereby ring-fencing the EC. The reason for this rule is understandable since allowing free flow of information to non-EC countries could result in circumventing the EC Rules that aim to ensure free flow of information without unduly affecting the individual's right to privacy.

The adequacy of the level of protection afforded by the third country is to be assessed by taking into account all the circumstances surrounding the data transfer. Particular account is to be taken of the following:
- the nature of the data;
- the purpose/s and duration of the proposed processing operation;
- the legislative provisions, general and sectoral, in force in the third country; and
- the professional rules complied with in the third country. (Article 26(2)).

It is not clear whether, in taking into account the legislative provisions and professional rules, due regard will be paid to the philosophical tenets on which the third country's legislation and other rules are based.

Where the third country does not offer an adequate level of protection which is likely to harm the interests of the EC or its member state, Article 26(4) empowers the Commission to enter into negotiations with that country to remedy the situation.[22] Of course there would be no obligation on the part of the third country to comply with the Commission's requests except in the interests of international comity and economic growth.

---

[21] The exceptions allowed under Article 26 are:
- subject, where appropriate, to Article 8(2)(a) the data subject has consented to the proposed transfer in order to take steps preliminary to entering into a contract;
- where the transfer is necessary for the performance of a contract between the data subject and the controller and the data subject has been informed of the fact that it is or might be proposed to transfer the data to a third country which does not ensure an adequate level of protection;
- the transfer is necessary on important public interest grounds; or
- the transfer is necessary in order to protect the vital interests of the data subject.

[22] See Chapter nine for Thomas Hoeren's comments on Articles 24 and 25 on data transfer to third countries as set out in the original draft directive.

The best way forward in these situations would be for the EC exporting party and non-EC importing party to enter into specific contractual provisions ensuring adequate protection of the data to EC standards in the importing country. The privity problem can also be circumvented if the data exporter stipulates that the contract is entered into on behalf of the data subject also.[23] Indeed Article 27 allows authorisation to be given by a member state for transfer, or categories of transfers, of personal data to a third country which does not ensure an adequate level of protection where the controller adduces sufficient justification. This justification could, in particular, be in the form of appropriate contractual provisions guaranteeing especially the effective exercise of the data subjects' rights.

The problem with allowing member states to determine the adequacy of the level of protection offered by a third country (Article 26(2)), or allowing the controller to adduce sufficient justification in contractual provisions guaranteeing the data subject's rights for transfer of information to take place to countries lacking adequate levels of protection means that there will be a lack of uniformity in approach amongst the member states. A way round this would be to provide extensive guidelines.

The revised draft directive goes a long way in harmonising the disparate laws of its member states and promotes the free flow of information, fully taking into account the right to privacy of the individual. However, what yet remains to be assessed is the cost to industry, especially small and medium sized organisations, and to the people, especially taxpayers and consumers, for introducing this piece of legislation. It may be premature to agree with the Commission that the directive will promote economic growth and create jobs in the private and public sectors.

3. Electronic Data Interchange (EDI) and Computer Crime

The term 'computer crime' is used to cover a multitude of sins. In most instances, it simply refers to the fact that a computer has been used in the committal of an offence which could have been carried out equally through other means. Just as murder can be committed by using a gun or a knife, so too fraud can be committed using a computer or paper. In such instances, the existing criminal laws are adequate for dealing with computer commissioned crimes.

---

[23] Such a clause, if suitably worded, may be effective in common law countries. See *New Zealand Shipping* v *Satherthwaite* [1975] *AC* 154 where the stevedore was allowed to take advantage of the exceptions and immunities in the contract of carriage to which he was not a party on the basis that the carriers had contracted on behalf of the stevedores. See Lord Wilberforce's judgment which stresses the need for taking a pragmatic approach to commercial transactions and not be constrained by legal technicalities.

However, there is a species of computer centred activity that has the potential of causing a great deal of harm, mostly economic, to the legitimate user but does not fall within the sphere of criminal law unless the meaning of existing criminal offences are strained to the fullest extent. Even where this is done it may prove inadequate.[24] It is this type of computer crime that poses a real threat to businesses, whether they are small scale or multi-national, since they are increasingly relying on EDI rather than on paper for carrying on their commercial activities. In this type of crime, the most frightening prospect is that some individual will interfere with the information, either to their benefit (be it economic or psychological) or to the financial detriment of the legitimate user. As many of those in charge of businesses do not operate computers, nor understand their operation, there is a certain amount of myth and hysteria about the likelihood of falling victim to such activities. The fear was certainly far less when paper was used since its weaknesses were clearly understood and accepted as unavoidable.

The further factor that increases the need for some kind of control is that computer crime does not obey national boundaries. An individual sitting at a computer terminal in State A may access and use a computer system located in State B, with the capacity to alter or obtain copies of data held in the accessed computer.[25] This ease of transborder computer activity has led international organisations to consider the problems related to computers and crime.

The level of the problem is difficult to ascertain since most reports tend to be sensationalised and lack the information which is necessary for a clear legal

---

[24] See *R v Gold and Schifreen* [1988] *AC* 1063 where through using a password issued to engineers the hackers obtained entry into the Prestel system - a data base service of British Telecom. They were charged under s.1 of the 'Forgery and Counterfeiting Act 1981' which states:
> A person is guilty of forgery if he makes a false instrument, with the intention that he or another shall use it to induce somebody to accept it as genuine, and by reason of so accepting it to do or not to do some act to his own or any other person's prejudice.

'Instrument' under s.8(1) of the Act includes any disc, tape, soundtrack other device on or in which information is recorded or stored by mechanical, electronic or other means.

The Court, however, came to the conclusion that the words 'recorded or stored' implied a degree of continuance and the password did not carry that degree of permanence since it was expunged once the computer had executed the checking task.

[25] See the business news section of *The Independent on Sunday* 6 June 1993. Citibank and a firm of private detectives are being prosecuted for allegedly hacking into the computers of Barclays and National Westminster to obtain details about a customer's wealth before his company was placed in receivership. The prosecution is reported as being brought by Mr Raymond Hill, a property developer.

discussion.[26] Where there are official statistics, as with all other criminal activity, they are not representative of the full problem. In the area of computer crime the problem is compounded because much of computer related crime is not separately recorded. This however may prove to be a blessing. Overprovision in this area is perhaps best avoided since it would discourage the use of traditional criminal laws wherever these are adequate to deal with the activity. Otherwise, the criminal law may become overspecialised and become less able to deal with more general problems.

In Britain, as in many other countries, traditional criminal laws seem unable to cope with certain kinds of computer related crime. This is a consequence of the intangible nature of information held on a computer. Much of criminal law protects tangible property and either cannot be used to cover computer crimes,[27] or their use strains the natural meaning of criminal law to its limits and extends the laws in unacceptable ways which might affect use in non-computer related offences.[28] Particular problems are encountered in respect of taking information. For example, if a disc containing information is stolen a prosecution for theft can lie and it may be legitimate to assess the worth of that item taking account of the information contained on it, but if the thing taken is only the information on the disc, then nothing has been stolen and the charge of theft will be unsuccessful.[29]

As far back as 1987, the Scottish Law Commission in its report recommended that one offence needed to be added to the criminal laws, namely,

---

[26] See Wasik, Martin (1991), *Crime and the Computer* Oxford: Clarendon Press, for an account of the scale of the problem.

[27] See *R* v *Gold and Schifreen (supra)* in which legislation passed partially with modern technology in mind, failed to cover the mischief committed.

[28] See *Her Majesty's Advocate v Wilson* [1984] *SLT* 116 where the crime of malicious mischief, normally attached to physical damage to actual property, was extended to cover interference with productive operation of machinery to make a profit. Also *Cox v Riley* (1986) *Cr App R* 54 in which the Criminal Damage Act 1971, used to protect property of a tangible nature (s. 10), was extended to cover interference with a computer program by saying that the owner was required to expend time and money in restoring it to its original condition. See also *R* v *Whiteley* (1991) 93 *Cr App R* 25

[29] See *Oxford* v *Moss* (1978) *68 Cr App R* 183 where a university student obtained the original of an examination paper which he returned after copying. The Court held that taking of confidential information was not theft. Of course, if he had kept the paper on which the examination questions were printed the course of events would have been different.

obtaining unauthorised access to a program or data stored in a computer where this is done in order to:

> *'inspect or otherwise acquire knowledge of the program or the data or to add to, erase or otherwise alter the program or the data with the intention:*
> *(a) of procuring an advantage for himself or another person; or*
> *(b) of damaging another person's interests.'* [30]

In 1989 the Law Commission for England and Wales report[31] recommended that unauthorised access should be an offence whether performed for its own sake or with another motive in mind thereby making hacking *per se* unlawful even if only done in order to experiment with the user's computer skills in overcoming any security devices. The Government did not initially act on the report but subsequently used a private member's bill as the basis of the Computer Misuse Act 1990.[32] The Act creates three offences:

- obtaining unauthorised access to a program or data held on a computer (s.1);
- doing the above with the intention to facilitate the commission of a further offence (s.2); and
- unauthorised modification of the contents of any computer (s.3).

Under s.17(2) a person secures access to any program or data held in a computer if by causing a computer to perform any function the person:

- alters or erases the program or data;
- copies or moves it to any storage medium other than that in which it is held or to a different location in the storage medium in which it is held;
- uses it; or
- has it output from the computer in which it is held (whether by having it displayed or in any other manner).

Use is interpreted under s.17(3) as anything which:

- causes the program to be executed; or
- is itself a function of the program.

From the above it is clear that minimal access will be enough to commit a s.1 offence provided the other elements are also present. So, simply turning the machine on would suffice since the program will be activated. Also the hacker need not succeed in gaining access; an offence will be committed merely be

---

[30] Scottish Law Commission No 106 *Report on Computer Crime* Cmnd. 174, 1987, London: HMSO, Part IV.

[31] Law Commission Report No 186, *Computer Misuse*, Cmnd. 818, 1989, London: HMSO

[32] This Act came into force on 1 August 1990.

accessing a security device on the machine. The other elements that need to be established for a s.1 offence are:
- the access must be unauthorised (s.1(1)(b));
- the user must know at the time of causing the computer to perform the function that the access is unauthorised (s.1(1)(c)).

The requirement of knowledge of unauthorised access on the part of the user would be easy to discharge where the user has to enter a password, or there is some other device indicating that the access is available only to authorised personnel. Unauthorised access will also arise in situations where access is permitted for certain purposes but not for others. It is not necessary to prove intent to access any particular program or data (s.2) so that the s.1 offence covers those who gain access purely for the intellectual exercise with no idea of what they might find there.

This section clearly covers the general hacker but as the section protects access to the program or to the data it may also criminalise the loading and use of an unauthorised copy of a computer program. Although this is not the intended target of the Act it may prove useful for software protection.

One of the problems with s.1 is that many items of every day use like compact disc players, cars, and telephones have small computers as part of their operation. S.1 would make an unauthorised use of these machines an offence. The actions which will fall under this section would, if carried out without a computer, be classed as theft or some other offence or may amount to civil wrongs such as trespass. It seems particularly unfortunate that the net has been cast so wide when other areas of the law would have proved adequate. This problem could be dealt with by giving definitions of key terms such as 'computer', 'program' and 'data'. But, understandably, the Act has left these terms undefined to permit sufficient flexibility to accommodate the rapid development of technology. However, it results in the peculiar situation where the unauthorised use of a compact disc player may be classified as a s.1 offence because it contains a microchip..

Another problem with s.1 is that it is so widely cast that it also covers the hacker who accesses files solely for the psychological thrill and neither intends nor causes any damage.[33] The reason for the width of the offence seems to be that the person or institution whose records have been violated may fear damage, and expend large sums of money in checking all the records or perform some other time consuming and costly procedure. But, would it not have been better to leave these problems to be dealt with by insurance thereby increasing the

---

[33] The *Fifth Report of the Data Protection Registrar* warned of this outcome saying that it would criminalise juveniles whose hobby was to access without causing harm, at pp 30-31.

pressure on the companies to install good security devices?[34] This provision unwittingly may encourage businesses to rely solely on the Act to serve as a deterrent and disregard sophisticated security devices for financial reasons. Of course, if s.1 offences can be monitored successfully it will manage to clog up the already over-burdened criminal justice system.

The above problems in relation to s.1 would not have arisen if the Scottish Law Commission's recommendation 'to make unauthorised access with intent to cause harm to the computer owner' had been accepted.

S.2 creates an ulterior intent offence, and occurs where the individual who gains unauthorised access to a computer intends to commit or facilitate a further criminal offence for which the sentence is fixed by law or where a first offender aged over 21 would be sentenced to a five year term of imprisonment. For the purposes of this section it is irrelevant whether it would be impossible to commit the further offence.

S.3 offence covers unauthorised modification of computer material, and would cover those who introduce a virus in another computer as well as anyone who alters or deletes information. It is the computer equivalent of criminal damage.[35]

The Computer Misuse Act recognises that computer crime transgresses international borders by allowing British courts jurisdiction where a 'significant link' with Britain can be established. A significant link is established for s.1 and s.3 offences where the user or targeted computer is located in Britain. Where the offence is a s.2 offence jurisdiction is permitted if it is established that the further acts intended are an offence in the country in which they were intended to take place.

At the international level the Council of Europe[36] has suggested that eight types of computer related activity comprising the minimum list should be incorporated in the criminal laws of Member States. These are:

    (1) computer related fraud;
    (2) computer forgery;
    (3) damage to computer data or programs;
    (4) computer sabotage;

---

[34] The Data Protection Act 1984 certainly seems to have cast the onus on the user to ensure adequate security measures are taken. The Eighth Principle requires that appropriate security measures are taken against unauthorised access to, or alteration, disclosure or destruction of, personal data and against accidental loss or destruction of personal data.

[35] So situations like those of *Cox v Riley (supra)* and *R v Gold & Schifreen (supra)* would be covered by s.3 now.

[36] The other international organisation that has done a lot of work in this area is the Organisation for Economic Co-operation and Development.

(5) unauthorised access;

(6) unauthorised interception of data transmission;

(7) unauthorised reproduction of a protected computer program; and

(8) unauthorised reproduction of a topography.

The Council also suggested that four other activities, comprising the optional list, should also be discouraged. They recommended that it might be advisable to criminalise these but left the method and extent of control up to individual states. These are:

(9) alteration of computer data or programs;

(10) computer espionage;

(11) unauthorised use of a computer;

(12) unauthorised use of a protected computer program.[37]

Some of these suggestions have already been incorporated in the British Computer Misuse Act 1990. In fact their fifth suggestion is narrower than s.1 of the Computer Misuse Act as it requires security measures to be infringed before the offence can be committed. This narrower protection was recommended by the Council in order to discourage managerial negligence in setting up suitable protection systems. As suggested earlier, this would appear to be an acceptable limit. As far as the other proposals are concerned British law leaves those to be dealt with through general criminal laws. Thus there is no new offence of computer forgery (although where the forgery is unsuccessful s. 2 provides a remedy).

Of particular interest is computer espionage in the optional list. Computer espionage would certainly cover eavesdropping, an activity where the electromagnetic signals around the visual display unit of a computer are picked up from outside the building using a video recorder and television set. The eavesdropper has no control on the kind of information which will be picked up and the activity therefore is passive. During the debate leading up to the Computer Misuse Act the question of making computer eavesdropping a criminal offence was considered but it was felt that it did not pose a serious threat. However one must agree with the conclusions reached by the Council of Europe that eavesdropping could become a real threat since much commercial and governmental communication is now carried out electronically and it is inevitable that the patient eavesdropper will come across sensitive material. It is time for the threat of computer eavesdropping to be given more serious consideration.

There is one crucial area which was not covered in either the discussion leading to the 1990 legislation or by the 1990 legislation itself, or by the Council of Europe. The omission relates to enforcement, probably the most important of

---

[37] Recommendation No R 89(9) *Computer Related Crime*

the aspects of computer crime to have been ignored. It is highly desirable to have these crimes on the statute book but if the means are not available to detect the offences the criminal law remains unenforced and becomes almost worthless. There was a little debate concerning detection in the parliamentary stages of the 1990 Act. The Act imparts powers of searching premises and seizure to the police under s.14, provided the circuit judge is satisfied by information on oath given by a constable that there are reasonable grounds for believing that a s.1offence has been committed or is about to be committed and that there is relevant evidence in the premises. Most unauthorised access, however, occurs by means of a telephone line and there are no provisions in the Act to allow the police to obtain details concerning telephone lines. Monitoring of telephone lines is routinely carried out by telephone companies and the police may request such information; it is up to the company to decide whether to provide the material or not. Without the power to make such searches of telephone data held by telephone companies it will almost be impossible to establish the 'reasonable grounds' necessary to obtain the warrant under s.14. However providing special powers to include automatic searches of telephone data by the police raises the question of whether there would be a serious breach of individual rights to privacy guaranteed under Article 8 of the European Convention on Human Rights. Certainly such important invasions of privacy should not be permitted simply on the perceptions of the phone company. On the other hand, to pass legislation of this sort without giving any means of detection to the police may give companies and individuals a false sense of security. Without powers of detection the Computer Misuse Act is likely to be a relatively useless piece of legislation largely relying upon chance rather than careful investigation for discovery. To offer true protection will necessarily involve intrusive detection methods which requires a serious consideration of the virtues of protecting the collective good as against the sanctity of the individual's right to privacy. Either one or the other has to be abandoned, or some compromise has to be reached.

4. Artificial Intelligence Applications in Law

Various researchers[38] have suggested that computers have the capacity for performing complex tasks in the legal sphere. Currently, at the simplest level computers are used for storing legal information, such as legislations and decisions, which can be accessed for reference purposes. A familiar example for most lawyers would be database systems such as LEXIS, JURIS where the user gains access to legal materials in a particular area through the use of subject specific search words. At this level, it must be admitted that the computer performs a highly desirable function for the legal researcher.

---

[38] See Susskind, Richard (1987), *Expert Systems in Law,* Oxford: Clarendon Press

However, as is well known computers are not purely storage facilities with the capacity to retrieve information through pattern matching. They can successfully perform 'intelligent' tasks like aircraft control, determining medical conditions and recommending drug dosages. This has led to the view that computers have the capacity[39] to perform significantly in a number of complex legal tasks. For instance:

(1) they could be used for legal diagnostic purposes whereby the system provides answers to legal problems in specific areas to either professionals or lay people;[40]

(2) they could be used to pass judgements thereby functioning in a judicial capacity;[41]

(3) they could be used to guide the decision maker in a court of law by providing information on the legal issue under consideration.[42]

At first sight these uses may be attractive to both litigants and practitioners. From the litigants' point of view such uses may prove to be financially beneficial. The practitioner might regard the speed of the legal process and the introduction of uniformity in the application of legal rules[43] envisaged by (2) and (3) above as advantageous.

However, such uses are fraught with questionable theoretical assumptions on the nature of legal reasoning and the purpose of law and hence extending these uses to the public sphere without due scrutiny may do more harm than good. It will therefore not be remiss to outline the jurisprudential assumptions made and the questions raised as a consequence of the functions ascribed to intelligent computer systems.

---

[39] Though most of the legal expert systems are in prototype form there are a few that are commercially available like Capper and Susskind's system on the Latent Damage Act.

[40] See Chapter Twelve *infra*.

[41] At present, to our knowledge, systems having the capacity to act as judges do not exist. However, John McCarthy, the guru of artificial intelligence is noted as saying that judges do not know anything that cannot be told to a computer and that it is perfectly appropriate for artificial intelligence to strive to build machines for making judicial decisions. See Weizenbaum, J (1985), *Computer Power and Human Reason*, Middlesex: Penguin Books, p, 207.

[42] See Hassett, Patricia (1992), *Using Expert System Technology to Improve Bail Decisions*, London: Institute of Advanced Legal Studies Research Working Papers

[43] For instance, Hassett (1992), at p,17 states that essentially similar cases produce a range of different bail decisions; this may partly be due to personal views held by the decision maker.

4.1. Assumptions and Resulting Questions

The first use suggested is that a computer system can offer legal advice on the basis of responses by the user to questions posed by the program - a function not dissimilar to that offered by a solicitor to a client. For this to be possible the system must contain the following components:

(1) a knowledge base that contains formalised knowledge about the area of law in which the system is to operate;

(2) an inference engine that is essentially a link between the knowledge base and the user; and

(3) an interface that allows the user to interact with the system.

The first issue relates to how the contents of the knowledge base are derived from a body of legislation (which in common law countries would consist of case law and statutory material). Many expert system builders appear to accept the highly questionable premiss that law can be easily reduced to rules.[44] Even if one were to accept this stance nonetheless the task of extrapolating the legal rules still remains. This poses problems both at the conceptual and the pragmatic level. At the conceptual level some of the questions that can be raised are:

(1) What is the nature of a legal rule? Is it the same as a scientific law? Does it exhibit qualities such as uniformity and rigidity that are to be found in scientific laws? Or, are legal rules always surrounded by a penumbra of uncertainty brought about by their linguistic content thereby disabling the process of deductive reasoning?

(2) Can it be applied mechanically to the case under consideration without taking into account human factors that may be present in the individual instance?

(3) Or, is law a set of 'loose rules' affected by human factors and linguistic content? If this is the case then how are these 'loose rules' to be logically expressed?

At the pragmatic level the formulation of legal rules from available legal material, generally regarded in the common law context to consist of case law and statute law, can prove to be a difficult task. At the case law level, a number of problems may arise. For instance:

(1) How should one discern the *ratio decidendi* of a case?[45] Does the *ratio* pertain only to a particular set of facts? Can the *ratio* be applied to a

---

[44] For a concise introduction to the theories on the nature of law, see Harris, J.W. (1980), *Legal Philosophies*, London: Butterworths

[45] There are different views on how the *ratio* can be determined. The general view is that the material facts taken into account by the judge in arriving at his conclusion determines the *ratio* - see Goodhart, A.L., (1931), *Essays in Jurisprudence and the Common Law*, Cambridge University Press. However, this view assumes that it is

situation where the facts do not correspond exactly to the set of facts in a case from which the *ratio* has been derived?

(2) What if there is more than one discernible *ratio* of a case? A situation that is likely to arise where more than one judgement is given.[46]

Against this context the task of providing a legal rule becomes highly individualistic or subjective, and is therefore largely dependent on the perception and understanding of the rule formulator.

A similar problem presents itself even where statute law, a medium preferred by expert system builders, is used as a source for deriving rules. Statutes give the appearance of being better ordered than case law by providing a body of legal knowledge and definitions as appropriate and therefore requiring no more than a translation of the material into a logical form that the computer would be able to recognise. As Susskind says '... it is likely that most researchers' preference for statute law is rooted in a recognition not of its central role in legal reasoning, but of its being apparently more amenable to computational treatment than case law'.[47] However, this preference for statute law as desirable material for building expert systems is based on questionable grounds. Even within statute law there are difficulties reminiscent of those within case law that need to be contended by the rule formulator. The Sale of Goods Act 1979 is one such statute. An illustration of the difficulties faced by the expert system builder will be provided by looking at s.14(2) of the Act. S. 14(2) states:

'Where the seller sells goods in the course of business, there is an implied condition that the goods supplied in the contract are of merchantable quality, except that there is no such condition -

(a) as regards defects specifically drawn to the buyer's attention before the contract is made; or

(b) if the buyer examines the goods before contract is made, as regards defects which that examination ought to reveal.

On the basis of this section it is possible to formulate the following rule (Rule A):

---

easy to ascertain which facts are treated as material and which not and this may not be always the case. The fact description may provide some clues regarding the materiality of facts ; however Julius Stone has argued, that facts can be material under an infinite range of fact descriptions. This has led him to regard the ratio as simply a 'category of illusory reference' - see Stone, J., (1985), *Precedent and Law*, Melbourne: Butterworths

[46] See *Hillyer v St Bartholomew's Hospital* [1909] 2 *K B* 820 where at least two *rationes* can be discerned. in relation to the duty of care owed by the nurses and porters to the plaintiff. See also *Gold v Essex County Council* [1942] 1 *KB* 293 and *Cassidy v Minister of Health* [1951] 2 *KB* 343

[47] Susskind (1987) *op cit.* p. 80.

In the absence of condition (a) or (b) if the seller sells goods in the course of business then he or she undertakes that the goods are of merchantable quality.

This rule presumably can be formulated in the required logical form for computer use. Nonetheless, the formulation of the above rule in itself is insufficient to tackle the legal problems in this area and apart from conditions (a) and (b) Rule A needs to be explicated further. The following needs to be addressed:

(1) the kinds of situation in which the transaction on the part of the seller will be regarded as having taken place in the course of business; and

(2) the criteria that needs to be satisfied for the goods to fulfil the requirement of merchantable quality.

(1) requires 'course of business' to be elucidated further. The Act provides a definition of business in s.61(1) according to which it includes 'a profession and the activities of any government department ... or local or public authority'. It does not provide a definition of 'course of business'. The use of common sense may be adequate to formulate the legal rule that a domestic user selling a pair of speakers will not be selling in the course of business whereas Dixon's of High Street selling hi-fi equipment with the aim of making a profit will be selling in the course of business. These illustrations are unproblematic and therefore clear cases; the problem arises where the situation falls between these two extremes. For instance, does the hairdresser who uses hi-fi equipment in his or her salon sell in the course of business if he or she sells a pair of speakers? So a rule is required that would be adequate to deal with the above fact situation. For this to be possible, the rule formulator, in the absence of provisions for interpretation in the statute will have to look outside it. The following possible moves, by no means exhaustive, are available:

- Are there any cases that have considered the phrase in the context of Sale of Goods Act?
- Is there any available case law on this phrase in the context of sale of goods prior to the passing of this Act?
- What was the aim of Parliament when it enacted the statute? For instance, was it to correct inequality of bargaining powers?
- Is the phrase used in any other statute and how has that been interpreted in the context of that statute?

Accordingly, in the absence of definitions within the statute that indicate adequately the kinds of situations in which a rule derived from a statutory rule is applicable, the task of the rule formulator is as interpretative as that of a case law rule formulator.

(2) requires elucidation of 'merchantable quality'. S.14(6) of the Act provides:

> *'Goods of any kind are of merchantable quality within the meaning of subsection (2) above if they are as fit for the purpose or purposes for which goods of that kind are commonly bought as it is reasonable to expect having regard to them, the price (if relevant) and all other circumstances.'*

The definition is ambiguous and inexhaustive and raises a number of doubts. For instance:

(1) The definition refers to 'purpose or purposes'. Does this mean that were the goods unfair for even *one* of their purposes the goods would be rendered unmerchantable? This goes against the decision in the House of Lords in *Brown v Craiks*[48] where it was held that goods that were unfit for *one* of their purposes did not make them unmerchantable provided the buyer would accept them without a special abatement in price. Does this mean that s 14(6) has changed the law in a substantial way? In order to arrive at some kind of conclusion the rule formulator will have to go beyond the actual wording to fathom the legislator's intentions.

(2) The definition states that the merchantable quality must be measured in terms of 'what is reasonable to expect having regard to ... the price and all other circumstances'. It is unclear what 'all other circumstances' is meant to include. Yet again an investigation is required.

Accordingly, it would not be an exaggeration to say that even legal rules derived from a statute, despite definitions, involve some amount of interpretation.

The task of interpretation in itself may prove to be a formidable one since it may not always be possible to discern a single principle from the decisions. And, even where an underlying principle can somehow be detected it may appear to go against some other well-established principle. The task of the rule formulator then becomes a highly individualistic one based on an understanding of the language, his or her perception of what the law is, and what it is aiming to do in a given social context.

The second use identified earlier suggests the possibility of ascribing judicial functions to intelligent systems. This assumes that judicial decisions are a consequence of rigid, non-discretionary application of legal rules. This, however, is a short-sighted view since there are many instances in English law where the judges have regarded their role not as one of rule following but as one of carrying out justice be it at the individual or the social level, and to this end they take account of principles extraneous to legal rules, and balance these in an arguably appropriate manner. The case of *Royal College of Nursing* v *Department of Health and Social Security*[49] provides a good illustration. In

---

[48] [1970] 1 *WLR* 752
[49] [1981] 1.*AER* 545

1967, when the legislature passed the Abortion Act permitting the termination of pregnancy by a registered medical practitioner in certain circumstances, only two methods of termination existed. These were the surgical and intra-amniotic methods and both these required the presence of a doctor. In 1971 a new extra-amniotic method had become current and this achieved termination by controlled introduction of a drug called prostoglandin over a period of 18-30 hours. The DHSS advised the Royal College of Nursing (RCN) that as long as a doctor approved and started the process the nurse could lawfully continue it by starting and regulating the supply of the drug. The RCN sought a declaration from the courts that this advice was incorrect and that the Act did not protect the nurses in their application of the extra-amniotic drug. The issue therefore before the court was whether the words 'registered medical practitioner' in the Act included ancillary staff in the medical profession.

The minority in the House of Lords thought that the words should be construed literally and that the Act was not one for purposive, liberal, or equitable construction. They were echoing Lord Denning's hesitation in the Court of Appeal to construe the words liberally since abortion is an emotion laden subject. Accordingly, they felt that it should be left to Parliament to implement further changes. The majority however felt that the policy of the Act was (a) to broaden the grounds on which abortion may be lawfully obtained and (b) to ensure that it was carried out under proper and hygienic conditions. A careful reading of the judgments suggests that the majority seem to have given precedence to carrying out social policy and ensuring that social ills, for instance, fewer abortions due to dangerous surgical methods, would not ensue.[50]

Accordingly, to ascribe judicial decision making capacities to the system, it will have to possess those abilities that are found in human judges which requires greater understanding of judicial decision-making as found within society.

The third use envisages computers as playing a very useful function by assisting the decision-maker in a court of law. The knowledge base in such a system is to be drawn from the factors taken into account by the decision-maker in a particular field. The justification for such a use is that it will introduce consistency and predictability in the judicial system.

Though the above idea is an attractive one, the biggest stumbling block that has to be tackled at the very start is one of methodology. Some of the issues that will have to be decided are:

---

[50] For more examples of instances where the judges have taken into account moral principles and social policies in arriving at a decision see Mahalingam, Indira (1991) Computers in Law - Hard Cases in Narayanan, Ajit and Bennun, Mervyn (eds.) *Law, Computer Science and Artificial Intelligence,* New York: Ablex Publishing

(1) Which factors taken by the decision-maker are to be regarded as relevant? Are the criteria for identifying these factors subjective ones (namely, those that the decision-maker him/herself regards as important) or objective ones (namely, those that are seen by others as affecting the decision-maker)?
(2) What is relevance? Is it determined by the factors and their relationship to the predictable behaviour of the accused? If so, is the link a causal one which can be determined by the observance of human behaviour?
(3) Does every human action have a strictly identifiable cause? Are human/social phenomena like physical phenomena?

The questions raised by the use of artificial intelligence applications in the legal domain are numerous, complex and varied.[51] The areas that have been identified in this section are essentially philosophical; nonetheless, they are most pressing if computers are to play the kinds of roles envisaged for them. Of course, from the point of view of legal philosophy, the introduction of 'intelligent' computers into the legal process gives many traditional questions a new and intriguing slant, as well as raising many new questions and problems.

5. Conclusion

The questions raised in this and the following chapters show that the existing framework of reference may prove inadequate to handle the vast number of legal issues that arise as a result of the introduction of computers in virtually all spheres of life. It is clear that a remoulding of traditional legal concepts, where possible, and the introduction of new concepts is required to accommodate the peculiarities of this technology. It is equally clear that this process of accommodation is urgently required since the new technology is already in place and is rapidly spreading.

---

[51] Many important legal questions such as the level of competence of software engineers and liability of defective software arise in relation to artificial intelligence applications, be it in law or other areas like aircraft control and medicine which could be reasonably dealt with by using contract law and tort law. Some of these issues are dealt with in Chapter Fifteen *(infra)*.

Part I
ELECTRONIC DATA INTERCHANGE: TECHNICAL AND LEGAL ASPECTS

2
Sergej H Katus
Three Types Of EDI Contracts

I. EDI Contracts

1.1. Introduction

Several independent organisations have drafted model terms for electronic data interchange (EDI) contracts. Reading the Standard Agreement made by the UK EDI Association,[1] the most recent version of the EC TEDIS European Model EDI Agreement,[2] or the Dutch Ediforum Contract,[3] one gets the impression that EDI contracts are agreements in which two or more *users* in the switching role of sender and addressee, undertake to communicate by electronic means according to the principles of EDI. Users, however, are not the only parties involved in EDI and their agreements alone are not the only kind of EDI contracts in existence.[4] Article 8 of all three model agreements states that the parties are liable for failures or omissions when using the services of an intermediary in order to transmit, log or process data.[5] This suggests that there are other kinds of EDI contracts apart from the obvious one between the users.

In this paper the different types of EDI contracts are compared through a classification of the EDI contracts and a general survey of the responsibilities of the various parties. The non-fulfillment of contractual obligations can lead to liability in an EDI environment.

1.2. Three Types of EDI Contracts

The three model agreements mentioned above, belong to a group of contracts that came to be known as Interchange Agreements. Similar regulations were

---

[1] Terms of the Standard Electronic Data Interchange Agreement of the EDI Association (hereafter referred to as: EDIA Agreement).
[2] European Model EDI Agreement (Final Draft), Commission of the European Communities' Programme TEDIS I (CEC/DG XIII/TEDIS), May 1991; (hereafter referred to asTEDIS Agreement).
[3] Ediforum 'De EDI Overeenkomst', *Nationale EDI Gids 91-92*, Woerden 1991, p.349-366 (hereafter referred to as: Ediforum Contract).
[4] R.E. van Esch, 'Electronic data interchange contracten' *Hoofdstukken Informaticarecht, F de Graaf (ed.), Samson H D Tjeenk Willink.* Alphen a/d Rijn 1989, p.263 (hereafter referred to as: Van Esch).
[5] Article 8 TEDIS Agreement.

drafted in North America such as the Model EDI Trading Partner Agreement of the American Bar Association and the Model Form of EDI Trading Partner Agreement of the EDI Council of Canada. Interchange Agreements were solely considered to be confined to EDI contracts in which trade partners undertook to communicate. However, other types of contracts appeared quickly where third parties provided special network services to facilitate electronic data interchange. Therefore these agreements made between users and intermediaries have also to be considered as EDI contracts.[6] Furthermore, other agreements now exist that do not deal with the communication as such. This is where third parties provide services to increase EDI fidelity such as security services, technical/logical support and independent monitoring services. Accordingly, there are three types of contracts that are related to the use of EDI:[7]

    (1) The *Interchange Agreement* between sender and addressee (users);
    (2) The *Network Agreement* between users and network providers (intermediaries);[8]
    (3) The *Third Party Agreement* between users or network providers and other third parties.[9]

As a basis for the model EDI contracts, the work of the International Chamber of Commerce is of great importance. With the help of users, the ICC drafted a code of conduct that can be incorporated by the parties in EDI contracts. In 1987 these Uniform Rules of Conduct for Interchange of Trade Data by Teletransmission (UNCID) were accepted and adopted by the United Nations Economic Commission for Europe as the legal basis for the UN/EDIFACT messaging standard.[10] The rules regularly serve as a basis for EDI agreements

---

[6] Hans B Thomson, 'Interchange Agreements', *EDI and the Law*, Blenheim Online Publications, London 1989, p.74 (hereafter referred to as: Thomson References to 'EDI and the Law' will be abbreviated to the title only). CEC/DG XIII/TEDIS. Papers *The TEDIS/EDI legal Workshop*, Brussels 24 July 1989, p.51 and 58 (hereafter referred to as TEDIS Legal Papers).

[7] In the original paper, these contracts were called: Interchange Agreements, Connection Agreements and Support Agreements. Due to the publication of two TEDIS Reports (notes 9 and 10) and the need for standardisation - also in terminology - these terms were changed.

[8] Compare: CEC/DG XIII/TEDIS, *The Liability of Electronic Data Interchange Operators*, doc. XIII/187/92.

[9] CEC COM(90) 473 def, November 1990; nr. 19. Also: CEC/DG XIII/TEDIS. *Trusted Third Parties and Similar Services*, doc. XIII/5/92 (hereafter referred to as TEDIS Doc 5/92).

[10] Nigel Savage and Ian Walden, 'International trade law and UNCID', *EDI and the Law*, p.71, Van Esch, p.260. WJ de Jong, 'EDI en normalisatie', *Informatic* 1990; 9, p.701.

made by other organisations, thereby gaining independent legal force themselves.[11]

1.3. Interchange Agreements

As indicated before, the Interchange Agreements are the best known EDI contracts they govern the rights and obligations in relation to the way data are interchanged using electronic means. They, however, should not be confused with agreements that are transmitted as EDI messages (transaction agreements). Interchange Agreements can either be made bilaterally (between users) or multilaterally (in which case the agreements are made for a larger group of users).[12] The primary intention of the parties to the agreement is the exchange of data according to the principles of EDI. Consequently, the main characteristic of this agreement is the point of communication; to the contracting parties (forming a network) it is essential that they create and use the means to transfer a message electronically because of the information it contains. During the exchange of messages, much may be at stake because data may contain information of great importance to the involved users. Accordingly, the Interchange Agreement is made to ensure efficient EDI in an atmosphere of legal security by regulating the rights and obligations of the users with regard to the technical requirements and legal issues.[13]

1.4. Network Agreements

The Network Agreements are not that well known. Network Agreements are closely related to the Interchange Agreements since they both deal with communications. However, the parties' intentions are not to communicate with each other by interchanging data but, from the users point of view, to make a connection to a network to enable communications with other users and/or to make use of value adding services provided by the intermediary.[14] These services may consist of, *inter alia*, protocol conversion, message routing, correction, (de)coding or store and forward facilities.[15]

---

[11] Van Esch, p.261. Thomsen, p.75 and 77.

[12] It is not unusual that in practice written Interchange Agreements do not exist. However, verbal agreements or agreements by habit are also Interchange Agreements.

[13] Thomson, p.80. TEDIS Legal Papers, p.54.

[14] In case such an entity provides more services than the mere transport of signals, the intermediary is known as a provider of Value added Network Services (VANS). See also TEDIS Report § 11.4.5.2.3.

[15] Report of the Nederlandse Vereniging voor Informatie en Recht (Dutch Association for Computer and Law), *Juridische aspecten van netwerken*, April 1990, p.41-42. A more complete survey can be found in Ph. E. de Roos, 'EDI en netwerkleveranciers', S.H. Katus (ed.), *EDI en België,* Die Keure, Brugge 1993, p. 117 and further (hereafter referred to as De Roos or *EDI en België* only).

One should make a distinction between intermediaries that are responsible for a nation's telecommunication infrastructure as a public task (national PTT's) and private network providers like IBM Information Network and GE Information Services. The latter will be affected by the principles of contract law and competition law and law concerning their status as a legal entity; whereas national network providers (possibly privatised) have a special legal status which makes them fundamentally different in commercial practice.[16]

Network Agreements exist in several forms as users sometimes contract network providers directly (GEIS or IBM IN) and sometimes they enter a certain user group by consenting with the by-laws (SWIFT).[17]

The Network Agreement could therefore be defined as an agreement that regulates the rights and obligations of users and intermediaries with regards to technical requirements and legal issues, to ensure an efficient passing of EDI messages in an atmosphere of legal security.

1.5. Third Party Agreements

Although a network provider is a third party when seen from the Interchange Agreement level, 'third parties' are the ones who are contracted by users and intermediaries to provide supporting services, like hardware, software, maintenance services and security services. Third Party Agreements can be regarded as sub-contracts that result from the other types of EDI agreements and do not necessarily focus on data exchange. Because of the wide range, it is not really possible to identify a general contractual aim here. However, it should be mentioned that an overlap may exist between the services that are provided by intermediaries and other third parties. As an example, one can think of a network provider who provides electronic notary services as well.[18]

2. Similarities

In all three categories of contracts, it is obvious that the parties intend to do something with EDI, either directed towards the process of communication or towards some kind of support. Consequently, the written EDI contract is a legal document in which terms related to the use of EDI can be found. This is most clear in the Interchange and Network Agreements. In both contracts rules are laid down for technical and legal matters with regard to the use of EDI. The Third Party Agreement, however, does not necessarily regulate these matters since a technical part may very well be missing.

---

[16] The *Wet op de Telecommunicatievoorzieningen (WTV)* in The Netherlands from 1989 or the Belgian Law of 21st March 1991.

[17] Articles 2.3.A.1. and 2.3.B.1, 2 and 3, SWIFT II Policy (1990).

[18] See: TEDIS Legal Papers, p.58, 130-150, CEC COM(90) 475 def. November 1990, nr. 19 TEDIS Dec. 5/92. De Roos, p. 129.

So, what are the terms that are typical for EDI? This is easy to answer because of the already mentioned UNCID rules, notwithstanding the fact that they are particularly made for the transfer of *trade* data. Since the definition of EDI is "transmission of data structured according to agreed message standards, between information systems, by electronic means",[19] the UNCID rules are applicable according to Article 3 UNCID. Except for the Third Party Agreement, EDI contracts regulate:[20]

    (1) That parties exchange EDI messages (Article 3 UNCID);
    (2) The agreements on the use of standards for data elements, message structure and similar rules and communication standards (Article 4 UNCID);
    (3) That parties are capable to receive data transfers (Article 5 UNCID);
    (4) That parties ensure the reliability of messages (according to the agreed standards) by regulating (Article 5-10 UNCID):
        (a) integrity - the messages should be correct and complete;
        (b) exclusivity - messages can be secured/protected (logically, physically or by encryption) against interference by unauthorised persons. Unauthorised changes of messages or disclosures to unauthorised persons are prohibited;
        (c) verifiability - identification, verification, acknowledgement, confirmation of content and storage of data.

Interchange and Network Agreements have a great deal in common. One could compare the situation with a railway network: the Interchange Agreement is to ensure that a train with A's message reaches station B from station A, whereas the Network Agreement is to ensure that A's message reaches B's station by passing pointman C, because C is responsible for an important part of the track. Also any D, E, and F can only be reached by having an agreement with C. All have to make sure that messages are exchangeable. Therefore, both users and intermediary need equipment, software and other means to transmit, pass and receive messages. Above all, they have to agree on what a message looks like (UNCID points 1, 2 and 3). Accordingly, Interchange and Network Agreements either contain these agreements themselves or, more commonly, they provide a framework agreement while the technical specifications are put in a separate User Manual/User Handbook/Technical Annex.[21] However, having a closer look at, SWIFT's General Terms and Conditions, one can see that:

---

[19] Article 1, 2nd definition, TEDIS Agreement.
[20] In my opinion, article 5b UNCID does not hinder the applicability to intermediaries.
[21] Cf. TEDIS Agreement, the EDIA Agreement, the Ediforum Contract, SWIFT II Policy.

(a) The SWIFT network enables the secure, confidential, and rapid transmission of **messages** (...) between financial institutions world-wide.

(b) The SWIFT network has four main functions:
- to **accept** messages (...)
- to **validate** messages (...)
- to **store** messages (...)
- to **deliver** messages (...)[22]

One cannot deny that the parties' intentions are not the same as in the Interchange Agreement, where the meaning of a message is essential. SWIFT plays the role of a postman instead of a user and is not interested in the information as such. If we look at GE Information Services, IBM Information Network or even the Dutch insurance network (ADN), they never claim interest in a message's content. ADN, for example, only connects 'participants' to the network, giving them the right to make use of the provided ADN services.[23] Consequently, contracts drafted by network providers will reflect other interests than Interchange Agreements (or Network Agreements where users played a more influential role of course).

Third Party Agreements most likely do not contain the first three UNCID elements since they are based on the realisation of Interchange/Network Agreements (although an overlap might exist between a support contract and any other EDI contract by providing support electronically). Therefore, Third Party Agreements will mainly be based on the fourth point of the UNCID regulations and may contain those elements themselves. For example: organisations that are contracted to store data files for verification, may be instructed not to disclose the information to unauthorised persons.

3. Responsibility Issues

3.1. Assignment

Users should be expected to be interested in the well functioning of EDI applications only, since they regard EDI just as a tool to communicate.[24] Since the whole facility simply has to work, users assign EDI related obligations that result from Interchange Agreements to third parties, as these new jobs presumably fit in the third party's daily business. The interests of the contracting parties, however, may differ too much to result in totally acceptable contracts to all of them. This is important since, for example, network providers usually have the position to impose their terms upon others. The interests of others may, therefore, be at risk.

---

[22] *Ibid.*, Chapter 11.1 (bold printing by SWIFT).
[23] Articles 2 and 5 ADN Aansluitingsovereenkomst.
[24] See also: TEDIS Report § 11.4.

The notion of 'derived responsibility' becomes relevant here. If high interests are at stake when data are interchanged between users only, each user has a responsibility related to the degree of their mutual interest to interchange data in a correct way. If the help of a third party is called in, this party not only has to handle data as carefully as the users are accustomed to, but as a specialist, this party would be expected to bear a heavier responsibility than the users in the old situation. If he or she does not intend to carry this burden, this should be made clear explicitly in the agreement.[25]

As an illustration: in the Netherlands banks make use of General Banking Conditions which create the possibility to make use of third party services to fulfil the obligations from a contract with a client. If something in the financial transactions goes wrong, Dutch banks accept liability, even when financial damage was caused by a third party.[26] It is, therefore, highly reasonable to assume that Dutch banks, being SWIFT members, have great trust in SWIFT by making use of its services. The amounts of money involved are large and banks do not like to take great risks. Evidently, SWIFT has the responsibility to make no relevant mistakes at all, while messages from all over the world are flashing through the SWIFT computers all the time.[27] Despite this, SWIFT never accepts *full* responsibility. Something its members are aware of.[28]

3.2. Interchange Agreement Obligations

Of course, parties do not automatically have responsibilities related to the use of EDI, these responsibilities are agreed upon by making contracts. The Interchange Agreement as a contract between users only, contains the descriptions of responsibilities with regards to the role of the sender and the addressee. We already know the general obligations of a user as described in the UNCID rules, but those rules are not sufficiently specific about the *allocation* of the parties' obligations.

As will be explained hereafter, it is important to recognise that the responsibilities in the use of EDI are mainly relevant when users are actually dealing with messages. From the sender's point of view, those are the moments of preparation and transmitting. From the addressee's point of view, those are the moments of reception and processing. Naturally, they both are responsible for their capacity of interchanging EDI messages. Accordingly, they have to

---

[25] IBM IN and GEIS included this in their contracts. See: paragraph IV. c.
[26] Article 3 and article 10 Algemene Bankvoorwaarden (Rabobank, December 1987).
[27] 1 million messages a day in 1990. See: B Petre, 'Network Providers' *Computer Law & Practice,* September/October 1990.
[28] *Ibid.*, p.18. Responsibility is limited for amounts that exceed 3 billion BEF for negligence, loss or omission in message transport, with an annual limit for 6 billion BEF. Furthermore, the loss of interest for late payments is limited to 50 million BEF.

provide themselves with the technical equipment, software and maintenance services required.

3.2.1. *Responsibilities of the Sender*

A sender has to transform data (which itself must be correct) into an EDI message, which means transforming the data into a message structured to agreed standards, in a computer readable format and capable of being automatically and unambiguously processed.[29] If agreed, these preparations additionally include any measure to secure the message against the risk of unauthorised access by any person, alteration, loss or destruction such as measures of encryption or adding authentication mechanisms. If agreed, the transmission itself needs control to ensure that the message is sent in the correct format. For evidential purposes, the sender (can be placed under an obligation to) keep a data log, a chronological record to store all EDI messages.[30]

3.2.2. *Responsibilities of the Addressee*

To establish its authenticity, the addressee receiving a message, will have to convert, decode and verify it. Sometimes verification may already (partly) have taken place by making use of special decryption keys. Verification can also be done by sending confirmations/acknowledgements to the sender. Furthermore, usage of authentication mechanisms enables the addressee to determine the message's authenticity as well. Received messages have to be registered in a data log. If the message contains confidential data, the addressee is not allowed to disclose the data to unauthorised persons.[31]

3.3. Network Agreement Obligations

In the Network Agreement, the intermediary temporarily plays the role of addressee and sender, at the same time. When an original sender transmits a message, it is received by the intermediary and from that moment, the intermediary is responsible. He or she processes the message as agreed (providing the value added services), then forwards the message to the real addressee, thus passing on the responsibility as well.[32]

The first responsibility of an intermediary in a Network Agreement is, of course, to connect a user to the network. Therefore, he or she needs the equipment and software required, making sure that maintenance will be done. In

---

[29] Article 1, third definition TEDIS Agreement.

[30] *Ibid.*, Articles 6 and 7.

[31] *Ibid.*. Regarding privacy issues see J. Dumortier 'Privacybescherming bij EDI' *EDI en België*, p. 199 and further (see footnote 15).

[32] Art. 21.5.1 SWIFT II Policy: 'SWIFT is responsible for the complete international network. Looking at it from the user's point of view, this means that SWIFT is responsible for the message from time it reaches SWIFT-owned equipment (...) to the time it leaves SWIFT-owned equipment.'

all cases, one may expect a certain level of expertise. Network Agreements may contain agreements on back-up facilities, availability, etc.[33] In order to ensure an efficient transport of messages, the intermediary may instruct the user to make use of specified hard- and software and/or messaging standards.

Since intermediaries are neither the original sender nor the addressee, their responsibility is limited to the 'envelope' of the message (ie, generally, they are not authorised to change the information it contains). Even repairs of damaged messages mean that their contents have to remain unaltered. When it is known, while making the Network Agreement, that exchanged messages may contain confidential data, an intermediary has to ensure that no unauthorised persons have access to any transmitted EDI messages.[34]

3.3.1. *Responsibilities of the Users*

The users' responsibilities are mainly those already described in the Interchange Agreement situation, except for the fact that they have to follow the instructions of the network provider.[35] Depending on the content of the Network Agreement, the intermediary may provide services that assign responsibilities from the user to him/herself. If, for example, an intermediary translates data transmitted by a sender into an EDIFACT EDI message, the sender no longer is responsible for the correct protocol conversion as long as this added service is acceptable to the parties in the Interchange Agreement (see below). Naturally, payments for such services are part of the users obligations.

3.4. Third Party Agreement Obligations

The Third Party Agreements show derived responsibility in *optima forma* since they are aimed at the assignment of responsibilities from the users/intermediaries to third parties. However, this does not mean that third party service providers only have the obligation of good performance of the assigned responsibility. As already made clear, Third Party Agreements may also contain responsibilities related to the provision of special services.

3.4.1. *Responsibilities of the Users/Intermediaries*

The users'/intermediaries' responsibilities, however, are twofold. On the one hand they may have the obligation to provide the facilities for the supporter to do his or her job (payments included). On the other hand the supportees have the responsibility towards other users/intermediaries to choose their third party service providers carefully since the supporter's services may affect the relations

---

[33] Compare TEDIS Report § 11.4.5-6-7 and § III 4.1.2.
[34] There seems to be a tendency for intermediaries to become increasingly involved in the content of messages. This is, for example, the case when *netting* services are being provided.
[35] Compare: TEDIS Report § III.4.1.1.

between message exchanging partners. Sometimes this is the reason why responsibilities cannot be delegated and personal performance by the party originally contracted is essential.[36] For example, assignment may raise problems with authentication or aspects of confidentiality.[37] A characteristic of the Third Party Agreement is that, although third parties fulfil obligations from the Interchange/Network Agreement, the user/intermediary normally remains responsible towards his or her parties in the original data exchange contracts.

4. Contractual Liability Issues

4.1. Breach of Contract

Knowing the responsibilities resulting from the EDI contracts, it may be clear that every party has the obligation to perform according to their responsibilities within reasonable boundaries. Not fulfilling the contractual obligations means breach of contract, which may cause damage to other parties.[38] With the exception of *force majeure*, one is normally liable to the injured party (having the obligation to compensate for the damage caused).[39] The main questions, therefore, are:

(1) Did the party perform insufficiently to fulfil his or her contractual EDI obligations?

(2) Did this non-performance cause damage to another contracting party?

4.1.1. *Interchange Agreement*

In the Interchange Agreement, liability is imposed only if a message lacks integrity and causes damage to another user because of a fault. Damage can either be caused in the transmission phase or in the reception phase of electronic data interchange. It is just a matter of checking the Interchange Agreement: did the guilty party act the way he or she ought to, according to his or her responsibilities as a sender or an addressee? Needless to say, mistakes that do not cause damage to another party are not relevant from the legal point of view. They just may be regarded as wrong but harmless messages, or mistakes that only affect the causing party.

4.1.2. *Network Agreement*

The Network Agreement places intermediaries in almost the same position as the users in an Interchange Agreement; they may be liable for mistakes in receiving

---

[36] Cheshire, Fifoot and Furmston, *Law of Contract,* 12th edition, Butterworths, London, Dublin, Edinburgh 1991, p.523-524 (hereafter referred to as *Law of Contract*).

[37] Thomsen, p.87.

[38] See TEDIS Report § 11.3.3.

[39] According to Article 6.74 Dutch New Civil Code (Nieuw Bargerijk Wetboek), article 1148 Belgian Civil Code.

and forwarding messages. Besides that, mistakes made in providing any other service (instructions included) are a reason for liability as well. As already mentioned, the services provided by the intermediary often imply that the connected users have fewer responsibilities than in the Interchange Agreement situation. Since the intermediaries usually are experts in EDI, this means that the risk of being liable is greater to intermediaries than to users.

4.1.3. *Third Party Agreement*

The Third Party Agreement is a sub-contract for performing contractual obligations by a third person. Generally, because of the privity of contract, any relevant mistake made by third party C, causing user A damage, makes supportee B liable since the delegation of his or her responsibilities never relieved him or her from the original contractual obligations. B, of course, can try to sue C for non-performance or defective performance of the support contract.[40]

4.2. Article 8

Article 8 of the TEDIS Agreement provides (as do other model agreements) that senders are liable for mistakes made by intermediaries, thus referring to the situation of the Third Party Agreement. This can be explained by the fact that in case individual parties in an Interchange Agreement delegate their responsibilities to an intermediary, to the other users the delegating parties just call in the help of a supporter. Furthermore, statutory law and case law often use the Reception Rule on contract formation, which says that senders are responsible for messages till the moment they are received by the addressees.[41]

One can ask, however, whether Article 8 regulates liability too much.[42] What if parties - maybe implicitly - agreed that they would both use a particular intermediary? Suppose user A prepares a message that is of no value to him or her and does so just as an extra service (for example providing stock information on interest rates). His or her interchange Agreement with B, however, contains an Article 8 clause. A sends the message to intermediary C as agreed, who makes a fatal, though not a very obvious error (minor alteration of interest rates), and forwards the message. Both A and B accepted C's standard Network Agreement independently, on a voluntary basis. It is stated there that C cannot be held liable for damages. It is too late, however, when B discovers that his or her computer system sold shares at a bad time. B suffers substantial damage and sues A since C is untouchable. Consequently, A is fully liable. Obviously,

---

[40] *Law of Contract*, p.523.
[41] See TEDIS Legal Papers, p.36. The Reception Rule is embodied in the Dutch New Civil Code (NBW), article 3.37, 3rd and 4th section.
[42] S H Katus, 'De Aansprakelijkheidsaspecten van het Ediforum Contract', *Computerrecht* 1992/2, p.59 and further (hereafter referred to as Katus).

this is a weak spot in a model agreement. Users generally are not professional lawyers and just choose model agreements in the belief that they increase the safety of EDI. Negotiations on this matter would result in a modification of such an article.[43] A and B could agree to share the risk where C makes mistakes.[44]

4.2.1. *Limitations of liability*
In general the restriction of liability by intermediaries is a well known phenomenon.[45] Exclusion of public network providers may even be based on statutory law, like the liability position of RTT-Belgacom in Belgium.[46] Of course, parties in EDI contracts are free to agree whatever they like, subject to the restrictions on such clauses in the law of contract. For all EDI contracts the parties will have to take into account that in court restriction clauses have to survive the test of reasonableness. The larger the scope of the restriction, the harder this will be.[47]

There are several aspects to this test. In the Netherlands the main question will be whether it was necessary, from the imposing party's point of view, to restrict liability. Necessity is missing it, for instance, at the time that the restriction was imposed, the possibility to insure the risk of damage existed, or when enough reserve funds were available. Also, the parties' relation towards each other will be considered. A strong party imposing liability restrictions on a weaker party must prove the reasonableness of such a clause.[48] In determining to what extent someone using restriction clauses can be liable, the use of standard contracts plays a role as well.

The test of reasonableness is interesting to study with regards to the slogan 'No EDI, no business'. This illustrates that parties can be forced to implement

---

[43] Unless other interests are involved of course. Compare: TEDIS Legal Papers, p.54.
[44] Article 5 EDIA Association deals with the integrity of messages. A sender is liable when errors are *not* reasonably obvious to addressees. Since this may often be the case in practice, the EDIA option underlines the liability position of the sender.
[45] Article 1.9 Algemene Bepalingen (General Terms) of IBM Nederland BV, related to the use of IBM Information Network services. Article 9 *EDI Express System Supplement to the Agreement for Teleprocessing Services of General Electric Information Services Belgium. TEDIS Legal Papers, Question 3, p.51.
[46] Article 64 Law of 21st March 1991.
[47] Sa'id Mosteshar, 'Liability issue of EDI', *EDI and the Law*, p.51.
[48] G J Rijken, *Exoneratieclausules* (diss), Kluwer, Deventer 1983 (serie Recht en Praktijk; 38) p.101.

EDI. In the Netherlands, contractual exclusion of liability may be invalid in these cases.[49]

5. Developments in EDI Contracts

5.1. International Efforts

We saw that the UNCID rules, being the first EDI regulations, were made in 1987. Other contracts appeared that started dealing with legal issues. As is shown by two recent TEDIS research projects,[50] people obviously got interested in other categories of EDI relations as well. However, all these different contracts confront us with the situation that on a worldwide scale, a lot of pluriformity exists. Because of its nature, EDI requires a standardised legal environment; however, in the current climate, its status may vary from partner to partner and from country to country. Additionally, the discussion on Article 8 illustrates that the creation of computer networks inevitably leads to social networks in which the legal position of participants gets interrelated.[51]

To solve this problem, international organisations have started introducing rules that are internationally binding. The ICC wanted to create a second version of UNCID that can be used like the commercial INCOTERMS.[52] Also the UNECE and the United Nations Commission on International Trade Law (UNCITRAL) deal with EDI. The first organisation wants to draft a true international Interchange Agreement, the latter recently produced a Model Law on International Credit Transfers and decided that it may be time to regulate EDI in particular (especially in finance).[53]

However, until now the UNCID rules have proved to be functioning well. We must not forget that EDI is a business matter where parties need the room to negotiate. Furthermore, EDI agreements like those of the EDIA, TEDIS and Ediforum are standardised already since they are based on UNCID, which is also part of the UN/EDIFACT standard. Everyone who accepts EDIFACT, accepts UNCID.

---

[49] S H Katus, 'Aansprakelijkheidsposities in een EDI omgeving', found in R.E. von Esch en C Prins (Eds.) *Recht en EDI: juridische aspecten von elektronisch berichtenverkeen,* Serie Recht en Praktyk nr, 68, Kluwer, Deventer, 1993.
[50] See notes 9 and 10.
[51] Katus, p.61.
[52] See R E van Esch, 'Interchange Agreements' in *EDI en België* (see footnote 15).
[53] *Ibid.* See for an interesting discussion on F-EDI intermediaries. Report of the UN Commission on International Trade Law on the Work of its twenty-fourth session, June 1991, General Assembly, Official Records: forty-sixth session, supplement No.17 (A/46/17) nrs. 55-61.

5.1.1. *Case Law*

UNCID is acquiring force on its own in legal practice. However, even without such model rules, it would not be true that parties are free to do whatever they like. Although it has so far been unnecessary to discuss Law of Torts, US case law has proved that this area is highly relevant. In a dispute between banks concerning electronic funds transfers, it was stated that 'operational errors' are no valid excuse for mistakes in computerised payments since this would defeat the goals of certainty, finality and reliability that exist in the banking system.[54] In England and on the European continent similar criteria exist.[55]

6. Conclusion

Obviously, a uniform legal standard increases EDI security from an international legal point of view. However, one can doubt the need in practice for such a thing. Contracts that are being used, make it easy to determine the allocation of EDI related responsibilities. Breach of contract means liability. Adding the consideration that many EDI partners want room to negotiate, a rigid legal system would not be preferable. Until now, EDI users have adapted Interchange Agreements to suit their own needs; there is no reason however, to expect that this will ever change.

The situation is markedly different where EDI partners lack any solid legal basis because they do not use EDI contracts at all. If a dispute were to arise some sort of legal basis should exist. It would not be sufficient just to increase the parties' awareness of the existence of rules like UNCID; a safety net would prove to be of better use. The best option, therefore, is to draft rules as statutory law which parties can vary by agreement. EDI practice then could benefit from the best that the two systems would have to offer.

---

[54] US District Court of Colorado Civil Action No.90-B-0771.
[55] UK: Supply of Goods and Services Act 1982, s.13 and *Tai Hing Cotton Mill Ltd* v. *Liu Chong Hing Bank Ltd* [1986] AC 519. For the Netherlands, see I P Michiels van Kessenich-Hoogendam, *Aansprakelijkheid van Banken*, Tjeenk-Willink, Zwolle 1987. Furthermore: TEDIS Report, § III.2-3. An evaluation of tortious law in the Netherlands can be found in S.H.Katus, 1993 (see footnote 49).

3
Corien Prins
The Need to Standardise in an EDI Environment: Balancing the Legal Conditions and Implications

1. Preliminaries[1]

Standardisation is one of the key issues in the use of electronic means of processing and communicating information. Network service suppliers are becoming critically dependent on the use of technical standards that are the same throughout the world since incompatible means of communication systems may constrain, or even block, the effective flow of information between trading partners. Next to the necessary capability of intercommunication between trading partners, the need for communication standards derives from the demand to share network facilities, software and specialists. This demand is inflated for instance by financial considerations, specialisation, and the wish to avoid duplicated research, and training.

As for the European Communities, the lack of standardisation may obstruct the continuing development of the single European market. Harmonisation of already existing standards and an effective strategy toward getting certain new communication systems accepted as international standards from the beginning is an essential component in the battle against the fragmentation of the European market. In 1992, the Council once again underlined the strategic importance of standardisation for the European market in a Resolution of 18 June 1992.[2]

Standardisation and the development of transnational networks has always been a priority issue in Community projects. Following the decisions taken in Maastricht in 1991, these issues have been given further attention. In a reaction to the goals set in Maastricht, the Commission has set out the Community R&D strategy beyond 1992.[3] One of the priority issues in the package of future R&D

---
[1] I would like to thank Gera P. van Duijvenvoorde, Frank A.M. van der Klaauw and Aernout H.J. Schmidt for their valuable comments.
[2] *Official Journal of the European Communities* (O.J.) 1992 C 173/1
[3] SEC (92) 682 final, April 9 1992.

is the continued growth of community-wide telecommunications services and standardised cross-border networks. However, despite the Community's ambitions, it takes more than a well thought out industrial strategy to assist industry to compete at an international level. Turning to transnational networks, whilst structural funds, the promotion of cooperation and the stimulation of the training and mobility of Community researchers are important aspects, the effective development of community-wide networks also depends on other factors. A healthy legal environment is a key factor in this respect[4] as the creation of common systems of interchanging data and the pressure to conform to, and to use, certain standards may be curtailed by legal mechanisms, such as intellectual property law and competition law. In other words, standardisation has its boundaries. Interestingly, however, there is also an influence in the reverse order: the boundaries of the legal mechanisms are influenced by standardisation interests. Recent developments show clearly that the development and use of standards challenges traditional legal concepts.

This article is an attempt to provide a glimpse of both effects. It will centre the discussion around Electronic Data Interchange. EDI is illustrative for the effects that may be gained by standardisation, and it will be our tool for the analysis as to what standardisation is about and to what extent the path toward creating and using standards may be continued. The neccesity to standardise is clearly shown by a study commissioned by the European Commission with respect to the use of EDI in the transport area. Of those 600 companies that participated in the study, one in three appeared to have problems with the interconnection of networks. Further, 20% of the companies mentioned the lack of adequate standards as a problem in implementing EDI.[5]

The paper begins in section 2 with a brief introduction to EDI. Section 3 considers some characteristics of standardisation, and EDI standardisation in particular. Subsequently, I will introduce in section 4 different types of networks used for EDI applications. I will then elaborate on two effects mentioned above (section 5 and 6). The paper closes with a few tentative conclusions in section 7.

2. EDI - What is it About?

Procedures, costs and risks in connection with business transactions can be reduced significantly when using the opportunities provided by information technology products. Hence, it is no surprise that for the last few years EDI has become an important tool in facilitating commercial partners to communicate

---

[4] Compare the statement of Sir Leon Brittan with respect to competition law: '...I do not believe we would have a successful industrial policy without an important competition policy...' (1992) 4 *CMLR*, Antitrust Reports,433, at 477.

[5] *Telecommagazine*, 9/1992, p. 83.

standardised messages instantly, instead of transmitting trade documents in paper form. Although definitions of EDI vary, it is generally understood as the electronic exchange of structured messages in recognised formats between (commercial) partners. EDI is distinguished from other forms of electronic passage of messages in that the content of the message and the conduct of the EDI partners are publicly oriented. EDI thus includes electronic contracting across enterprise as well as organised boundaries, but excludes electronic passage of messages between individuals intended for purely informational purposes.

The advantages linked to EDI are shown by an European Commission report which estimates that the costs in completing paper documents, results in delays and mistakes, etc. could be equivalent to up to 10% of the cost of the exported product.[6] However, although for business reasons there is a growing interest in electronic contracting, the underlying legal problems hinder this opportunity from becoming a widely accepted means of business transaction. An EC report notes three key legal obstacles to EDI. First, the obligation imposed in certain areas of law to issue or preserve documents on written paper. The required written document constitutes particularly a major problem with: transport (bill of lading), means of payment (bill of exchange) and the settlement of disputes (arbitration clauses in writing). A second legal obstacle is the transience of information transmitted by EDI and the consequent difficulty of producing evidence of the transaction. Third, there is the difficulty of determining the moment and the place at which the transaction effected by EDI was concluded.[7]

Because EDI is considered essential for economic activities, priority action is given to legislative measures that solve problems such as the aforementioned. Within the European Communities such legal projects are initiated and coordinated under the TEDIS programme. After the finalisation of the first phase of the Tedis programme (1988 to 1989)[8] it was clear that there was still a large diversity and fragmentation of EDI initiatives taken at national level. Hence, the second phase of the programme was launched in the summer of 1991, involving 25 million ECU for a period of three years.[9] The important objectives of the second TEDIS phase in the legal field are: first, to finalise the European EDI agreement, which is to govern the exchange of EDI messages between parties; second, to undertake a thorough legal analysis of media and means of storage and the electronic signatures for EDI messages; and third, to analyse the problems of data protection which could arise with the development of EDI.

---

[6] COM (86) 662, final 1 December, 1986.
[7] See: *The Legal Position of the Member States with Respect to Electronic Data Interchange*, DG XIII, Commission of the European Communities, 1989.
[8] O. J. 191 L 285/35.
[9] O..J. 191 L 208/66.

Besides these objectives, a key issue within TEDIS is the standardisation of EDI messages and techniques.

3. EDI: Standards and Networks

3.1. Standardisation

Speaking of standardisation in relation to EDI, we may generally state that EDI standards are uniform specifications or communication procedures of the structure and format of data as well as the transmission methods of the formatted data. Standards may, however, also apply to certain security procedures and even contract terms. Presently, work is being done under the auspicies of the International Chamber of Commerce to develop standards of legal EDI messages and contract terms. These standards, the so-called LEGMES (LEGal MESage), would contain a set of codes that refer to the most frequently used contract terms of interchange agreements.[10]

I mentioned earlier that the reasons for standardisation are multiple. Consequently, standards may be established for different reasons, by different bodies, having a different status.[11] Generally, the following distinctions are made when speaking about standards:

(1) *Open versus closed*: With closed standards participation in developing and updating is limited to a restricted group of organisations, people, etc, whereas this is open to all with the first-mentioned standard.

(2) *Public versus non-public*: Public standards are those of which the results of the standardisation process are publicly available. With non-public, or private, standards the results are restricted to the closed group that participated in the development of the standard.[12]

(3) *De facto versus official*: The latter, also called formal standards, are those that have been developed by the national and international standardisation institutes. They are both open and public. Contrary to an official standard, a *de facto* standard does not originate from a standardisation institute. It is developed in a private business environment, that is usually closed. De facto standards are, e.g., programmes that have been created initially by a single manufacturer and that in the course of

---

[10] See: Piette-Coudol Th., 'What can EDITERMS's position be among other legal instruments authenticating EDI?', *ICC Document* 460-10/Int. 57.

[11] In this paper I shall not discuss the legal status of standards (binding/non-binding) and their legal character (dynamic/fixed reference).

[12] It has been contended that to speak of a clear distinction between public and non-public (private) standards is misleading, because it would underestimate the closeness of the working relationship between the public and private sectors while setting standards. See: Salter L., *Conceptual Issues in Standards. The Case of Communication and Information Technology Standards* (to be published).

time have become an industry standard (e.g. as a result of its commercial success).

It is important to note that the outcome of a certain standardisation decision may not always be the best solution. With *de facto* standards, the industry may agree on a certain standard because a market leader was successful in using his or her dominant position. Also, the adoption of a standard in a particular field may be just the result of chance events. Why, for example, did the DOS operating system develop into a *de facto* standard operating system for personal computers? Certainly not because it was the best option available. It is more likely, arbitrary occurrences highly influenced the outcome. But also with formal standards the prevailing solution may not always be the best. For within standardisation bodies, the standard accepted for a particular need may be dictated by the various interests that have to be compromised (e.g. regional /national business interests versus European).

At a minimum, however, standards should be transparent, reliable, simple and mostly internationally agreed upon.

3.2. Levels of EDI Standardisation

In looking at the stages of the EDI message's journey we note that standardisation can be established at different levels. Here, I shall discuss the two principal levels: 1) the message level and 2) the communication level.

3.2.1. *The Message Level*

To communicate is to understand. In order to effectively exchange information, people have to use signs, symbols and sounds that are known to them. As with the traditional means of communication, such as speech and writing, it is essential that the EDI trading partners structure their message according to agreed message protocols and that the formatting of the data into logical strings is done on a uniform basis.

Various groups have become involved in message standardisation, or try to influence the standardisation process. Governments, being aware of the economic and political importance of the applications of information technology, are very keen on a close participation in standardisation activities. The initiatives of the European Communities are a prime example in this respect.

Over the past years, message protocols have been developed by various user groups and governmental organisations both on a national and on an international level. Examples of sectoral standards are Swift (used in the banking world), CEFIC (the chemical industry), and Odette (the automobile industry). On a national level, the American X.12 standard established by the U.S. national standards institute, ANSI, is widely known. What is apparently becoming the number one worldwide standard is Edifact (Edi for Administration, Commerce and Transport). The Edifact standard was developed in the Working

Party 4 of the UN Economic Commission for Europe (ECE),[13] in cooperation with the ISO (International Standards Organisation).[14] Sectoral standards such as Swift and Odette claim to adapt to Edifact. Note also that Americans appear to sacrifice their ANSI X.12 standard for Edifact.

3.2.2. *The communication level*

The transmission of the message is carried out by means of computer equipment, software and services including communications services. To take the maximum advantage of the applications and the systems that exchange data, international communication networks, open interfaces and technical conventions are a prerequisite. Thus, the emphasis is on open computing, integration and international standardisation, meaning that suppliers of the communication equipment are forced to integrate and open their systems. The work programme as set out in Annex 1 of the Council Decision of July 22, 1991 establishing the second phase of the Tedis programme calls upon the Community to encourage the use of standardised communication protocols for EDI in underlying services.[15] In this respect mention is made of P-edi (Protocol for EDI), X.400 (1988) and X.500.

Various communication protocols for compatibility and inter-connectivity of networks are already in use. Although standards have been set by particular suppliers, such as IBM (SNA) and Digital (VT-100), the most widely used standards have been developed by the international standardisation institutions. In this respect it is interesting to note that it is the users' business requirements rather than the industry strategies which strongly influence the business policies and developments. Contrary to IT applications such as electronic mail and messaging systems, where decisions are normally taken by providers rather that by users (e.g. DEC's All-in-one or IBM's Office Vision), with EDI users' interests have allied to bring about changes in the market.

Probably the number one data-communication standard is the X-family, developed by the International Telegraph and Telephone Consultative Committee (CCITT), in which various national PPT's cooperate. This standard is based on the ISO seven-layer model (Reference Model for Open Systems Interconnection = OSI Reference Model). The key idea of this model is to create a model for connecting open systems that are independent of the particular hardware and software used. The ISO has produced standards for all seven layers, which have

---

[13] Working Party 4 (WP.4) is the ECE's Working Party on Facilitation of International Trade Procedures.

[14] The members of this non-treaty organisation are the national standards institutes, from over 80 countries.

[15] O.J. 1991 L 208/66.

been published as separate international standards.[16] For example, the X.400, being the seventh layer on OSI Reference Model, is based on the ISO standards for Message Handling networks (DIS10021 and DIS9594). Another standard of the X-family is the X.25, that takes care of the lower layers of the OSI Reference Model. Unlike the X.400, this standard has no mail-box facilities.[17]

4. Networks

With EDI, an order for material can be transmitted over a telecommunication link from one computer to another.

This can be done in different manners. The trading partners may use a point-to point network service, often provided by national telecommunications authorities (PTT's), or they can transmit their message through the facilities of a third party, a Value Added Network (VAN) service.

When looking at the path from sending-partner to recipient-partner, we observe several stages. Generally speaking, after the data relating to the order has been structured by an agreed message standard, the sender's computer transmits the message of the network-service connection point (also named the network-service node). Subsequently, the message is transmitted in the network itself to the recipient's network-service node, after which it is sent to the recipient's computer. Depending on the type of network used, the message will be received immediately by the recipient, or will be stored ('called forward') in his or her network service mailbox. User needs with regard to networks greatly depend on the size of the user-company, financial considerations, service activities and the area of application. To meet the different needs of users a wide range of network types has emerged.[18]

For the purpose of this article I shall separate between competitive, co-

---

[16] The seven layers are: the physical layer (concerned with transmitting raw bits over a communication channel); the data link layer (that sees to transforming a raw transmission facility into a line, appearing free of transmission errors, to the network layer); the network layer (that controls the operation of the subnet); the transport layer (accepts data from the session layer and passes them correctly to the network layer); the session layer (enables users on different machines to establish sessions between them); the presentation layer (that sees to finding a general solution for often requested functions, thus preventing each user from having to individually solve the problem); the application layer (that contains an area of protocols that are commonly needed). See for more details: Tanenbaum A.S., *Computer Networks*, Prentice-Hall, Englewood Cliffs, 1989, pp.14-21.

[17] Meaning that the trading partners have to send and receive the message at the same time. Thus, the data cannot be stored. An example of the X.25 standard is Datanet-1 of the Dutch PTT.

[18] Users may opt for a private or public network, a local area or a wide area network, etc.

operative and public networks.

(1) *Competitive networks*: With this type of network the initiative lies with a big company that requires its suppliers to use EDI. Competitive networks usually work on either a 'power model' or a 'fragmentation (closed) model'. In the first situation, the basis for taking part in the EDI network is force. An example in this respect is the automobile company Chrysler which forced its 3500 suppliers to use EDI. Some hundred companies that did not fulfil this demand were written off as suppliers. Within a 'fragmentation model' (also called 'closed model') a restricted number of companies take part in an EDI network, while excluding others in the branch. An example of a network where users tried to deny access to certain users can be found in the field of computer reservation systems for air-transport services.[19]

(2) *Co-operative networks*: This type of network is established within a certain industry sector or user group to provide a common infrastructure for electronic trading activities. The essential characteristic here is that this network facility is open, meaning that it is accessible to anybody who wants to participate. Hence, co-operative networks are based on a 'participation or open model'. Usually, the decision as to which standard will be applicable may be mutually selected by the parties. An example of such a network is Swift, used in the banking world.

(3) *Public Networks*: This type of network is based on a 'participation model'. The characteristic of public networks is that they are generally accessible. If access and usage conditions (e.g. regarding tariffs or frequencies) are set, they must be objective, transparent and non-discriminatory.[20] Examples of public networks are the networks maintained by the different national PTT's.

5. The Boundaries of Standardisation

As said, the extent of standardisation is determined by various factors, among them legal mechanisms. The creation of common systems of interchanging data and the pressure to conform to, and to use, certain standards may be curtailed by legal mechanisms, such as intellectual property law and competition law.

5.1. Competition Law

Coming to the legal boundaries of standardisation, a first area of attention is

---

[19] Here the denial of access to this system by Sabena to London European resulted in a qualification of abuse of a dominant position, covered by art. 86 E.C. Treaty, *London European* v *Sabena* , O.J. 1988 L 377/47.

[20] See in this respect the 'Council Directive establishing the internal market for telecommunications services through the implementation of open network provisions' of June, 28, 1990 O.J. 1990 L 192/1. The *ONP Directive* is intended to facilitate the access of private companies to public telecommunications networks and services. Also, it aims to achieve harmonisation of technical interfaces and to ban divergencies of tariff principles and usage conditions.

competition law. In case a number of organisations decide to transfer their business transactions through electronic means, several decisions have to be made. It will not come as a surprise that while making these decisions careful consideration should be given to the rules and practices of E.C. competition law. Articles 85 and 86 of the E.C. treaty are of special importance in this respect.

A first business decision to be made is whether to opt for a public, a co-operative or a competitive network. In case the parties decide to use the last, the question arises: what partners will be allowed to participate? At this point, the freedom of the EDI partners to exclude certain companies may be profoundly restricted by the application of the E.C. competition rules and practices. In general we may say that the Commission is anxious to ensure that membership is open to all potential network users. The block exemption for computer reservation systems for air transport services shows that the mere refusal of access to a network is not permitted.[21] In general, non-objective and discriminatory access criteria will certainly raise competition law problems.[22] An example of a situation in which an applicant may nevertheless be denied access to the network is where he or she uses particular hardware and software which is of such an inferior quality that it may be feared that the whole network system will go down.

At this point, it is interesting to draw attention to the Council Directive of 28 June, 1990 on the establishment of the internal market for telecommunications services through the implementation of open network provisions (ONP).[23] The ONP Directive concerns the harmonisation of conditions for open and efficient access to and use of public telecommunications networks and services. Such conditions may include harmonised conditions with regard to: technical interfaces; usage conditions (including frequencies); tariff principles. In case such open network provision conditions are set, they must comply with the following basic principles. They must be: on objective criteria, transparent, published in an appropriate manner, guarantee equality of access and non-discriminatory. Member states may restrict access to the public telecommunications network for the following reasons: the security of the

---

[21] Commission Regulation No. 2672/88 of 26 July, 1988 on the application of Art. 85(3) of the Treaty to certain categories of agreements between undertakings relating to computer reservation systems for air-transport services, O.J. 1988 L 239/13. Compare also: Council Regulation No. 2299/89 of 24 July, 1989, O.J. 1989 L 220/1 and the Commission's Explanatory Note on the EC code of conduct for computer reservation systems. O.J. 1990 C 184/2.

[22] It should be mentioned that the denial of access to certain parties may also lead to a qualification as abuse of a dominant position as covered by Art.86 EC. Treaty. Compare in this respect the *London European* v *Sabena, supra,* note 19.

[23] *Supra,* note 21.

network operations; the maintenance of network integrity; and, in justified cases, for the inter-operability of services and data protection. What may happen is that the ONP generate a certain influence in relationships outside those with public telecommunications services. In other words, ONP are of indirect importance for EDI-relationships between private companies. For, contracting parties may use the ONP as necessary conditions for an adequate functioning of their network. An example is the conditions as regards technical interfaces, and security. There have been situations in the Netherlands where the private parties involved agreed upon a network-service contract that included a reference to the ONP.

Once the parties have decided on the type of network to be used, a second decision relates to what data-communication standard this network should be based upon. It is risky to develop a standard which is out of line with already recognised standards. But if the use of a widely accepted standard is preferred, should the partners adopt one set by a particular supplier (IBM's SNA, Digital VT-100), or is it preferable to opt for a data-communication standard developed by an international standardisation forum (such as the CCITT's X-family)? What if a standard adopted by the parties is officially changed, or modified as a result of a new release or version? What is to happen with future developments and competitive new concepts for communication services? Will the decision whether and when to change to the new standard be made on a mutual basis, or are merely a restricted number of the partners permitted to make this decision? Major users may set standards, but then again, organisations involved with the development and strategy decisions affecting the standard can acquire and maintain a leading edge over the competition. If one or several of these organisations maintains a dominant position in the relevant market, abuse of this position by curtailing competitors' freedom and forcing them to consent to support new standards may lead to an infringement of Article 86 of the E.C. Treaty. The same issues will arise with respect to the decision as to what computer equipment and software the network participants will have to work with.

In conclusion, we may state with respect to the earlier discussed types of networks both Articles 85 and 86 of the E.C. Treaty influenced standardisation in such a manner that, strictly speaking, networks working on either a 'power model' or a 'fragmentation (closed) model' are not allowed.

5.2. Intellectual Property Law

Various issues come to the fore when considering intellectual property right issues in relation to standards. I will concentrate on copyright and discuss the restrictive influence of copyright law on the use of standards.

A first aspect when considering copyright issues in relation to standards, is that strictly speaking certain types of standards no longer exist. The European Software Directive, for instance, bans non-public standards. As mentioned, with non-public standards the results of the standardisation process are restricted to the closed group which participated in the development of the standard. However, the Directive recognises in Article 6 the right to de-compile the program (standard) under certain conditions, even where the developer of the program (standard) has chosen not to reveal to third parties the specification of the standard.[24] Hence, even if a limited group decided not to reveal the standard information to others, certain acts will nevertheless be available to all third parties (public) in case they want to develop (competitive) products that are inter-operable with the standard.

A second aspect is the troublesome position of certain standards under intellectual property law. Specifically, as regards *de facto* standards the question arises as to whether the developers of these standards should acquire a property right. According such a right could establish a legal and factual monopoly on something that has become so widely used that it has become an industry standard. No doubt a leading example of this problem is *Lotus Development Corp.* v *Paperback Software International*, decided by the Massachusetts district court on 28 June 1990.[25] In this case, filed in 1987, the defendant argued that the command structure of menu hierarchy of the Lotus 1-2-3 spreadsheet program had become an industry standard and hence a *de facto* standard. Since the public interest requires that the software industry is able to write interoperable programs which comply with this industry standard, it was claimed to be lawful to copy these standards. Judge Keeton, however, found:

> *'that the more innovative the expression of an idea is, the more important is copyright protection for that expression. By arguing that 1-2-3 is so innovative that it occupied the field and set a **de facto** industry standard, and that, therefore, defendants were free to copy plaintiff's expression, defendants had flipped copyright on its head.'*

Thus the court gave recognition to the fact that even in a case where a program sets a *de facto* industry standard, others are not allowed to copy it for compatibility and standardisation purposes. The opinion that industry leadership and a *de facto* industry standard are of no relevance for the decision as to whether copying is permitted or not, is viewed as very worrying by the cloning industry.

However, in case European courts rule in line with the above Lotus 1-2-3 decision, the troublesome effect of such rulings can be tempered by two possibilities which try to balance innovation and protection. A first balance may be established by the reverse engineering possibility laid down in the European

---

[24] Council Directive of 14 May 1991 on the legal protection of computer programs. O.J. 1991 L 91/250.

[25] Lotus Development Corp. v. Paperback Software International, 740 F Supp. 37, 15 U.S.P.Q.2d, 1517, [1990] (D. Mass. 1990)

Software Directive. As discussed earlier, software developers have access to the information necessary to achieve interoperablility of their independently created program with other programs (*de facto* standards). A second balance may be found in applying the rules and practices of competition law.

Of importance in this respect is the 10 July 1991 judgment of the European Court of First Instance in the *Magill* case.[26] The Court upheld a decision of the European Commission regarding the abuse of U.K. broadcasters' dominant position on the market of radio and television programme listings.[27] Since the radio and television programme listings were protected under British copyright law the broadcasters had a legal as well as factual monopoly over these listings. The Commission had found the refusal of the broadcasters to grant licences for the publication of the listings to be an infringement of E.C. competition law. Consequently, the Commission ordered the broadcasters to make the listings publicly available on a non-discriminatory basis. In its decision the Court held that the Commission had rightfully ordered a compulsory license.

When applied to the information technology industry, the outcome of this decision may act as an important barrier against the abuse of a market position as established by an ownership right to a *de facto* standard. In this respect it is also noteworthy to remember what is said in the Software Directive regarding the relationship between intellectual property rights and competition law. Although the final Directive, contrary to its initial draft,[28] does not contain separate conclusions dealing with this issue, the explanatory memorandum emphasises that the provisions of the Directive are without prejudice to the application of Articles 85 and 86 of the E.C. Treaty. If the dominant supplier refuses to make information available which is necessary for interoperability as defined in the Directive.[29] Also, it is made clear that the rights given under the Directive are without prejudice to Community regulations relating to standardisation in the field of information technology and telecommunication.

---

[26] *Magill TV Guide* v *ITP, BBC and RTE*, July 10,1991 IP/91/668.

[27] *Magill TV Guide* v *ITP, BBC and RTE*, Decision European Commission, O.J. 1989 L78/43.

[28] See: Commission conclusions decided on the occasion of the adoption of the Commission's proposal a Council Directive on the legal protection of computer programs.O.J. 1989 C 91/16: 'under certain circumstances, the exercise of copyright as to the aspects of the program, which other companies need to use in order to write compatible programs, could amount to (...) an abuse (= an abuse of a dominant position - C.P.)'.

[29] In the so-called European IBM case, which did not lead to an official Commission decision, the Commission accused IBM of delaying the access of competitors to certain technical information about the interfaces to System/370. The Commission considered this practice an abuse of a dominant position, contrary to Article 86. IBM responded by promising to publish the necessary information regarding interfaces.

6. The Boundaries of Legal Concepts

The above shows that the use of EDI standards may be curtailed by legal mechanisms. But next to this, we note an influence in the reverse order. The development and use of standards challenges traditional legal concepts. Although these challenges are not necessarily specific to EDI, it is vital to understand them when initiating and supporting standardisation activities.

6.1. Competition Law

As is known, the concept of the Single Market is intended to establish a free flow of persons, goods, services and funds. With respect to EDI services, we noted earlier that in this light the Commission is anxious to ensure that membership is open to all potential network users. E.C. competition law does not permit the mere refusal of access to a network. Also, standardisation agreements which involve several parties may have pro- as well as anti-competitive effects, meaning that such agreements are covered by Article 85(1).

Nevertheless, it appears that standardisation interests sometimes prevail over E.C. competition law principles. Individual exemptions are readily available for standardisation agreements which restrict competition. At the time of writing, no specific decisions have been issued with regard to the position of EDI projects,[30] and EDI standardisation in particular, under EC competition law, case law on joint creation and exploitation of EDI standards. The three Commission decisions given below may prove pertinent.

The first is *X. v Open Group* decision of 15 December 1986, dealing with a common development project based on the use of UNIX.[31] Access to this project was not automatic. The members of the Group decided upon applications for membership, taking into account whether certain access conditions provided for by the members of the Group had been fulfilled. Although in principle this practice might result in a distortion of competition covered by Article 85(1) of the E.C. Treaty, it becomes clear from the Commission's decision that it is willing to accept certain criteria by which membership applications can be judged. One of these criteria is the need for the preservation of a good working relationship between the participants whereby they may expect some quality input of the members. Hence, the Commission tolerated an exemption to its general policy (under Article 85(3)) in the interest of the preservation of the qualitative and quantitative aspects of the joint development of industry

---

[30] The only EDI-related decision in this respect deals with the joint venture Eurolog that was established between Eucom and Digital Equipment BV, with Eucom again being a joint venture between France Télécom and the Deutsche Bundespost Telekom. Eurolog was established to offer value added services. Case no. IV/M.218, Eucom/Digital, *Bull. EG*, 5-1992, 26.

[31] *X. v Open Group*. O.J. 1987 L 35/36.

standards.

As well as *X. v Open Group*, there are two other decisions of the European Commission which provide us with factors relevant to the Commission while determining whether certain agreements or practices between companies in the information technology industry are permitted under competition law, as implemented by the Commission. Both *Olivetti v Canon*[32] and the *Konsortium ECR 900* cases[33] make clear that the following factors (benefits) are of major importance in the decision as to whether an agreement is a candidate for an exemption under Article 85(3):

(1) the advance of technical and economic progress;
(2) the stimulative effect on innovation;
(3) the public benefit (e.g. users benefit from open industrial standards);
(4) the sharing of the financial risks and development costs (individual companies would, due to the huge anticipated financial expenditure refrain from developing the product on their own).

Although these cases do not in themselves warrant that the existence of the above factors will in all situations meet with a positive attitude from the Commission towards granting a negative clearance, they nevertheless seem to provide an expectation that the Commission will rely on the same factors while deciding on joint projects for the development, creation and exploitation of EDI standards. The ratio under the block exemption for computer reservation systems for air-transport services makes equally clear that arguments such as public benefit and financial considerations are decisive in the decision to tolerate certain agreements.[34]

Although individual exemptions are readily available for standardisation agreements which restrict competition, the procedure under Regulation 17/62 is very cumbersome, involving costs, lengthy procedure and uncertainty. To circumvent these problems, a block-exemption for standardisation agreements should be adopted.[35] Although it has been argued that the Commission cannot

---

[32] *Olivetti v Canon*, O.J. 1988 L 52/51. Decision issued on 22 December 1987. The purpose of the cooperation agreement between Olivetti and Canon was to establish a mutual subsidiary which was to develop and produce, among other things, laser printers.

[33] *Konsortium ECR 900*. O.J. 1990 L 228/31. Decision issued on 27 July 1990. The agreement dealt with the creation of a joint venture by three European companies for the development, manufacture and distribution of a pan-European high-capacity and multi-functional digital cellular infrastructure for mobile telecommunications (Groupe Speciale Mobile - GSM system).

[34] *Supra* note 22.

[35] See Duijvenvoorde G. van. Prins C., Schiessl M., 'Linking Competition Law and IT Standardisation. Why the Commission Should Use Regulation' 2821/71.' [1992]

rely on enough experience to issue such a block exemption,[36] the extensive case law in the field of standardisation agreements proves the contrary.[37] The main characteristics of such a regulation should be the following:

(1) participation in a standardisation agreement should under certain circumstances be open to all interested parties. Access to standardisation activities is especially needed when parties are operating within a standardisation body or group. Nevertheless, access to an agreement between two small enterprises would go too far. Restrictions on membership which are indispensable for the achievement of the group, may be justified on fair and equal grounds. An appeal procedure before an independent arbitrator should be provided in case membership has been refused.

(2) the results of the standardisation process must be made publicly available immediately after the adoption of the standard. If intellectual property rights are involved, licences must be granted on a non-discriminatory basis under adequate conditions.

(3) a market share requirement should be established in the interests of SME's. Such a requirement should be analogous to the solution recently proposed in the amendments to the block-exemptions in the field of R&D agreements and in the field of specialisation regulations.

(4) the regular revision of standards is necessary to prevent a standstill of technological innovation. This obligation for such a revision can be established through the limitation of the block-exemption's effective period.[38]

6.2. Intellectual Property Law

Concentrating again on copyright law, it can be said that standardisation affects and challenges this body of law in two respects. First, it is clear that the overall need to interface with other (EDI) products requires an attitude toward the copyright's protective scope which conflicts with traditional copyright thinking. Voices are heard against exclusive rights to certain, in principle, copyrightable products because this may act as an obstacle to innovation. An example of this attitude can be found in defendant's arguments in the earlier discussed *Lotus* case.

In my view it is not sustainable to argue that a supplier whose product holds a sizeable market share must give way to competitors. The fact that a product

---

ECLR, no.5.
[36] See Vollmer A.N., 'Product and Technical Standards under Article 85', [1986] *ECLR*, p.402.
[37] *Supra*, note 36.
[38] *Supra*, note 36.

turns out to be a commercial success to which the market adapts does not by definition imply that the producer must surrender its rights to competitors. Of course the scope of copyright protection influences the process of standardisation. But this does not mean that the need for standardisation and compatibility should be an overriding goal, dismissing traditional rights to protection. The mere fact that customers have grown accustomed to the program's aspects, making certain that, from a technical perspective, arbitrary programming choices are no longer arbitrary from a commercial point of view does not by definition imply that these aspects may no longer be held protective. The issue should be decided by the business strategies, not by limiting the traditional scope of the law. In case there is abuse of position by the holder of the property rights in the standard, competitors can always take action on the basis of competition law regulations and practices.[39]

Second, standardisation not only influences the scope of protection, but also the *contents* of copyright. Traditionally, the copyright system did not provide for the possibility to freely use a work for the creation of another work. However, an additional exception to author's rights was considered necessary to enable the creation of programs that will interoperate with *de facto* standards. Manufacturers are concerned about the market for their product where a popular system of the large industries establishes a *de facto* standard. Although copyright principles dictate that anyone may freely use ideas, principles, and concepts, thus leaving the free flow of information undisturbed, computer programs in object code, contrary to most types of copyrighted works, do not disclose their essentials and ideas on inspection. Thus, it is claimed that standardisation and interoperabilty require an exemption to author's rights permitting reverse engineering. As is known, the European Software Directive followed this line and introduced this new limitation on the traditional contents of copyright. This rule, however, only applies to the European Communities and the seven EFTA (European Free Trade Association) members. Whether or not a reverse engineering provision will be accepted on a worldwide basis remains to be seen. Proposals have been made to include this rule within the framework of the Berne Convention. The Memorandum prepared for the November 1991 meeting of the Committee of Experts on a possible Protocol to the Berne convention proposed the adoption of a reverse engineering right. [40]

However, discussions during the November meeting showed widely differing opinions. While a number of delegations suggested that the provision to be included in the Protocol should be as much in harmony with the E.C. Directive,

---

[39] Compare the earlier discussed *Magill TV Guide* case, *supra* notes 26 and 27.
[40] Committee of Experts on a possible protocol to the Berne Convention for the protection of literary and artistic works. First Session, Geneva, 4 - 8 November 1991, Doc, nr. 7004D/CPL/0459D

other delegations, particularly the U.S. delegation, highly opposed the proposal to establish a worldwide rule that allows free decompilation.

Apparently this view is part of a campaign launched by the U.S. organisation CBEMA (Computer and Business Equipment Manufacturers Association), backed by several large U.S. software companies (IBM and Digital), in order to 'isolate Europe' as regards reverse engineering. Now that the U.S. companies have lost the reverse engineering battle on the European continent they are trying to prevent this rule from being introduced on a worldwide scale. It is no surprise that the delegations at the World Intellectual Property Organisation meeting could not agree on the reverse engineering subject (as well as on the other issues relating to the protection of computer programs). Thus, matters relating to this subject were postponed for possible later consideration by the WIPO Committee.[41] In the meantime, the U.S. companies continue their anti-reverse engineering campaign, which in the end is likely to influence the pace of EDI standardisation.

At this point it is finally interesting to mention that in the field of standardisation and intellectual property rights, major problems will arise when it comes to the question of the extent to which a company's right to a patent or copyright can be overridden in the public interest. Among the organisations affected by this matter is the European Telecommunications Standards Institute (ETSI). ETSI published in March 1993 its long-awaited policy on resolving potential conflicts between standardisation and the rights of intellectual property owners. A highly criticised 1992 draft of this 'Intellectual Property Rights Policy and Undertaking' waived copyright in standards and introduced compulsory licensing of patents in return for an equitable remuneration. After the European Commission had taken a critical approach towards this proposed policy, ETSI abandoned the compulsory licensing approach in the final (March 1993) version of the Policy. Various provisions of the final text, however, testify to the fact that ETSI still continues to pursue its strategy of enhancing the effectiveness of standardisation at the cost of the relevant intellectual property rights. Also, ETSI's strategy raises doubts as to their compatibility with competition law principles.[42]

7. Conclusion

From the topics discussed above, EDI standardisation raises other legal issues. For instance, should the liability of the standardisation institutes be dealt with in

---

[41] World Intellectual Property Organisation, Doc. BCP/CE/1/4. 19 November 1991, pp. 12-14.
[42] See Prins, C and Schiessl, M, (1993) 'The New European Telecommunications Standards Institute Policy: Conflicts Between Standardisation and Intellectual Property Rights', 8 *EIPR*.

case the use of an official standard leads to losses? Does the use of standards, or the reference to standards in a contract, influence the rights and obligations of the contracting partners? What is the position of standards with respect to products liability and services liability? All these questions are worth further consideration.

In this paper I have restricted the discussion to only a few competition law and copyright law aspects of standardisation. We noted that both these legal rules influence the boundaries of standardisation. Competition law does not allow the use of certain types of networks in the strict sense of their meaning (power and participation models). Further, a newly introduced copyright provision bans non-public standards under certain conditions. But other boundaries are challenged as well. The need for standardisation affects certain legal concepts. Examples of this are the introduction of a reverse engineering possibility (thus restricting author's exclusive copyrights) and the proposed block exemption for standardisation agreements.

The boundaries of space only permitted tentative steps in examining both the above mentioned trends. Further study will certainly reveal other considerations to be taken into account and determine how far the path to standardisation should, and can be followed. Nevertheless, I hope to have shown that careful analysis is necessary as to what EDI standardisation is about, how far it must be taken, and what effects it may have on traditional legal concepts.

Part II
ISSUES IN COMMERCIAL LAW

4
Maria-Chiara Malaguti
Liability for Fraud and Mistake in Electronic Transfers of Funds

1. Introduction

The application of electronic innovations in the banking sector has had a number of significant and far reaching legal consequences. In particular, the introduction of electronic transfer mechanisms in the payments system raises troublesome and challenging legal issues. Payments may be totally or partially processed through electronic means. By means of check truncation, payment data carried on a check may be transmitted by banks through electronic networks. Wire transfers may be ordered or executed electronically. Deposits or withdrawals of money may be carried out by customers through automated teller machines (ATMs). Finally, electronic points of sale (POSs) may permit direct transfers from the buyer's account to the seller's account.[1]

These several kinds of transfers are often described collectively as electronic fund transfers (EFTs). The main feature distinguishing EFT's from paper instrument payments is the elimination of any element of negotiability, if transfers concerning bills of exchange and debit transfer instructions are excluded. Aside from this common feature, there are a number of substantial differences: retail wire transfers (such as ATMs or POSs) raise issues of consumer protection which do not arise in corporate wire transfers. This term includes large value transfers of funds ordered by companies rather than consumers. Corporate wire transfers undertaken by banks can be effected through a normal chain of bank transfers or settled directly through an organisation that effects common settlement on a daily basis. In fact, these networks do not always offer the same kind of service. Not all of them offer a settlement procedure (as Swift, for international payments) and those that do, may effect settlement either on a bilateral basis (as in Fedwire in the USA) or on a multilateral basis (as in CHIPS in the USA).[2]

---

[1] For a complete overview on electronic innovations in payment systems, see Hitachi Research Institute, *Payment Systems - Strategic Choices for the Future*, F.I.A. Financial Publishing Co., Tokyo, 1993

[2] For a description of the possible ways to clear and settle inter-bank transfers, see C. Borio, D. Russo and P. Vanden Bergh, 'Payments Systems Arrangements and Related

The kind of transfer that starts with a payment order and is effected through a wire transfer is now recognised in the United States as a unique method of payment among EFT's.[3] Its fundamental characteristic is that it is a pay order, meaning that it starts from the debtor (the Sender), who gives the bank the order to execute the payment. The creditor (the Beneficiary) receives funds through the banking system along with the order. Such transfers are clearly differentiated from draw orders, like cheques or credit cards, where the payer orders a transfer that does not occur simultaneously. In the former situation, the electronic transfer not only communicates the order, but also effects the transfer automatically.[4]

The application of electronic innovations in the banking sector has had a number of significant and far reaching legal consequences. In particular, the introduction of electronic transfer mechanisms in the payments system raises troublesome and challenging legal issues. Payments may be totally or partaially processed through electronic means. By means of check truncation, payment data carried on a check may be transmitted by banks through electronic networks. Wire transfers may be ordered or executed electronically. Deposits or withdrawals of money may be carried out by customers through automated teller machines (ATMs). Finally, electronic points of sale (POSs) may permit direct transfers from the buyer's acount to the seller's account.[5]

The statutory law regulating EFTs remains relatively limited. None of the statutes that have been adopted to regulate this area refer expressly to electronic transfers. There is no rule that applies only to electronic transfers (if consumer protection issues are excluded). However, it is commonly recognised that Article 4A of the U.S. Uniform Commercial Code (UCC) was drafted to regulate electronic wire transfers, and that the United Commission for

---

Policy Issues: A Cross-Country Comparison', *Proceedings of the Workshop on Payment System Issues in the Perspective of European Monetary Unification*, Bank of Italy Publications, November 1991

[3] 'There is some resemblance between payments made by wire transfer and payments made by other means such as paper-based checks and credit cards or electronically based computer payments, but there are also many differences. Article 4A [of the U.S. Uniform Commercial Code] excludes from its coverage these other payment mechanisms. Article 4A follows a policy of treating the transaction that it covers - a funds transfer - as a unique method of payment that is governed by unique principles of law that address the operational and policy issues presented by this kind of payment', Official Prefatory Note, Article 4A-101(1).

[4] H. Scott, (1993), 'Corporate Wire Transfers and Uniform Payment Code', 83 *Colombia Law Review*, p. 1664.

[5] For a complete overview on electronic innovations in payment systems, see Hitachi Research Institute, (1993), *Payment systems - Strategic Choices for the Future*, F.I.A., Financial Publishing Co., Tokyo.

International Trade Law (UNCITRAL) Model Law approved on 15 May 1992 is designed to regulate in principle international electronic transfers.[6]

Article 4A is dedicated to *fund transfers*, while the UNCITRAL Model Law is only concerned with international *credit transfers*. This distinction has been justified by the consideration that a general law must regulate all aspects of a single fund transfer, whether electronic or non-electronic. The fact that a transfer is electronically executed does not seem to have any recognised relevance under the existing and proposed statutes.[7] However, it appears clear from the analysis of these laws that some of their rules were intended to concern EFTs, and indeed can be justified only in the light of electronic transfers.

The determination of whether electronic fund transfers could be considered to be an autonomus payment is beyond the scope of this chapter. In order to conform to existing bodies of law, thsi paper will deal with fund transfers, meaning the execution of the whole chain of operations needed to make a payment final, whether retail wire transfers or corporate wire transfers, the single payment order being either electronic or non-electronic (see Figure 1). However, since the scope of this chapter is to identify how liability for fraud and mistake are allocated when electronic means are employed, I shall focus specifically upon electronic transfers.

The fact that this method of payment is generally executed through electronic means and its execution is potentially instantaneous makes the failure to complete the transfer and the consequential liability for payments of major importance. Failure may occur, in particular, because of mistake or fraud.[8] The

---

[6] See *infra*.

[7] In fact, Article 4A was extended to funds transfers under the factual assumption that only a very few transfers are completely executed via electronic means: 'In most cases, the payment order of each bank to the next bank in the chain is transmitted eletronically, and often the payment order of X to its bank is also transmitted electronically, but the means of transmission does not have any legal significance. A payment order may be transmitted by any means, and in some cases the payment order is transmitted by a slow means such as first class mail. To reflect this fact, the broader term 'funds transfer' rather than the narrower term 'wire transfer' is used in Articlae 4A to describe the overall payment transaction', Official Prefatory Note, Article 4A - 101 (1). However, the UCC already regulates collection and processing on paper based transfers at its Article 4. Therefore, Article 4A can still be considered to regulate electronic funds transfers as an autonomous instrument of payment.

[8] Credit risk is also involved in the execution of transfers. Banks normally participate in netting schemes (either bilateral or multilateral) which permit settlement at discrete times. In such a way, the receiving bank is informed of the transfer at real time, but receives the settlement only at discrete time and only for the net position. Especially in cases of wholesale transfers, the receiving bank makes the sum available to the client since it receives information about the transfer, while it is exposed to credit risk due to

legal issues raised by failure in EFTs relating to fraud and mistake are discussed with reference to the rules of existing statutory law. In so doing, I will seek to compare European domestic laws (none expressly regulating fund transfers), and agreements commonly in force between banks and clients with the rules implemented by Article 4A of the UCC and the UNCITRAL Model Law Rules (see Appendix).

2. Overview of Existing Statutory Law on Fund Transfers

In the USA, the challenges created by the introduction of electronic means of payment led Congress to introduce regulatory legislation. Since Article 4 of the UCC did not explicitly concern paperless transfers, in 1978 Congress enacted the Electronic Fund Transfers Act (EFTA), in order to protect consumers. EFTA covers POSs, ATMs and transfers by telephones, but excludes corporate wire transfers.[9]

In 1989, in order to remedy this situation, the National Conference of Commissioners on Uniform State Laws produced a draft of Article 4A to be added to the UCC, concerning fund transfers (Article 4A). Article 4A covers only credit transfers and excludes transfers to or from a consumer account. By 23 October, 1992, Article 4A had been adopted in 12 U.S. States.[10]

The approach in European countries has been different: no specific legislation covers EFTs. The civil law systems of Europe have led judges and academic commentators to consider the new means of payment under existing legal principles.[11] Wire transfers have consequently been subjected to uncertain juridical principles seeking to ascertain whether they are contracts and, if so, what kind of contracts they are. The majority of courts and commentators have found them to be mandates (orders to pay).

The same issues arise in the kinds of agreements banks enter into with their clients. In the United States, not only do banks often have standard contracts for wire transfer services, but large corporations also elaborate their own agreements to propose to banks. In Europe, most agreements are general service contracts not expressly drafted with EFTs in mind, though more modern

---

the possible insolvency of the counterparty at the time of settlement. When the banks participate in multilateral netting schemes, they also bear a so-called *'systemic risk'*, due to their general exposure to credit risk which can also be caused by banks with which the single bank has not directly dealt.

[9] EFTA, 903 (6)

[10] See 'Symposium: Revised UCC Article 3 & 4 and New Article 4A', *Alabama Law Review*, Vol. 42, Winter 1991.

[11] For an analysis of electronic transfers in Italy, see E. Giannantonio, 'Trasferimenti Elettronici dei Fondi e Autonomia Privata', *Giuffrè*, 1986; for France, see M. Vasseur, 'Le Paiement Electronique. Aspects Juridiques', *La Senaine Juridique*, 1985, p. 3206.

standard contracts are used in Germany and France. This issue must be taken into account, since the lack of exhaustive legislation on the matter has meant that most issues have been resolved by private agreement. This issue is especially important in international transactions, where the application of different legal principles may result in different and incompatible solutions.[12]

In 1986, a Working Group on International Payments was established by the United Nations Commission for UNCITRAL to elaborate a model law for international EFTs. A final draft, extended to international credit transfers, was adopted on 15 May 1992 (the Model Law).[13] Rather than taking the form of a convention, The Model Law is addressed to legislative bodies in the hope that national statutory laws will be adopted. The Model Law, while limited to international transfers, represents the first attempt to harmonise domestic rules on EFTs. Like Article 4A, it excludes consumer protection issues from its scope.[14]

Article 4A and the Model Law are for the time being the only statutes intended to regulate (even if not limited to) EFTs. On 24 September, 1990, the EC Commission published a discussion paper on *Making Payments in the Internal Market* (the 'Paper'). A section of the 'paper' deals with EFTs. Although the 'paper' was deemed to be only a first document to open a debate on the issue at European level, it provoked a great deal of comment and led the Commission to institute two working groups charged with identifying and solving the major legal issues arising in cross-border payments. The two advisory groups reported to the Commission for the first time in February 1992. The Commission subsequently produced its second report, entitled *Easier Cross-Border Payments: Breaking Down the Barriers*. The report is meant to be a working programme for improving cross-border payment systems and will lead to new comments and working projects, included in the field of EFTs.

Following the adoption of the Model Law, the EC Comission also formed a working party to evaluate the possibility of a draft law for wire transfers for European Member States. This working paraty should reach some conclusions by the end of 1993 concerning whether a binding community measure should be issued and what should, most properly, be its scope, which some would extend to debit transfers. However, severe opposition exists on the part of scholars of sveral Member States to adopt domestic provisions similar to those adopted under the Model Law. Also, in case of implementaation of a binding measure of

---

[12] Dobbins, Gottlieb and Grace, *'Wire Transfer Customer Agreements'*, 1985.

[13] See E. Bergsten, 'UNCITRAL Model Law on International Credit Transfers', *Journal of International Business Law*, No 7, 1991, p. 276.

[14] Therefore, the Model Law has a wider scope than Article 4A, since it also applies to retail wire transfers, while not derogating to existing domestic consumer protection acts.

wire transfers, its content may strongly devate from ecisting bodies lf law.[15]

Interest in Europe has been renewed with respect to the issue of payments in other institutions. Electronically executed transfers receive special attention, both from commentators and from regulatory bodies (such as central banks). It is, therefore, to be expected that new statutes on EFTs will be developed in Europe, providing considerable scope for contributions from lawyers and bankers alike.

3. Mistake

Although EFTs are designed to improve the speed and safety of transactions, some risks of delay and mistake remain. The use of automated data processors, where human involvement is reduced, involves certain risks.

3.1. The Economics of Mistake

The most obvious kind of mistake consists of erroneous transmissions of orders by clients. After such an order is given, data are processed through machines which verify the order on the basis of memorised instructions. Several different types of accident may occur at either of these stages. Since humans check EFTs infrequently, it is often difficult to identify the person who committed the original mistake in the process of the transfer, or indeed the exact nature of the mistake itself. Moreover by the time the mistake is discovered, the payment may already have been effected. Finally, an interruption of communication facilities may occur which can delay or avoid the transfer.

When negligence resulting in a delay or failure to transfer an order is easily detected, the liability for resulting damages may easily be attributed to the wrongdoer. Frequently, however, it is difficult to identify negligent behaviour. Thus, the first question to ask before analysing the issue of liability for mistakes in wire transfer is: who should bear the risk of loss?.

One of the most common approaches of economic analysis in the United States, frequently applied to torts, places the risk on the 'Best Avoider' - the party which is best able to avoid the risk should bear the loss, when it occurs.[16]

---

[15] M. Vasseur, 'Les Principaux Articles De La Loi-type De La Cnudci Sur Les Virements Internationaux Et Leur Influence Sur Les Travaux De La Commission De Bruxelles Concernant Les Paiements Transfrontaliers', *International Business Law Journal*, No 2, 1993, p. 155.

[16] G. Calabresi, 1970, *The Costs of Accidents: A Legal and Economic Analysis*, New Haven, Yale University Press. Another Approach (also described by G. Calabresi) consists of the *loss spreading approach* which seeks to minimize costs to each party by spreading losses as widely as possible. The selection of this approach instead of the *best avoider* approach would, of course, modify the allocation of liability among operators see D. Menge, 1990, 'Legal and Regulatory Reform in Electronic Payments: an Evaluation of Payment Finality Rules', in *The US Payment System: Efficiency, Risk*

In this way, the possibility of bearing the loss works as an incentive to reduce the risk. Since the bank chooses the means for its services, it might be suggested that it should in principle bear the risk of loss.

Should a bank, however, bear any kind of loss for any reason? When the error arises in the transmission of the order by the customer, he or she is usually informed of the necessity of respecting procedures. Moreover the bank is not usually informed of the content of the message, nor the reason for the payment. Thus, it cannot foresee the damages that might occur in case of failure or mistake. This means that, at least when the mistake consists of misspelling data, it may be more efficient to place the risk of loss on the customer.

Since both parties must have the incentive to employ electronic means correctly, however, another approach would be to share the loss between the parties. Such an outcome often happens by agreement: the bank and the client can define the standards of care requested from the bank and in this way divide the risk of loss by reference to these standards. Again, parties can agree on different levels of security procedures and allocate the risk commensurate with more or less costly procedures, which the client has the opportunity to choose.

3.2. Private Agreements

As to the legal framework on liability in fund transfers, the first question concerns the duties that the bank owes to its client while providing services. In the United States, under the UCC, the bank is under a duty to the client to effect proper payment (4-401). While effecting payments, it is under the duty of the ordinary care (4-202;4-212). The bank is, however, not liable for events beyond its control: in case of events that could not be foreseen, the bank is discharged of all liability, but it bears the burden of proving that it exercised due care under the circumstances.

The most common causes in standard bank contracts in the United States detail the procedures and controls that the client must follow in making transfers and discharge the bank for responsibility of losses beyond its duty of ordinary care, including everything beyond its reasonable control. Ordinary care is presumed when the bank follows the procedures stated in the contract. Moreover, where both the client and the bank are negligent in following these procedures, the client's negligence totally discharges the bank from its own lack of ordinary care. Until recently, that is before the adoption of Article 4A of the UCC, the only law applicable to EFTs in the United States was to be deduced form the above-mentioned general rules contained in the UCC on the duty of care, which in fact allows banks to determine by agreement the standard of care applicable and transfer the risk to the client within the limits of reasonableness.

---

and the Role of the Federal Reserve, ed. by B. Humphrey, Kluwer Academic Publishers, p. 145.

US courts have often tried to enlarge the boundaries of the standard of care required of banks in the supply and control of the electronic system. The result has been a general trend towards a heightened duty of compliance on the part of the bank.

In Europe, the same kind of causes can be found in agreement covering wire transfers. These clauses are very often criticized by civil law courts for their potential incompatibility with the spirit of the applicable codes. In several European countries, the codified rules on the allocation of liability and duty of care do not differ substantially from those stated in the UCC. Yet courts have often affirmed the underlying principle in most civil law codes that an enterprise must bear losses not attributable to the negligence of any particular party, assuming the risk inherent in the activity it exercises. An agent offering services is a free *entrepreneur*. As a result, banks must in principle be considered liable when executing their mandates, if they do not execute orders correctly, regardless of the cause of the failure.

This presumption does not prohibit private parties from signing contracts discharging the bank, even if courts often strongly limit their validity to partial discharge. Although in effect the agent of a mandate has to assume the risk of its own activities, the freedom of private agreement with respect to the allocation of loss must be respected. The only limit imposed on such freedom may consist in the untransferability of risk of loss arising from gross negligence of intentional wrongdoing.

In summary, it can be said that in Europe there is a general presumption that a bank is liable for the consequences of its own negligence in affecting EFTs, but this liability can usually be limited through private agreement. As in the United States, the fairness of clauses limiting the bank's liability is often discussed, although an overview of the approaches of different European courts provides no certain or clear conclusions. It must nevertheless be noted that, notwithstanding possible judicial trends towards a heightening of banks' duty of care, the clauses commonly used in wire transfers allocate a significant part of the risk to the client. This occurs especially through the allocation of the burden of proof of negligence to the client. Since the real issue in the case of mistake in EFTs is in fact the difficulty of identifying the wrongdoer, allocating the burden of proof in practice has the same effect as allocating risk.

3.3. Article 4A of the UCC

With respect to the existence of security procedures, Article 4A seeks to favour their implementation as much as possible and provides for an elaborate structure concerning mistake. It considers separately the possibility of erroneous or duplicate payment orders and the possibility of erroneous execution of payment orders.

In the case of erroneous payment orders, Article 4A-205 applies. This article only concerns cases in which the bank has installed commercially reasonable security procedures. When no security procedures are installed, the general principles of duty of care apply. By contrast, under Article 4A-205, the Sender can rely on the liability of the bank only if it is able to prove that the mistake could have been avoided under the existing security procedures. The Sender must then prove the bank's lack of compliance with the procedures and its own compliance.

This rule does not modify the usual allocation of risk in fact effected through agreements. An interesting issue is, however, regulated in Article 4A-202(c), which deals with the concept of 'commercial reasonableness of a security'. This concept must be evaluated on the basis of the 'wishes of the customer expressed to the bank', the 'circumstances of the customer known to the bank', including size, type and frequency of payment orders, 'alternative security procedures offered to the customer, and security procedures in general used by customers and receiving banks similarly situated'.

Subsection (c) of 4A-202 clearly reflects a common practice in the United States; the bank installs different levels of security which vary considerably depending on the price of the services. It is up to the client to choose the security service it prefers. In this case, the client has to assume the risk of its choice. Since corporate wire transfers do not concern consumers, there is no inequality of bargaining power involved in the choice of security system, and agreement is supposed to be the best manner of allocating risk. This solution works as an incentive for both parties: the bank is stimulated to offer better security systems in order to be more competitive in the wire transfer services offered. The client is given an incentive to consider the level of damages that would be incurred in the event of failure and to plan the consequent level of fees that he or she is ready to pay to insure the transfer.

If the error is not in the order, but in its execution, the bank is held liable for its failure, unless it shows the absence of negligence. In this respect, Article 4A does not allow for modification by agreement.

The most significant change introduced by Article 4A to the present contractual allocation of losses is the separation of the two events of erroneous order and erroneous execution. In the first situation, the risk is in principle on the customer, who must pay attention to the order and weigh the security procedures necessary. In the second case, the bank bears the risk of loss, unless it shows an objective inability to foresee the event, and unless the Sender fails to exercise ordinary care in reporting the erroneous execution.[17] It is thus motivated to control and carefully maintain its EFT procedures. It must also be noted that, under Article 4A, the bank is not obliged to accept an order. It can always refuse

---

[17] For this aspect, see section 4 on Fraud.

to execute the order, and for any reason. When accepted, the order must be properly executed, i.e. with due care and in accordance with the indications given by the Sender. The allocation of losses among the members of the banking network systems is not covered by Article 4A. This matter is usually regulated by internal rules (if at all).

3.4. Model Law

Under Article 5(5) of Model Law, the Sender bears the risk of mistakes in the order, unless i) bank and client agreed upon a procedure for detecting erroneous transmission and ii) the correct use of the system by the bank would have permitted it to detect the mistake. The burden of proof is on the Sender.

The rule in Article 5(5) of the Model Law is very general. It neither defines a security system nor requires that such a system be 'commercially reasonable'. These elements are supposedly dealt with by domestic laws.[18]

Under Article 8, the receiving bank must properly execute the order and is liable for failure to execute it.

In substance, where a security system has been implemented, the two regulations do not differ. However, since the rules on Article 4a liability apply to each relationship in transfer chain, the result is that, for the purpose of allocation of liability, each sending bank is deemed to be a Sender and each receiving bank is under a duty to comply with the order. By contrast, the Model Law differentiates between the original sender and the intermediary banks and imposes a general duty of assistance that obliges each receiving bank to assist the originator in completing the transfer (Article 13). There is no sanction for failure to observe the duty of assistance. In the case of non-completion of the transfer, banks retain the right to be refunded (the 'money back guarantee', Article 14), so that the transfer goes back to the originator through the same chain. While the party which bears the loss is directly opposed to the one which suffered it under Article 4A, under the Model Law, the money-back guarantee leaves the original Sender to deal with any wrongdoer.

4. Fraud

Besides the risks involved in making mistakes, banks which effect orders of payment are exposed to the risk of unauthorised transfers. A Sender is bound by the transfer it makes, but if the bank executes a transfer which was not sent by the presumed Sender, the bank cannot debit the Sender's account.

4.1. The Economies of Unauthorised Transfers

Spurious payment orders can occur in several cases: the sender has never trans-

---

[18] Note that the Model Law applies to all credit transfers, either corporate or retail wire transfers. The observations in relation to the choice of security systems under Article 4A cannot apply here.

mitted an order, or someone else may fraudulently have altered the order actually transmitted. Alternatively, the bank may receive an authorised order to revoke a previous instruction, the latter order not in fact being sent by the Sender. In all these events, the bank effects an order that the client does not intend. On the other hand, the bank may not have been able to recognise the alteration, even though it met the required standards of care in verifying and processing the order.

Because of the difficulty in recognising the alterations, and the fact that a great number of operations involved in the process of verifying the Sender's authorization occur without human control, it might once again be difficult to recognise negligent behaviour by one of the parties. Moreover, both parties might have reasonably followed all the necessary procedures to avoid the transmission of spurious orders.

Once again, the question is who should bear the risk of loss? Both courts and commentators in Europe have always preferred to presume that in these circumstances responsibility must fall on the bank. Since the bank installs the system and offers the service, it has to bear the risk of failure. Since at least in corporate wire transfers both the parties are enterprises, however, it may be reasonably argued that in this event the sending firm has to assume the risk of its own message.

In Europe, the bank's responsibility is generally related to the above-mentioned concept of mandate. In order to be valid under European civil codes, a mandate must normally be authorised. If the mandator is able to show the lack of authorization, the agent is held liable and the bank should bear any loss. Even applying this principle, it can be argued that the elements of an 'apparent mandate' may be present in certain cases. When the agent is able to show that the circumstances indicate that authorization exists, the agent is discharged from liability. As for an authorised order of payment, the bank could demonstrate that its control procedures did not suggest the presence of any alteration. This approach has not generally been followed by European courts.

At the other extreme, the client could be held totally liable for any misuse of the means of transmission under the theory that he or she is the 'best avoider' of losses in the case of unauthorised order. However, it has been demonstrated by numerous famous cases of fraud that it is not always the access code which is manipulated.

4.2. Private Agreements

All clauses commonly in use for bank-to-client agreements indicate that bank and client usually share responsibility for fraud: the client is liable for any unauthorised order for breach of security rules of misuse of its secret code by its agents or representatives, while the bank is supposed to be liable for alteration by its employees. However, the bank is usually discharged from any responsibility for unauthorised orders once it has complied with the stated procedures and no liability can be attributed to any of its employees. As a result, the client in fact bears any loss other than losses clearly proved to have been caused by fraud of the bank's employees.

It has often been suggested that these clauses are incompatible with European civil codes because they usually state that the bank's records concerning the payment orders received are presumed to be correct and have evidentiary value. While the courts usually assume that limitations on types of evidence are permissible, judges are generally required at least to verify the level of security at which these records are stored.

Moreover, these clauses often limit the period of time during which a client may challenge his or her bank's records. With respect to time restraints, some clarifications must be made. The bank usually sends statements of account to its clients on a regular basis. The clients have the duty to communicate discrepancies or objections within a certain time period. Despite some criticism from commentators, courts usually consider such clauses, limiting the times during which a client can bring an action as legitimate, at least so long as the client is not totally deprived of its right to challenge.

Beyond the issue of time limit constraints, doubts may also arise concerning the legitimacy of these clauses to the extent they purport to discharge a bank from *any* liability. *Ex post* negligence by the client frequently discharges the bank from its own negligence. Article 4-406 of the UCC states that if the bank can establish that the customer did not respect its duty to report an unauthorised signature, it is precluded from opposing the lack of authenticity of the signature. The client can still show lack of ordinary care by the bank, and if both parties are negligent, the bank ultimately bears the risk. However it would be in practice very difficult for the client to prove the bank's negligence.

In fund transfers, on the other hand, agreements often provide that a client has no right to challenge the bank's lack of ordinary care. This means that negligence in the verification of the statements of account can prevent the client from action even if it was totally diligent during the transmission of the order.

From the point of view of the best allocation of the risk of loss, the complete assumption of liability by the client when it fails to check its statements of accounts on a timely basis cannot be justified in order to provide an incentive for the parties to *prevent* the risk, since the client discovers the fraud only after it has happened.

4.3. Article 4A

Article 4A tries to resolve this issue by distinguishing between cases of fraud in which security procedures have been followed and those in which no such procedures have been followed. When no security system is implemented, the bank bears the risk of loss (4A-202(a)).

When security procedures are implemented, the Sender can recover only after the Court has found that the security system was not 'commercially reasonable'. Once the Court has judged a system to be 'commercially reasonable', the bank has the burden of proving that it complied with it. Therefore, while in the event of erroneous transmission of an order the client has the burden of proving that the bank did not comply with the security procedures, the burden of proof is on the bank when unauthorised payments can be demonstrated. As we have seen, the allocation of risk on the basis of 'commercial reasonableness' in subsection (c) of Article 4A-202 states that the reasonableness of the security procedures depends on the choice made by the client.

Under Article 4A, the Sender also has the duty to report unauthorised or erroneous payment orders. Article 4A-202 applies only to cases of unauthorised payment orders which the client is not obliged to pay. As mentioned above, this situation can arise where the bank is held negligent in complying with its security procedures, but the client's lack of timely notification absolves it of liability.

In this situation, when the bank has in good faith honoured several subsequent unauthorised orders, the client might be held liable for any order subsequent to the reception of the statement which could have avoided such further fraudulent orders through a timely notification by the client (4A-202). Although in principle the bank is still responsible for unauthorised orders in this situation, this gives the client the incentive to constantly verify his or her financial transactions, without bearing the full risk of orders diligently sent.

4.4. Model Law

Article 5 of the Model Law enunciates principles similar to those of article 4A. In principle, the Sender is liable only for orders sent by it. However, if an authentication procedure other than a mere comparison on signatures is implemented, the Sender is bound if (i) the procedure was commercially reasonable and (ii) the bank complied with it. Therefore, once the bank is able to demonstrate its compliance with the procedure, the Sender bears the loss.

In return, if the Sender is able to demonstrate that the fraud was perpetrated by someone connected with the bank, it is discharged, unless the bank can demonstrate that the fraud resulted from an act of someone in connection with the sender. The most important feature of this mechanism of allocation of proof, is that, in case no one is able to identify the wrongdoer, the burden of loss will be allocated on the basis of the bank's compliance with the authorisation system, and in the end to the Sender if the bank can show its own compliance.

5. Conclusions

The fundamental policy differences adopted between the two sets of rules established to deal with mistake and fraud, common to the Model Law and

Article 4A, may be clearly identified at this stage. In the case of mistake, each party is responsible for its own action. In cases when the wrongdoer cannot be identified, the loss is allocated according to the principles of the 'best avoider' theory, which allocates the loss on the basis of the parties' effective opportunities to avoid the loss. In the case of fraud, however, the action of the third party is decisive. Bank and Sender have no direct power to avoid fraud, except for the implementation of very sophisticated authorisation systems. Both UCC and the Model Law then allocate the loss in principle to the bank. In this way, banks are encouraged to implement high standard systems of verification. Of course, the real issue at this stage will be what standards the courts will consider to be 'commercially reasonable'.

Except for the above-mentioned regulations, the legal framework regulating EFTs today often appears confused and likely to create uncertainty for network users. Moreover, legal principles applied to traditional means of payment cannot satisfactorily solve all issues raised by EFTs.

An overview of these two issues arising in connection with EFTs suggests that in electronic transfers the strength of the traditional connection between negligent behaviour and consequent liability is tempered. It is in fact often difficult to allocate responsibility or liability in the event of a failed EFT where both parties have been diligent in the discharge of their respective duties.

Two solutions exist. On the one hand, courts usually allocate this risk through a flexible interpretation of the boundaries of standards of duty of care that the bank must meet. This solution is a strong guarantee of the selection of reasonable standards, whilst giving the parties legitimate freedom to regulate the issue by agreement.

This approach does not resolve the real substance of the problem, however, since the risk of unreasonableness in the allocation of risk does not rest only on the standards of care applied, but also on the allocation of the burden of proof between parties. As long as the burden of proof is in principle on the client, any broad standard of care will not protect it.

On the other hand, the solution underlying Article 4A, relating to the standards of ordinary care to security systems, can be more helpful. A party is discharged from liability when it can show that it complied with the procedures agreed upon.

In this case two assumptions must be made. First, the client must be granted the choice of selecting a security procedure from the range offered by the bank. Once it has made this conscious choice, it must then bear the risk it has knowingly assumed. Second, in the case of absence of security procedures, the liability of the bank must be presumed since the use of such systems can be considered usual practice for banks. Moreover, when clauses providing that banks are presumed to exercise ordinary care are assumed to be legally binding, the courts must be free to verify the economic reasonableness of the security system.

The choice of this general policy does not eliminate the issue of the burden of proof as a key element of an efficient allocation. Leaving the parties totally free to shift the burden of proof could result in an inefficient outcome. Even if they have equivalent negotiation powers, in theory, the previous analysis has demonstrated that the actual burden of proof is not equally distributed.

Accordingly, a legislative act establishing the framework of this matter must be strongly supported. The presence of comprehensive legislation could also avoid the clearly inefficient outcome resulting from the coexistence of bank-client and bank-to-bank agreements, in particular with respect to the negligence of intermediary banks.

Finally, it is surely time for Europe, where EFTs are dealt with in the same way as traditional methods of payment transfer, to develop legislation which is capable of addressing the complex issues involved, and to enable orders of payment to receive consideration on the basis of their distinctive characteristics. It will soon be seen whether such a result will be obtained through Community action.

Appendix: *Rules Implemented by the Uncitral Model Code and Article 4A of the UCC*

FRAUD	
UNCITRAL	**ARTICLE 4A UCC**
Article 5. Obligations of sender	**201. Security Procedure**

(1) A sender is bound by a payment order if it was issued by the sender or by another person who had the authority to bind the sender.
(2) When a payment order or an amendment or revocation of a payment order is subject to authentication other than by means of a mere comparison of signature, a purported sender who is not bound under paragraph (1) is nevertheless bound if:
    (a) the authentication is in the circumstances a commercially reasonable method of security against unauthorised payment orders; and
    (b) the receiving bank complied with the authentication.
(3) The parties are not permitted to agree that a purported sender is bound under paragraph (2) if the authentication is not commercially reasonable in the circumstances.
(4) A purported sender is however not bound under paragraph (2) if it proves that the payment order as received by the receiving bank resulted from the actions of a person other than
    (a) a present or former employee of the purported sender, or
    (b) a person whose relationship with the purported sender enabled that person to gain access to the authentication procedure.
The preceding sentence does not apply if the receiving bank proves that the
	'Security procedure' means a procedure established by agreement of a customer and a receiving bank for the purpose of:
	    (i) verifying that a payment order or communication amending or cancelling a payment order is that of the customer; or
	    (ii) detecting error in the transmission or the content of the payment order or communication.
	A security procedure may require the use of algorithms or other codes, identifying words or numbers, encryption, callback procedures, or similar security devices. Comparison of a signature on a payment order or communication with an authorised specimen signature of the customer is not by itself a security procedure. orders issued to the bank in the name of the customer as Sender will be
	202. Authorised and verified payment orders.
	(a) A payment order received by the receiving bank is the authorised order of the person identified as Sender if the person authorised the order or is otherwise bound by it under the law of agency.
	(b) If a bank and its customer have agreed that the authenticity of payment orders issued to the bank in the name of the customer as Sender will be verified pursuant to a security procedure, a pay-

FRAUD (cont.)	

payment order resulted from the actions of a person who had gained access to authentication procedures through the fault of the purported sender.	ment order received by the receiving bank is effective as the order the order of the customer, whether or not authorised, if:
	    (i) the security procedure is a commercially reasonable method of providing security against unauthorised payment orders; and
	    (ii) the bank proves that it accepted the payment order in good faith and in compliance with the security procedure and any written agreement or instruction of the customer restricting acceptance of payment orders issued in the name of the customer.
	The bank is not required to follow an instruction that violates a written agreement with the customer or notice of which is not received at a time and in a manner affording the bank a reasonable opportunity to act on it before the payment order is accepted.
	(c) Commercial reasonableness of a security procedure is a question of law to be determined by considering: the wishes of the customer expressed to the bank; the circumstances of the customer known to the bank, including the size, type and frequency of payment orders normally issued by the customer to the bank; alternative security procedures offered to the customer; and security procedures in general use by customers and receiving banks similarly situated. A security procedure is deemed to be commercially reasonable if:
	    (i) the security procedure was chosen by the customer after the bank offered, and the customer refused, a security procedure that was commercially reasonable for that customer; and

FRAUD (cont.)

(ii) the customer expressly agreed in writing to be bound by any payment order whether or not authorised, issued in its name and accepted by the bank in compliance with a security procedure chosen by the customer.

(f) Except as provided in this section and in section 203(a)(1), rights and obligations arising under this section or section 203 may not be varied by agreement.

203 Unenforceability of certain verified payment orders

(a) If an accepted payment order is not, under section 202 (a), an authorised order of a customer identified as sender, but is effective as an order of the customer pursuant to section 202(b), the following rules apply:

(1) By express written agreement, the receiving bank may limit the extent to which it is entitled to enforce or retain payment of the payment order.

(2) The receiving bank is not entitled to enforce or retain payment of the payment order if the customer proves that the order was not caused, directly or indirectly, by a person:

(i) entrusted at any time with duties to act for the customer with respect to payment orders or the security procedure; or

(ii) who obtained access to transmitting facilities of the customer or who obtained, from a source controlled by the customer and without authority of the receiving bank, information facilitating breach of the security procedure,(...)

MISTAKE

UNCITRAL
Article 5.

(....)
(5) A sender who is bound by a payment order is bound by the terms of the order as received by the receiving bank. However, the sender is not bound by erroneous duplicate of, or an error or discrepancy in, a payment order if:
    (a) the sender and the receiving bank have agreed upon a procedure for detecting erroneous duplicates, errors or discrepancies in a payment order; and
    (b) use of the procedure by the receiving bank revealed or would have revealed the erroneous duplicate, error or discrepancy.

ARTICLE 4A UCC
205. Erroneous payment orders.

(a) If an accepted payment order was transmitted pursuant to a security procedure for the detection of error and the payment order (i) erroneously instructed payment to a beneficiary not intended by the sender, (ii) erroneously instructed payment in an amount greater than the amount intended by the sender, or (iii) was an erroneously transmitted duplicate of a payment order previously sent by the sender, the following rules apply:
    (1) if the sender proves that the sender or a person acting on behalf of the sender pursuant to section 206 complied with the security procedure and that the error would have been detected if the receiving bank had also complied, the sender is not obliged to pay the order to the extent stated in paragraphs (2) and (3) (...)
    (3)(b) If (i) the sender of an erroneous payment order described in subsection (a) is not obliged to pay all or part of the order, and (ii) the sender receives notification from the receiving bank that the order was accepted by the bank or that the sender's account was debited with respect to the order, the sender has a duty to exercise ordinary care, on the basis of information available to the sender, to discover the error with respect to the order and to advise the bank of the relevant facts within a reasonable time, not exceeding 90 days, after the bank's

MISTAKE (Cont)	
	notification was received by the sender. If the bank proves that the sender failed to perform that duty, the sender is liable to the bank for the loss the bank proves it incurred as a result of the failure, but the liability of the sender may not exceed the amount of the sender's order.

5

Diana Faber
Shipping Documents and EDI

1. Introduction

Many shipping documents can be replaced by electronic messages without difficulty, however electronic bills of lading give rise to legal and technological problems. This paper tackles the legal issues leaving the technology to computer experts to tackle. It is divided into four sections. First a review of the most important documents currently in use. Then a summary of the technical advances in the shipping industry. Thirdly a review of the problems raised by EDI bills and lastly developments which may solve these problems.

2. Shipping Documents and Their Functions

Shipping documents exist to facilitate international trade. Therefore it is logical to consider first the sale agreement itself. This contract describes the goods to be shipped, it provides for the price to be paid and the method of payment, and either expressly or by implication it provides who bears the risk at each stage of transportation and when property in the goods passes. Letters of credit are often the method used for payment in international sales. In the course of their operation not only sellers and buyers but also banks hold various shipping documents.

To carry goods from one country to another the buyer or seller or their agent charters a vessel or books space on one. There are numerous different forms of charterparty. Under time charters vessels are hired for a period of time and the use of ship and crew is paid for at a daily rate. Such contracts are analogous to the hire of a car and driver. The time charterer pays for fuel and has the right to direct the shipowner as to the use of the vessel. Voyage charters give the charterer the right to load goods on board for carriage to a certain port or number of ports which, once nominated, cannot be changed. The voyage charterer pays a lump sum for the voyage, is allowed a specified amount of time to load and discharge the goods and pays damages known as demurrage for exceeding that time. Charterparties are also used by liner operators who offer regular services carrying goods from port to port. They will use not only their own ships, if they have any, but also chartered vessels.

It should be noted that the person with whom the shipper contracts for the carriage of his or her goods may not be the owner of the ship upon which they are carried. That person, known as the carrier, could be a time charterer, voyage charterer, liner operator, freight forwarder or other participant in the transport industry.

2.1. Bills of Lading

The 'bill of lading' is the document at the heart of international trade. Its functions are threefold. It is a receipt for the goods, it is evidence of the terms of the contract of carriage and it is a document of title. Traditionally a bill of lading comes into existence after goods are loaded on board ship. At that point the Captain or ship's agent issues a document which sets out information given by the shipper (the name of the shipper, that of the consignee and the party to be notified of the arrival of the goods at the port of destination); it also describes the goods received, shows the ports of loading and discharge, contains or refers to the carrier's contract terms and is signed by or on behalf of the Captain. The bill is then handed to the shipper. A document in the form of a bill of lading can be issued at the point of receipt by the carrier or his or her agent before the goods are loaded on board ship. Such documents are known as 'received for shipment' bills to distinguish them from the traditional form evidencing loading on board.

As it is impossible to hand over payment in return for the goods where the buyer and seller are in different countries the bill of lading is used to represent the goods so that the buyer pays the sale price in return for receipt of the bill of lading. If prior to issue of the bill of lading the seller knows the identity of the buyer his or her name would appear as consignee on the bill. However, if the identity of the buyer is not known at the time of issue of the bill and it is to be used to obtain payment for the goods, a flexible mode of indicating the person entitled to take delivery has to be used. Thus the consignee is 'to order' or 'to AB or to his order', AB being the seller, his or her agent or bank. Once the buyer is identified and has paid for the goods, the bill is endorsed in the buyer's favour. This means the seller or their agent or bank either writes the buyer's name on the bill and signs it or merely signs it, such being known as endorsement in blank. Banks are involved where letters of credit are used as the means of payment. In that situation, the bill is passed to the buyer's bank or confirming bank together with the other documents required for the operation of the credit. It may be endorsed to the bank and by the bank to the buyer.

For the seller to obtain the best price for the goods it could be necessary to offer them for sale in more than one place at a time. Thus the practice grew up of issuing three original bills all signed by or on behalf of the carrier which the seller could use for this purpose. This is known as a set of bills.

The above is an outline of the practicalities of the issue and use of bills of lading. It is by no means comprehensive as there are as many different procedures for issuing and using bills as there are different types of goods traded internationally. What this paper has so far not explored are the legal effects of bills of lading upon buyers, sellers, banks and shipowners.

Between the seller and the buyer the bill is a transferable document of title. It can be used to pass ownership of the goods from one to the other. It only has this effect however if it is intended to do so. For example the fact that it is endorsed to a bank playing a part in the letter of credit chain does not mean that the bank owns the goods. The bank only acquires special property as a pledgee enabling it to sell the goods in the event that its customer fails to pay the debt owed to the bank. Indeed the bank does not even acquire this special property if, before it receives the bill the ownership of the goods has passed from the buyer to the seller. Where a set has been issued and one part of the set has been endorsed from seller to buyer with the intention of passing ownership the other parts of the set cannot be used to pass ownership.

Let us deal now with the rights and obligations of the shipowner. The bill of lading is evidence of the right to possession of the goods. The shipowner is obliged to deliver the goods at port of destination to the person who produces the original bill of lading. In this sense the bill is a document of title. If a set of originals has been produced, delivery of the goods to the holder of one of the set renders the rest null and void. Provided that when the shipowner delivers to the holder of one of the set he or she has no notice that someone other than that person is entitled to the goods, the shipowner cannot be sued for wrongful delivery. The bill loses this document of title function once the goods have been delivered to the person entitled to receive them. When the bill is issued it is evidence of a contract between the shipowner and shipper. Prior to the Bills of Lading Act 1855 only the shipper could sue the shipowner for breach of that contract. This resulted in injustice to the buyer who had paid for the goods in full but who received goods which had been damaged in transit. Such a buyer could not sue the shipowner for loss and if the buyer also bore the transit risks under the sale contract the seller would not pay compensation either. The 1855 Act gave a right of action to such a buyer provided that his or her acquisition of ownership of the goods was causally connected either with being named as consignee or with the endorsement and delivery of the bill of lading to him or her.

2.2. Sea Waybills

These are documents issued by the shipowner or their agent which evidence receipt of the goods, show the port of loading and discharge and the shipper and consignee. They evidence a contract of carriage between the shipper and shipowner under which the shipowner promises to deliver the goods in accordance with the instructions of the shipper. Those instructions can be changed by the shipper at any time up to the point of delivery and need not involve delivery to the consignee named on the waybill. Possession of a sea waybill does not amount to evidence that its holder is entitled to possess the goods because it is not a document of title. To determine who is entitled to delivery of the goods, the shipowner demands identification to be produced by the person seeking delivery to establish that this person is the one to whom the shipowner has been ordered by the shipper to deliver the goods. Thus there is no need for the waybill to be transferred to the port of discharge, it can remain in the hands of the shipper. Transfer of the sea waybill is not used in transferring ownership under a sale contract. Because they are not transferable documents of title, their use reduces the risk of fraud - there is no temptation to issue fraudulent documents if they cannot be used to raise money. Thus where it is not necessary to transfer ownership of the goods while they are at sea the use of a sea, waybill is preferable to use of a bill of lading.

2.3. Delivery Orders

These words are used by those engaged in international trade to apply to a number of different types of documents. First a true ship's delivery order which is issued by or on behalf of the carrier and constitutes a promise by the carrier to deliver the goods described to the person mentioned in the document. An example of the use of such a document is where there is a bulk cargo, one bill of lading has been issued to the seller who in the course of the voyage sells parts of the cargo to a number of different buyers, payment for the goods is to be made against delivery orders, the seller surrenders the original bill to the shipowner and asks in return for a ship's delivery order for each parcel of cargo which has been sold, the delivery orders are passed to the individual buyers as they pay for their parcels and they present the delivery orders to the ship to obtain delivery at the discharge port.

The term 'delivery order' is also applied to orders to ships given by merchants as to the delivery of goods on board. These are of no legal effect unless the shipowner has attorned to them, i.e. acknowledged that the goods are being held on behalf of the person named in the order, or promised to deliver to that person.

3. Advances in Technology: Effect on Shipping

At the same time as radical advances in computer technology are taking place the transport industry has itself been making great strides technologically. From 1997 British Ports and Customs will accept EDI messages from shipping companies and importers to effect clearance of goods. It was the development of containerisation which led to the introduction of EDI into the world of shipping documentation. Container transportation is multi-modal. One journey can be made by a combination of means of transport. Ships, trains and lorries can be specifically designed to carry containers. Purpose built vessels carry hundreds of containers. This has led carriers to use computers to record the information necessary for an efficient transport service. Containerised goods are rarely sold at sea. They are often carried from one sister company to another. Thus there is no need for a document of title to be issued for them. Such voyages are often very short so that use of bills of lading leads to delay in delivery. A sea waybill is the best form of documentation for such a trade as it does not have to be presented at the discharge port. In these circumstances the use of computerised waybills has become widespread. The initial booking information is given to the carrier by the shipper's computer. The sea waybill is issued by the carrier's computer and need never take the form of a piece of paper. Delivery instructions are given by computer. These developments have increased the speed at which business can be done and the accuracy of the information passing between those involved. Sea waybills are the most popular form of transport document in the modern shipping world in part because their absence from the discharge port does not delay the delivery of goods. Their use also avoids the risk of fraud arising from the issue of multiple original negotiable bills.

However in some trades a negotiable bill of lading must be issued. A sea waybill is not negotiable and is therefore inadequate. The speed and convenience of electronic communication have led to efforts to introduce systems for electronic production of negotiable bills. These can broadly be categorised into two types: the depository system and the notification to carrier system. The first involves the deposit of the paper bill with an independent person who is then notified. Since the right to the possession of the goods is changed by electronic transfer he or she keeps a register of the changes to which the carrier can refer to ensure that delivery is made to the correct party. A number of similar schemes have been devised but all rely upon the existence of a bill of lading whether paper or, as in one case, programmable plastic rather like a credit card. The second system, which has been adopted by the Comite Maritime International (CMI) is one of notification to the carrier. It is entirely electronic and does not require the existence of a bill of lading. Using electronic messages the carrier issues an electronic bill to the shipper together with a private code or 'key' possession of which entitles the holder to control the goods. This right of control is passed to other interests after notification by the shipper to the carrier who cancels the original key and gives a new private key to the new person who is entitled to control the goods. It is intended that the key holder should have the same rights as a bill of lading holder. Neither type of scheme is currently in widespread use. New schemes are being developed by a number of organisations and banks.

4. Obstacles to the use of EDI

The rest of this paper considers the implications of replacing paper bills of lading by electronic messages. Most people, when asked to consider the replacement of bills of lading by computerised communications, immediately ask

'What happens when it goes wrong and what about hacking'? These queries arise from the widespread view that electronic communication is unreliable and easy prey to fraudsters. However, fraudulent practices using paper bills of lading are quite common and, statistically, it may well be that the incidence of computer fraud is rarer.

There are currently several practical obstacles to the use of EDI: for example the requirement of Customs and Excise authorities for the production of paper bills of lading; the absence of the requisite technology from many parts of the world; the lack of compatibility between computer systems and, even in countries where the technology exists, the need for it to be in every port or agent's office. Whilst such problems remain the CMI solution is to provide for the issue of a paper bill to replace the electronic message, should a party to the contract of carriage desire it.

Before turning to specific issues of law it is necessary to consider a particular obstacle to the use of EDI which is partly commercial and partly legal. This is the problem of authenticating the EDI bill of lading. How can banks, shippers and, in the event of a dispute, courts verify who actually issued the bill? There will be no written signature to be examined by handwriting experts. There is only an electronic message. This is obviously an issue for computer experts to examine. However there are systems already in use which are based upon digital cryptography. The sender has a secret numerical cipher which is used to encrypt all message. The receiver has access to the public key which can be used to decrypt the sender's messages. It is not possible by use of the public key to work out the sender's secret cipher. If a fraudster tried to create an electronic bill of lading or to alter one already created by a sender it would not be possible to decrypt the message using the public key because the secret numerical cipher known only to the sender would not have been used to create the message. For a judge to test an electronic message the sender could give the judge the plain text message and the enciphered message and the judge could apply the public key. If the message produced were different from the plain text, the judge would know that the enciphered message was a fraud. Provided a sufficient number of digits are used, forgery of a numerical signature is statistically more difficult than forgery of a written one.

Turning now to specific issues of law we find that as a matter of current technology it is possible to create an electronic message to replace a paper bill of lading. However, would English law treat such a message in the same way as a paper bill of lading or other document of title? English statutes and English judges do recognise other means of conveying information than written documents. There are plenty of examples: the definition of 'writing' in the Interpretation Act 1978 includes typing, printing, lithography, photography and other modes of representing or reproducing words in a visible form,'; Mr Justice

Vinelott held in *Derby & Co* v *Weldon (No 9)*[1] that the database of a computer's on-line system which is recorded in the backup files is a document for the purposes of the High Court rules governing discovery of documents; section 10 of the Civil Evidence Act 1968 (dealing with the admissibility of hearsay evidence) defines 'document' as including 'any disc, tape, sound-track or other device in which sound or other data (not being visual images) are embodied so as to be capable (with or without the aid of some other equipment) of being reproduced therefrom'; the Copyright (Computer Software) Amendment Act 1985 provides for the application of the 1956 Copyright Act to a computer programme in the same way as it applies in relation to a literary work. (This is re-enacted in the 1988 Copyright Designs and Patents Act). These examples demonstrate that English law is prepared to treat modern technology as performing the same function as paper documents.

However there is also the issue of signature of the bill of lading. No statute or decided case expressly requires a bill to be signed but references to the signing of bills appear in all the leading text books and in many judgements. The absence of a manual signature complicates the application of English law to electronic bills of lading.

In the absence of an express statutory or judicial definition which provides that electronic messages can be bills of lading or documents of title there is a risk that they would not be treated as such. In the Carriage of Goods by Sea Act 1992 (to which further reference is made below) there is express provision for regulations to be brought in to extend the application of its provisions to cases where telecommunications systems are used. No such regulations have yet been enacted and even when regulations are enacted they will not resolve all the problems resulting from the failure to recognise electronic messages as bills of lading. These problems are firstly that banks would not accept them as security for their loans and this would effectively prevent letter of credit sales and amount to a significant obstacle to international trade. Secondly, it would not be possible to pass property in the goods using an electronic bill. Thirdly, the holder of an electronic bill would not be able to establish title to sue the carrier. The fourth potential problem concerns the incorporation into the contract of carriage of internationally recognised rules governing the rights and liabilities of the parties.

5. Practical and Legal Developments

This part of the paper is divided into two sections. The first deals with published proposals for dealing with the problems raised by EDI bills and the second highlights areas that still require consideration.

---

[1] [1991] 1 *WLR* 653.

5.1. Published Proposals

5.1.1. *CMI Rules for Electronic Bills of Lading*

The CMI Rules are supposed to work by incorporation into the contract of carriage. As mentioned earlier, they operate by notification to the carrier of any change in entitlement to control the goods. After the carrier has received the goods such receipt is notified to the shipper in a message addressed to the shipper's electronic address giving the name of the shipper, the description of the goods, the date and place of the receipt of the goods, a reference to the carrier's terms and the private key to be used. After the shipper has confirmed this message, he or she becomes the holder of the private key and the Rules provide that the information is to have the same force and effect as if the message were contained in a paper bill of lading. The private key gives the holder the right to claim delivery and direct the carrier as to the identity of the consignee or any other subject as if he or she were the holder of a paper bill of lading. To pass the 'right of control and transfer' the current holder of the private key notifies the carrier of its intent to transfer, accompanying such message by use of the private key, the carrier confirms the message and transmits all the information apart from the private key to the new holder. Once the new holder has accepted the right of control and transfer the last private key is cancelled and a new one is given to the new holder. The transfer of the private key is intended to have the same effect as the transfer of rights of control and transfer under a paper bill. Delivery of the goods is made according to the instructions given to the carrier by the holder of the private key and delivery in accordance with those instructions automatically cancels the private key. At any time prior to delivery of the goods the holder of the private key can demand a paper bill of lading and the same option is given to the carrier. The issue of such a paper bill cancels the private key. The Rules further provide that the parties agree that the transmission of electronic data is to satisfy any requirements of national or local law and that the contract is to be evidenced in writing and signed.

The CMI proposals make no reference to authentication of the electronic bills. Their Private Key is to be used by shippers and others in giving directions to the carrier as to the disposal of the cargo. For authentication purposes, to replace a signature, a public key system should be adopted. This means that the carrier will use a secret code to encrypt the electronic bill and the shipper will have to use the public key appropriate to that carrier's messages to decode it, the same will apply to messages from the shipper. This scheme has met resistance from carriers and cargo interests because it requires the carrier's involvement in sale contracts.

5.1.2. *Carriage of Goods by Sea Act 1992 (COGSA)*

This Act deals with title to sue and replaces the Bills of Lading Act 1855 in relation to documents issued after the 16th September 1992. It covers bills of lading including received for shipment bills but excluding bills which cannot be transferred. It applies to sea waybills which are defined as documents which are not bills of lading but do contain or evidence a contract of carriage by sea and which identify the consignee even in a way which allows the identity of the consignee to be varied after issue. Non transferable bills of lading would probably fall within the definition of sea waybills. The Act also applies to true ship's delivery orders. This paper sets out (below) examples of problems encountered by cargo interests under the old law and solutions under the new.

1) Bills of Lading

Examples of situations in which the requirements of the Bills of Lading Act 1855 prevented recovery by cargo interests are as follows:

Example 1

Buyers of part of a bulk cargo received the endorsed bill of lading for their part during the voyage. They took delivery of their cargo but there was a shortage. The Sale of Goods Act 1979 prevented them from owning the cargo until it had been separated from the rest, therefore they could not claim for shortage because the endorsement and delivery of the bill did not pass ownership to them.

Example 2

Buyers were named as consignees in the bill of lading which was delivered to them during the voyage. They took delivery of the goods to the seller's order and could not claim for damage done during the voyage because ownership of the goods did not pass to them until long after discharge.

Example 3

In accordance with arrangements contemplated both in the charterparty and the sale contract an oil cargo was delivered, not against a bill of lading but in return for a letter indemnifying the shipowner against the consequences of delivering without bills of lading. There was a shortage and the receivers were not able to sue the shipowner for the shortage because they obtained ownership in the course of the voyage, but the bill was not endorsed and delivered to them until sometime after discharge.

Under the new Act (COGSA), by virtue of taking possession of the bill of lading in good faith, the holder obtains all the rights of suit under the contract contained in or evidenced by that bill as if he or she had been a party to that contract. The claimants under Example 1 would now have the right to sue the shipowner. They became the holders of their bill by endorsement and delivery of the bill to them, under COGSA the fact that this did not pass ownership of the goods to them is irrelevant. The Example 2 claimants, being named consignees in possession, would also have the right to sue.

It will be recalled that once goods have been delivered to the person rightfully entitled to them, the bill of lading for those goods ceases to be a document of title. It is not evidence of the right to possess the goods and cannot be used to transfer ownership. This was part of the problem in Example 3. Where someone becomes the lawful holder of a bill of lading after it has ceased to be a document of title they will not obtain the COGSA right to sue unless their possession of the bill results from contractual or other arrangements made before the bill ceased to be a document of title. Since the buyers in Example 3 received the bill after taking delivery of the goods, but pursuant to contractual arrangements made long before the goods were loaded, they would have title to sue the shipowner for the shortage.

2) Sea waybills and delivery orders

Formerly the use of a sea waybill could give rise to injustice in that the person who took delivery could suffer loss and be unable to sue the carrier for the breach which caused the loss because he or she was not party to the contract of carriage. The Bills of Lading Act 1855 did not apply to sea waybills. The mere possession of a delivery order did not necessarily give the holder a right of action against the shipowner. The document does not necessarily evidence any contract between the shipowner and the holder although it may operate to give some rights by way of estoppel. However the effect of such a delivery order will depend very much on the facts of the particular case.

Under COGSA people who take delivery of goods under sea waybills or true ship's delivery orders have rights of action against the carrier; (in the case of a delivery order for part of a cargo the right relates only to that part).

It should not be concluded that the Act is useful only to cargo interests; it does assist carriers in a number of respects but they are outside the scope of this paper.

There are different methods that could be adopted to render the 1992 Act applicable to electronic data interchange. It states that regulations are to be used for this purpose. The simple method used in the Copyright (Computer Software) Amendment Act 1985 might be adopted by saying 'this Act shall apply in relation to the electronic communication of information as it applies in relation to paper documents'. Then lawyers and the Courts would be left to deal with the problems arising on a case by case basis. Alternatively such regulations could actually redefine the words found in the Act. Such redefinition could be done in two ways. First a set of Rules such as those devised by the CMI could be scheduled to the Regulations and redefinition could be on the basis of the procedure set out in the CMI Rules. For example a bill of lading could be defined as: *'a receipt message as described in Rule 4'*

One objection to redefining the terms by reference to an annexed set of rules is that EDI systems might evolve and require further amendment of the Statute. Another is that the CMI system is based on notification of the changes in entitlement to the goods being given to the carrier whereas at least one of the

Shipping Documents and EDI

new schemes currently being developed involves notification to a bank. Therefore it may well be necessary to define the terms by reference to more general words, for example a bill of lading could be defined as:

> *'including an electronic message sent by or on behalf of the carrier containing such information as is provided by a documentary bill of lading'*

This would be inadequate in that the carrier could, for example under the CMI system send the message to someone who does not accept it and is not given the private key. Thus the definition must refer to the extant key or its equivalent. The redefinition of endorsement may present problems. Under the CMI system it involves notification to the carrier that the holder intends to transfer, confirmation by the carrier to the holder, transmission of the message without a key by the carrier to the proposed new holder, acceptance by the new holder and the carrier giving him or her a private key. A definition incorporating all these processes would be unwieldy and may not suit other EDI systems. Whichever regulatory scheme is adopted 'document' will have to be expressly redefined so as to include electronic data whether or not it has been printed.

5.1.3. *Insurance Against Technical Malfunction*

A technical malfunction in an EDI system could cause financial loss to any of the users whether a carrier, bank, seller or purchaser of goods. If the problem can be attributed to the fault of the system provider then the user will be able to sue the system provider under the contract. Not all the users of a particular system will necessarily be in contractual relations with the provider of the system and, furthermore, the fault may lie with the suppliers of the hardware or the software with whom the users will not have a contract under which to sue. In the absence of privity of contract with the provider or supplier a user may have no recourse for any financial loss following from a technical malfunction. It may well be difficult or prohibitively expensive for a system provider or a hardware or software supplier to obtain insurance cover against claims from all those who might suffer loss as a result of his or her fault; thus he or she may be insufficiently covered by insurance. From the point of view of individual users, it makes commercial and legal sense for each to be insured against their own prospective losses. Obviously it would be open to users to come to their own contractual arrangements as to who among them is to pay for such insurance. Although this issue has been addressed by users of EDI systems there are still significant gaps in the available insurance cover.

5.2. Developments Not Yet Subject to Published Proposals

It is necessary to recall here the functions played by bills of lading in international trade. They are as follows:

(1) receipt for the goods loaded on board ship,

(2) evidence of the terms of the contract of carriage,
(3) document of title. This third function results in three uses of bills of lading:
- passing the right to possession of the goods i.e. the right of physical control over them,
- use in the course of passing ownership of the goods,
- use as security given to lenders.

The CMI Rules could be used to cover the practicalities of the receipt function, evidence of the contract terms and passing of the right of physical control. When COGSA 1992 is extended to cover EDI bills it will strengthen the security given by such bills to banks. However those measures do not assist on the issue of whether the Hague, Hague-Visby and Hamburg Rules can be incorporated into a computerised bill of lading contract. Nor do they resolve all the problems arising from the use of an EDI bill to pass ownership of goods or as security.

5.2.1. *Hague-Visby Rules and Hamburg Rules*

Under this head the issue is whether the terms of the contract of carriage set out in these treaties will be applied to EDI bills of lading. In England the Hague-Visby Rules are enacted in the Carriage of Goods by Sea Act 1971 which applies them compulsorily to bills of lading or similar document of title. If the EDI message is not as a matter of law a bill of lading or a document of title then in the absence of an express contractual incorporation of the Rules into the EDI contract they would not apply. Even if the contract expressly incorporates the Rules it could fall for construction in a jurisdiction which does not recognise such incorporation. The absence of the Rules from EDI bills would result in uncertainty as to the terms of the contract of carriage. Thus the Rules require amendment to cover EDI documents in all contracting states. Amendment of the Rules would have to be by international convention. It could use a general provision such as that used in the Copyright Designs and Patents Act or it could be by reference to a specific system of EDI such as the CMI system or it could redefine the relevant words in the Hague-Visby Rules so as to apply them to any EDI system.

The Hamburg Rules also require a 'document'. However Article 14.3 provides:

> *'The signature on the bill of lading may be in handwriting, printed in facsimile, perforated, stamped, or in symbols, or made by any other mechanical or electronic means, if not inconsistent with the law of the country where the bill of lading is issued.'*

At first glance this would appear to obviate the Hague-Visby regime uncertainty relating to EDI bills. However the provision is expressly made subject to the law of the country of issue. To be compulsorily applicable to all EDI bills the Rules require amendment.

5.2.2. *Contracts of Sale*

Does the contractual incorporation of such rules into the contract of carriage suffice to preserve the negotiable character of the bill of lading? As previously mentioned, the transfer of a bill of lading will operate to transfer property in the goods if it is intended to do so. The contract of sale is the governing contract for the purposes of determining the parties' intentions in this respect. Thus that contract will have to provide specifically for EDI to replace a paper bill. The International Chamber of Commerce in the Incoterms 1990 rules for FOB (Free on Board), C & F (Cost and Freight) and CIF (Cost, Insurance and Freight) sales has made provision for the transport document to be replaced by an 'equivalent electronic data interchange (EDI) message' where the seller and buyer have agreed to communicate electronically. They have also adopted UNCID which consists of practical rules which are to be applied in the event that the parties do agree to electronic communication.

Logically, although the Sale of Goods Act 1979 does not affect negotiability, its references to bills of lading should be amended to cover EDI. The Factors Act 1889 operates where mercantile agents and buyers of goods in possession of the goods or documents of title sell them on without the authority of the owner of the goods. Its provisions protect innocent third party purchasers. Its references to "documents of title" should be expressly defined to include electronic data.

5.2.3. *Security for Banks*

To merely incorporate the EDI rules into the contract of carriage would not be sufficient to bind the banks. The Uniform Customs and Practice for Documentary Credits should be suitably amended. For example, Article 2 in defining 'documentary credit' refers to payment against 'stipulated documents'; the words 'or electronic message' could be inserted after that phrase. Alternatively it may be desirable to produce a set of Uniform Rules relating solely to EDI as was done in the case of Combined Transport Documents.

After amendment of the UCP there would be no reason why an EDI bill of lading could not be used in the same way as a paper bill; for example, under the CMI system the bank could hold the private key in the same way as it formerly held paper bills of lading. Under COGSA 1992 the bank does not undertake any liabilities to the carrier merely by holding the bill of lading. It will not undertake such liabilities unless it actually makes a claim against the carrier or tries to take or actually takes delivery of the goods. In that event it would incur liabilities, but they would be no greater than under the existing law.

Perhaps it would be possible technologically for computers to take over the process of checking the documents. If the letter of credit requirements are transmitted electronically and the 'documents' submitted to satisfy the letter of credit requirements are electronic messages why should not the computer carry out the checking process? Of course there remains the practical problem that other documents necessary to satisfy the letter of credit requirement may not be transmitted by electronic means and delays in their posting could hold up the process.

6. Conclusion
The legal problems that arise out of the replacement of paper bills of lading by electronic messages obviously require further detailed consideration by the shipping, trading and banking industries and their legal advisers. It is hoped that the suggestions presented in this paper will facilitate this process.

Part III
ISSUES RELATING TO INTELLECTUAL PROPERTY

6
Andreas Wehlau
Software Protection under European Community Law

1. Protecting Computer Programs

The protection of computer programs from illegitimate copying has been a legal issue for many years. The debate was intensified[1] when the Commission of the

---

[1] Betten, Jürgen (1990), LES (Licensing Executive Society). Tagung zur EG-Softwareschutz-Richtlinie, *Computer und Recht* 809. Colombe, Michel/Meyer, Caroline (1990a), Seeking Interoperability: An Industry Response, *European Intellectual Property Review* 79. Colombe, Michel/Meyer, Caroline (1990), Interoperability Still Threatened by EC Software Directive: A Status Report, *European Intellectual Property Review* 325. Emmerich, Torsten (1991), *Rechtsschutz für Standardsoftware*. (Wissenschaftliche Beiträge an europäischen Hochschulen, Reihe 2: Rechtswissenschaft, 14). Diss. Göttigen. Ammersbeck bei Hamburg. Goldrian, Hans (1990), EG-Richtlinienentwurf für den Urheberrechtsschutz von Computerprogrammen, *Computer und Recht* 556. Heussen, Benno (1991), Rechtsvergleichung und Softwareschutz. Das Bespiel Deutschland/Italien, *Computer und Recht* 385. Holzinger, Ernst (1991), Können Objektprogramme urheberrechtlich geschützt sein? Kritische Anmerkungen zu Schulz, GRUR 1990, 103 und König, GRUR 1989, 559, *Gewerblicher Rechtsschutz und Urheberrecht* 366. Lehmann, Michael (1990a), Nutzung von Computersoftware in Öffentlichen Bibliotheken. Kurzgutachten erstellt im Auftrag des Deutschen Bibliotheksverbandes, *Bibliotheksdienst* 1477. Lehmann, Michael (1990b), Portierung und Migration von Anwendersoftware. Urheberrechtliche Probleme, *Computer und Recht* 625. Lehmann, Michael (1991b), Die Europäische Richtlinie über den Schutz von Computerprogrammen, *Gewerblicher Rechtsschutz und Urheberrecht International* 327.Limberger, Gerhard (1991), Der rechtliche Rahmen für den europaweiten EDV-Markt 1992, Goebel, Jürgen W. (Hrsg.): *Rectliche und ökonomische Rahmenbedingungen der deutschen EDV-Branche*. Grundlagen, staatliche Förderung, Europarecht, Arbeitsrecht, Wettbewerbs- und Kartellrecht, Urheber- und Patentrecht, Technologie-transfer, Telekommunikation, Datenschutz. (*Informationstechnik und Recht*, 1). Köln. P.33. Mehrings, Josef (1990), Der Rechtschutz comptergestützster Fachinformationen. Unter besonderer Berücksichtigung von Datenbanken. *Fundamenta juridica*, 12. Baden-Baden. Miller, Clifford G. (1990), The Proposal for an EC Council Directive on the Legal Protection of Computer Programs, *European Intellectual Protection Review* 347. Müller, Harald

European Communities issued a proposal for a directive on copyright for software.[2] This proposal was - after a controversial discussion and several official amendments - finally passed by the Council of Ministers on 14 May 1991.[3] It will be implemented into national law by the Member States of the European Community according to Art. 189 EEC-Treaty before 1 January 1993, resulting in a harmonised legal basis for the protection of computer software throughout the EEC.

The directive uses copyright as the means to protect software. However, this is not necessarily the only possible answer to the urgent need for legal protection. In theory, a patent could be granted for software together with the hardware on which it is used, if the requirements of novelty, inventiveness and susceptibility of industrial application were fulfilled. Yet most programs do not pass this test; its courts consider them only as new ways of using the same machine (a computer). Some states even expressly excluded isolated software from the scope of its patent laws. Nevertheless, where a patent can be obtained for a technological application, it offers a reliable and safe protection for the producer which is probably preferable to copyright. Recently, the importance of

---

(1990), Brüsseler Bedrohung der freien Ausleihe von Software. Stellungnahme zum Gutachten von Prof. Dr Lehmann, *Bibliotheksdienst* 1490. Oppermann, Bernd H. (1991), Urheberrechtlicher Schutz und Substantiierungslast im Softwareprozeβ, *Computer und Recht* 264. Opperman, Bernd h. (1991) Urheberrechtlicher Schutz und Substuntiierunglast im Software prozess, *Computer und Recht* 260. Reed, Chris (1991), Reverse Engineering Computer Programs without Infringing Copyright, *European Intellectual Property Review* 47. Scheinfeld, Robert C./Buttler, Gary M. (1991), Using Trade Secret Law to Protect Computer Software, *Rutgers Computer & Technology Law Journal* 381. Soltysinski, Stanislaw (1990), Protection of Computer Programs: Comparative and International Aspects, *International Review of Industrial Property and Copyright Law* 1. Stone, Peter (1990), *Copyright Law in the United Kingdom and the European Community*, (European Community Law Series), London. Sumner, John P./Plunkett, Dianne (1988), Copyright, Patent, and Trade Secret Protection for Computer Software in Western Europe, in *Computer/Law Journal* 1. Walter, Charles (1988), Defyning the Scope of Software Copyright Protection for Maximum Public Benefit, *Rutgers Computer & Technology Law Journal* 1. Waltl, Peter (1990), *Geschutzte undnicht geschulzte Computerprogramme*. Diss Fu Berlin.
[2] Comp. *Official Journal of the European Communities* (1988) C 91/4. The plans for the Directive were first mentioned in the Commission White Paper 'Completing the Internal Market', COM 85, 310, and later in more detail in the Commission Green Paper on 'Copyright and the Challenge of Technology', COM 88, 172.
[3] *Official Journal of the European Communities* (1991) L 122/42; for an overview of the history of the Directive see Berkvens/Alkemade (1991) 476. Berkvens, J. M./Alkemade, G. O. (1991), Software Protection: Life after the Directive, *European Intellectual Property Review*, 476.

patents for software related inventions seems to be gaining ground.[4] Alternatives are offered by the law of unfair competition, which prohibits the identical use of the achievements of a competitor for commercial purposes.[5] This means of protection appears to be appropriate particularly for programs which are not really innovative or creative, but mere results of effort and working time. Furthermore, in certain sectors a trade secret protection might be suitable to prevent the knowledge about details of the software being spread and misused. Finally, suggestions for a new, *sui generis* protection through a program right were made, in order to allow for a legal concept which is equipped to handle the new and delicate issues, which cannot always adequately be dealt with by copyright and patent law.

If at the moment the copyright approach is prevalent, this is mainly because a protection within the pre-existing copyright laws draws on the already well-established international recognition of copyright, as enacted in the Revised Bern Convention. This convention is designed to guarantee authors from other countries the same treatment as nationals of a state. Such an effective system of protection would not be available for a newly created program right.[6]

When protecting rights of software producers, one has to strike a reasonable balance between giving incentives for producing new programs by protecting the programme's achievements from being copied by competitors, and keeping competition and innovation in the market possible by allowing free use of the underlying ideas of non-patentable products by competitors which would

---

[4] Comp. European Patent Office (1990) Report: Patentability of Computer Related Inventions, *International Review of Industrial Property and Copyright Law*, p.187; Anders, Wilfried (1991), Patentability of programs for data processing systems in Germany: is the case law undergoing change?, *Internaational Review of Industrial Property and Copyright Law* p.475. Jander, Dieter (1991), Zur Technizität von Computersoftware, *Mitteilungen der deutschen Patentanwälte* 90. Koch, Frank A. (1991), Rechtsschutz für Benutzeroberflächen von Software, *Gewerblicher Rechtsschutz under Urheberrecht* 180. Wenzel (1991) *op. cit.* Freed, Roy N. (1985), Legal Interests Related to Software Programs, *Jurimetrics Journal* 347. Hauptmann, Gunter (1991), Schutz von Computersoftware durch das U.S. Patent Law, *Computer und Recht* 592.

[5] Wenzel (1991), *op. cit.* 109.

[6] Freed (1989), Legal protection of software - a global view from Japan *Yearbook of Law Computers and Technology* 71. Dreier, Thomas (1991b), The Council Directive of 14 May 1991 on the Legal Protection of Computer Programs, *European Intellectual Property Review* 319. Erdmann, Willi (1991), Schutz von Computerprogrammen - Rechtslage nach der EG-Richtlinie, *Gewerblicher Rechtsschutz und Urheberrecht* 877.

otherwise be completely blocked in actively competing in this field.[7] Additionally, workable competition can only be achieved by ensuring open standards and interoperability between different, possibly competing programs. This will potentially make necessary some limits of protection as well.

Since the recent directive has already been adopted by the Council, we will mainly focus on this instrument, which chose copyright as the means to protect software (section 4). The need for legal harmonisation will be understandable after a brief look into national European Community law (section 3). Nevertheless some fundamental problems concerning the use of copyright in this context will have to be addressed (section 2), and we shall see that they cause considerable problems for the interpretation and application of the directive (section 5). Finally an attempt will be made to resolve some of these difficulties by a systematic and restrictive interpretation of the directive (section 6).

2. Fundamental Problems of Using Copyright for Software Protection

2.1. Free Idea - Protected Expression

Even though major industrial countries like Japan, the United States, and many European countries have chosen copyright as the main way to protect software, there are fundamental issues which suggest that this approach faces difficult problems. This is because copyright has developed historically and is mainly applied to artistic and literary works such as paintings, novels or poems. (This, as a matter of course, does not mean that scientific articles or technical reports cannot be subject to copyright protection). However, it illustrates that copyright is a means to protect a specific expression of thoughts or ideas and not the information content of a work. This distinction between protected mode of expression and free ideas and principles is one of the central tenets of copyright law;[8] even if some countries, such as the United Kingdom do not focus so much on it. It is a necessary distinction, because protecting an idea expressed in a piece of writing would render any discussion on that topic illegal and would therefore block free speech and writing in politics, science and technology, as well as in the arts.

---

[7] Lehmann, Michael (1991a), Der neue Europaische Rechtsschutz von Computerprogrammen, *Neue Juristische Wochenschrift* 2112. Lehmann, (1991b), *op.cit.* Sugiyama, Keiji (1991), Reverse Engineering and Other Issues of Software Protection in Japan, *European Intellectual Property Review* 395.

[8] Radcliffe, Mark F. (1991), The Future of Computer Law: Ten challenges for the Next Decade, *European Intellectual Property Review 358.*

2.2. Copyright as Secrecy Protection?

It has been argued concerning computer programs that it is not really the mode of expression in code form or programming language that needs protection, but the underlying valuable ideas and principles, developed by the software producer in the course of developing the program.[9] Obviously, copyright cannot be of much use in that case, since it only protects the expression, not the idea. It appears, in other words, that the software industry is more in need of a secrecy protection than of a legal instrument that merely protects the mode of expression.

2.3. Is Software Literature?

Moreover, the categorisation of software as literary work is highly questionable, because even if it contains certain information, it certainly does not contain readable language like a book or a poem. The fact that one can read a program does not speak against this finding, since a circuit diagram could also be read without being a work of literature or language.[10] The word 'language' for a set of rules and symbols used for programming might have caused this confusion. One has to understand this concept as a protection 'like literary works', even if the wording of a statutory instrument might stage 'as literary words'. This leads to the fact that the structure and format of a program are not really a part of the mode of expression in the sense used in connection with spoken languages; structure and format are actually information itself.[11]

2.4. Few Alternatives for Expression

Another problem is connected with the fact that software is written in a formal language which allows - strictly speaking - only one expression for one idea. Programming languages do not offer the choice of different expressions as spoken languages do. Choosing a different way to implement a solution to a problem is in itself strictly considered already another idea, another solution to the problem.[12] This could have the consequence that a person who wants to write a program tackling the same task is prevented from doing so, because the

---

[9] Staines, Ian A. (1989), The European Commission's Proposal for a Council Directive on the Legal Protection of Computer programs, *European Intellectual Property Review* 183.

[10] König, Michael (1991a), Computerprogramme sind kiene Sprachwerke. Teil 2, *Jur-PC* 1122. Cornish, W. R. (1990), Computer Program Copyright and the Berne Convention, *European Intellectual Property Review* 129.

[11] Freed, Roy N. (1989), *op. cit.*

[12] Junker, Abbo (1988), *Computerrecht Gewerblicher Rechtsschutz, Mängelhaftung, Arbeitsrecht*, (Schriftenreihe Recht und Praxis), Baden-Baden. Junker, Abbo (1991), Die Entwicklung des Rechtsschutzes für EDV-Leistungen in den Jahren 1988 und 1989, *Neue Juristische Wochenschrift* 2117, and Konig (1991a), *op. cit.*

only sensible solution has already been done and is now protected by copyright law. One could say that such a solution is not too bad since it protects the achievement of the better competitor; however, this is not in line with the underlying principles of copyright law, which is to protect expression whilst keeping free the use of the ideas and principles behind it. Only under the restrictive preconditions of patent law such a monopoly for a, technical, idea is granted. Of course one could argue that copyright law sometimes does protect ideas, for example the plot of stories or characters of novels, which cannot be copied freely by other authors for other purposes such as films.[13] But then again we face the possibility that ideas could be monopolised in a key industry, hindering a further rapid development in this field.

2.5. Division of Interests in Software Copyright

Finally, the interests and economic powers of the parties concerned with software protection are quite different from the traditional situation envisaged in copyright cases.[14] In publishing the economically weak author who fears exploitation at the hands of a powerful publisher is at least partially protected by the copyright provisions which gives the author exclusive rights in his or her work. Compare this with the software producer, software protection seems to lie more with protection against infringing competitors, and is less concerned with authors who are deprived of the benefits of their works.

All these issues cause some doubt, as to whether copyright is really the appropriate way to ensure that legitimate interests of authors and producers of software are respected. Yet the EC has decided to step forward by enacting software protection rules under a copyright regime.

3. Differing Protection in France, Germany and the UK

The scope of protection for computer programs is quite different at the moment. A brief outline of the scope of only France, Germany and the United Kingdom alone already clearly illustrates this. Whereas software is treated as literary works in Germany and the UK by statutory provision, France has enacted a special regime for computer programs which treats them differently in many respects such as moral rights and royalties. Also the duration of copyright varies. While France only affords a period of protection of 25 years from the date of creation onwards,[15] British law provides for the international minimum

---

[13] Comp. Freed (1989), *op. cit.*
[14] Haberstumpf, Helmut (1991), Neue Entwicklungen im Software-Urheberrecht, *Neue Juristiche Wochenschrift* 2105.
[15] Law No. 85-660 Relating to the Rights of Authors, Performing Artists, Producers of Sound Recordings and Video Recordings and Audio-visual Communication Enterprises of 3 July 1985; see Dreier, Thomas (1989), Copyright Protection for

of 50 years, beginning from the death of the rightholder.[16] Germany, moreover, has enacted a 70 years rule,[17] also beginning with the death of the rightholder.

The main difference, however, is to be seen in the question of which programs are actually copyrightable. British law requires originality, meaning that the work must be an original product of the author.[18] Additionally, only a non-trivial result of normal intellectual work must have been produced, exhibiting some skill, judgement and labour. Hence, an innovative or aesthetic character is not prescribed for copyrightability of software in Britain.[19] In contrast, French law insists on originalité, interpreted by the courts as demanding an independent personal effort beyond a mere expression of automatic and constraining logic.[20] This might already be more difficult to attain for a programmer, especially since in addition to that, an expression of the author's personality must have taken place. Even if this criterion might appear somewhat diffuse, it indicates a higher level of aesthetic creativity than the one required by British law. Yet, even stricter are the criteria of the German Federal Court: a program can only be copyrightable in German law if it clearly exceeds the average programming activity shown in the industry.[21] This leaves probably

---

Computer Programs in Foreign Countries: Legal Issues and Trends in Judicial Decisions and Legislation, *International Review of Industrial Property and Copyright Law* 820.

[16] Sec. 12(1) Copyright, Designs and Patents Act 1988; see Cornish (1989b), *Intellectual Property* 2nd ed., London: Sweet and Maxwell, p.283. Ehricke, Ulrich (1991), Softwareschutz in England, *Computer und Recht* 321.

[17] § 64 Urheberrechtsgesetz.

[18] See sec. 1(1) CDPA 1988; comp. Dreier (1989) *op.cit.*; Flint Michael (1990), *A User's Guide to Copyright,* 3rd. ed., London: Butterworth, p.21.

[19] Ehricke (1991), *op.cit.*

[20] Law No. 85-660 of 3 July 1985; comp. Dreier (1989), *op. cit.*; see also Terrisse, Marianne (1988), *Protection of Computer Software in France and the UK,* (LLM-Diss), Exeter.

[21] BGH CR 1985, 22; BGH CR 1991, 80; comp. also Kindermann, Manfred (1991), Copyright Protection of Computer Programs in Germany: Nixdorf v. Nixdorf, *European Intellectual Property Review* 296. Holländer, Günther (1991b), Urheberrechtsschutz nur für weit überdurchschnittliche Computerprogramme?, *Computer und Recht* 715. Haberstumpf (1991), 2105 *op. cit.*. Dreier (1991b), *op. cit.,*.320. König, Michael (1991b), Fallen Comptprogramme unter das Urheberrecht? 'Überdurchschnittliche' Programmierleistungen schützt der Bundesgerichtshof mit dem Betriebssystem-Urteil, *Frankfurther Allgemeine Zeitung,* 20, August 1991, p.T6. König, Michael (1991c), Urheberrechtsschutz von Computerprogrammen, *Computer und Recht* 584. Holländer, Günther (1991b), Urheberrechtsschutz nur für weit überdurchschnittliche Computerprogramme?, *Computer und Recht,* 715.

90 percent of the software without copyright protection.[22] The restrictive approach is based on a reasoning which stresses the above mentioned fundamental problems of copyright for software and which emphasises the peculiarities in software writing, where the expression of creativity is limited by the formal character of the medium and the need for technically clear solutions.[23]

Without judging the merits and flaws of the different national approaches, it is apparent, that whether one favours copyright for software or not a harmonisation is necessary, in order to avoid distortion in the trade and production of software within the EC.

4. The 1991 EC Directive on Copyright for Software

The directive on the protection of computer programs is a legal instrument which in itself is only obligatory for the Member States of the EC, which are under a legal duty to implement the terms of the directive into their national laws.[24] In doing so, Member States only have to achieve the prescribed result, generally they are not bound to use a specific means to apply the directive.[25] However, some provisions in Directives require the precise adoption of the formulation because otherwise the result could not be attained. In practice, therefore, discussing the meaning and the objective of a directive means more or less broadly talking about the future law of the country.[26]

---

[22] Radcliffe (1991), *op. cit.* 362. Meijboom, Alfred P. (1990), Software Protection in 'Europe 1992', *Rutgers Computer & Technology Law Journal,* 407, at 432. Germany is, however, not the only Member State with strict precondition on copyrightability of Software, for Denmark see Arnadottir, Erla S. (1990), Datenverarbeitung und Urheberrecht in Dänemark - Die erste nordische Urheberrechtsnovelle im Vergleich, *Gewerblicher Rechtsschutz und Urheberrecht International,* 290.

[23] Junker (1991), *op. cit,* 2118.

[24] Lasok, Dominik and Bridge, John W. (1991), *Law and Institutions of the European Communities.* 5th ed. London: Butterworths, 137. Kapteyn, Paul J., Verloren van Themaat, Pieter and Gormley, Laurence W. (1989), *Introduction to the Law of the European Communities. After the Coming into Force of the Single European Act.* 2nd ed. Deventer, 193.

[25] Hartley, Trevor C. (1988), *The Foundations of European Community Law,* (Clarendon Law Series), 2nd ed.,OUP, 99. Lasok/Bridge (1991), *op. cit.* 138. It has been suggested that there is no need for legislative action, where the meaning of the Directive is already contained in a general clause of the national law, because in such a situation it is up to the courts to comply with the Directive directly, comp. Erdman/Bornkamm (1991), *op. cit.* 877.

[26] On the influence of the directive on French law comp. Lucas, André (1992), The Council Directive of 14 May 1991 Concerning the Legal Protection of Computer Programs and Its Implications in French Law, *European Intellectual Property Review*

The directive obliges the Member States to protect software as literary works according to the terms of the Bern Convention, which lays down common international principles of copyright law (Article 1(1)). The individual creations of software authors are protected (Article 1(2)); ideas and underlying principles, however, are expressly excluded from protection[27] (Article 1(3)). The intention is to harmonise the differing scopes of protection in the Member States at the moment,[28] which have been depicted briefly above. It seems, however, that this objective will not be arrived at since the detailed requirements for the test of copyrightability are only set out in the preamble of the directive. This preamble is not legally binding on Member States or national courts.[29] It has therefore been forecast, that the differences between the national laws will continue to exist, or even, that the restrictive test might be applied in all Member States in future.[30] In the end this will be decided by the Court of Justice of the European Communities, which has the last say on questions of interpretation of EC law according to Article 177 of the EEC Treaty. Even where the directive has been implemented into the national copyright laws, the Court of Justice will determine the meaning of the wording through the underlying continuing legal force of the directive.[31]

The directive regulates the question of authorship, but it leaves it to the Member States to decide whether legal entities such as firms can acquire authorship themselves (Article 2(1)). In those countries where only natural persons can hold copyrights this will not be possible. If a programmer writes a program under a contract of employment, it is the employer who will hold the right in the software (Article 2(3)). Again it is left to the Member States as to how this result is achieved. It could be done by giving the actual authorship and direct copyright to the employer; it could also be implemented by providing for a statutory legal license for the programmer to the employer.

---

28. For German law see Lesshaft, Karl and Ulmer Detlef (1991), Urheberrechtsschutz von computerprogrammen nach der Europäischen Richtlinie, *Computer und Recht* 519. And Erdmann and Bornkamm (1991), 877.
[27] Comp. Lesshaft and Ulmer (1991), *op. cit.* 519, 522.
[28] Lehmann (1991b) *op. cit.* 327; (1991a) *op. cit.* 2112.
[29] Comp. Bleckmann, Albert (1987), Probleme der Auslegung von EWG-Richtlinien, *Recht der internationalen Wirtschaft* 929. 931. And Lasok and Bridge (1991), *op. cit.* 143. Dissenting: Erdmann and Bornkamm (1991), *op. cit.* 878.
[30] Hoeren, Thomas (1991), Urheberrechtsfähigkeit von Software. Die EG-Richtlinie zum Softwareschutz und die Rechtsprechung des Bundesgerichtshofes, *Computer und Recht* 463. Dissenting: Erdmann and Bornkamm (1991), *op. cit.* 878.
[31] Lasok and Bridge (1991), *op. cit.*143. Kapteyn, Verloren van Themaat and Gormley (1989), *op. cit.*195.

Article 4 lists certain acts which may be performed only with the consent of the rightholder. These embrace mainly the reproduction, translation, adaptation or arrangement and the distribution of programs. Furthermore, it is provided, that the sale of a copy leads to an exhaustion of the rightholder's power to control further commercial acts with that particular copy.

In order to ensure that the rightholder does not abuse the strong position granted by the directive, Article 5 provides for some exceptions to the rightholders power to authorise restricted acts. These exceptions apply only for lawful acquirers of a program. The correction of errors in the program, the making of back-up copies and the intended use of the program are acts which do not need prior authorisation by the rightholder even if they include acts generally forbidden by Article 4. Also the observation and testing of the program by the lawful acquirer in order to determine its underlying ideas and principles cannot be restricted. However, such rules appear more or less superfluous, a clause that prohibits the use of the program by the buyer will be held void by national courts, anyway.

Furthermore, the reverse translation of software from its machine code form into readable form does not require prior permission by the rightholder, if this is necessary to obtain information about interfaces which are indispensable to achieve interoperability of a new program with the translated program (Article 6). Information obtained through this process may be used only for the purpose of attaining interoperability; however, it appears somewhat doubtful how this restriction could be enforced in practice.

Member States are obliged to enact provisions in their national laws which safeguard the observation of these rules (Article 7). This includes measures against devices or software which are especially designed to circumvent the copy protection of programs. The possession of an infringing copy by a private person for non-commercial purposes is not included in the list of prohibited acts in the directive. Nonetheless, Member States cannot be forced to implement criminal penalties, since the Community has no power to legislate in criminal law.[32] The directive itself, therefore, leaves the way of enforcement to the discretion of the Member States.

The duration of the copyright will be a minimum period of 50 years, beginning with the death of the author (Article 8). Thus it appears that France will have to change its above mentioned shorter period of protection. The directive does not regulate anything concerning moral rights of authors such as the right to be named as the creator. This is left to a general harmonising measure on EC level, which is still under way.

---

[32] T Oppermann (1991), *Europarecht Ein Studienbuch* (Juristische Kurzlehbucher), Munich: Beck 432.

5. Inconsistencies and Contradictions Within the Directive

5.1. Restricted Access to Free Ideas?
As mentioned above, the directive excludes ideas and principles from protection. At the same time it restricts the access to these ideas and principles by prohibiting reverse translations of the code of software.[33] This is contradictory, because an idea which may not be read or known is not free but protected. The maxim set out in Article 2(2), that underlying ideas and principles are outside the scope of the protection, is one of the very principles of copyright law. Therefore, the restrictions on reverse translations will have to be overridden by a systematic and goal oriented interpretation of the directive. Reverse analysis has sometimes been outlawed in literature as a form of software piracy. However, if we consider software in the context of copyright, we have to keep in mind that reverse analysis is nothing more than the actual reading of a program. It is comparable to reading a book or looking at a picture, which certainly is no infringement of copyright only because a temporary reproduction of the text is formed in the memory of the reader.[34] If we insist on protecting software under copyright law, we are not entitled to block the access to the ideas and principles which are outside the scope of the protection and are only accessible through reverse analysis. Opponents of this opinion frequently use the term 'reverse engineering' for reverse translations of a program in order to stress polemically the potential misuse of the knowledge about the program structure, which could be utilised to plagiarise a similar, infringing program.[35] However, this attitude is comparable to a publisher who tries to keep a novel secret fearing somebody could make a film of the plot without asking for permission. It is absurd to restrict access to information content if a means of protection for the particular mode of expression does exist. However, if it is the idea, or the underlying principles, which need protection, the copyright is the wrong legal instrument.

5.2. Overriding Force of Article 1(2)
From the formal character of programming languages it follows that certain ideas in a program are inseparable from the mode of expression. Another expression would be another program, which might be slower, potentially more complicated and therefore unreliable. In such cases the only optimum solution could not be granted copyright protection, because the principle that ideas are not protected must prevail (Article 1 (2)).[36] Otherwise, a protection would

---

[33] Junker (1991) *op. cit.* 2119.
[34] Cornish (1990) *op. cit.* 130, 131.
[35] Cornish, W. R. (1989a), Interoperable Systems and Copyright, *European Intellectual Property Review* 391.
[36] Comp. Freed (1989), *op. cit.* 76; Hart, Robert J. (1991), Interfaces, Interoperability and Maintenance, *European Intellectual Property Review* 113.

result in a monopolisation of crucial programming solutions which would distort competition between software houses and slow down innovation in the software sector. It is only logical in such cases not to grant copyright protection. Where the author has no choice to express his or her idea in different ways, there is only a non-copyrightable idea and no copyrightable expression. In other words, the author only repeats a necessary rule, or an algorithm, which in itself does not merit protection.[37]

5.3. Access to Interfaces

The permissibility of reverse analysis is connected with a need for the analyser to obtain knowledge about interfaces to a program which are indispensable for writing an interoperable program.[38] This interoperability therefore is considered highly important for a functioning competition between software houses, and for the achievement of open standards, which are in the interest of not only the user but also of the industry as a whole. Only a powerful software producer, controlling large parts of the market, could gain something from inaccessible interfaces.[39] It has, however, been pointed out that potentially every part of a program can be considered as an interface for another program, depending on what sort of interaction is intended by the programmer of the new application.[40]

Moreover, how does the rightholder intend to gain the information about the source code of the allegedly infringing program? A reverse translation, if unlawful, would make him or her a potential infringer as well, in case it comes out that the program has not been copied illegally.

5.4. Conflicts with other Industrial Property Rights

Another problem in the directive is the fact that it contains no provisions on conflicts between different ways of protection. Is a patented program application protected by copyright after the lapse of the patent? Or are both rights exclusive with the result that patent and copyright cannot occur in the same object?[41]

---

[37] This is prevailing opinion in the USA and Germany. However, in the UK the contrary is held by the courts; comp. Ehricke (1991), *op. cit.,*.324; Flint (1990), *op. cit.*, 319.

[38] Cornish (1989), *op. cit.,*391. Dissenting: Kindermann, Manfred (1990), Reverse Engineering von Computerprogrammen. Vorschläge des Europäischen Parlaments, *Computer und Recht* 638.

[39] Junker (1991), *op. cit.*, 2117.

[40] Hart (1991), *op. cit.* 112; Lake, William T., Harwood II, John H. and Olson, Thorn P (1989), Seeking Compatability or Avoiding Costs? A Reply on Software Copyright in the EC, *European Intellectual Property Review*, 431 at 432.

[41] Comp. Wenzel (1991), *op. cit.*110; Radcliffe (1991), *op. cit.* 361.

Furthermore, the directive contains no rule on how to decide the difficult issues in connection with the use of software libraries or computer aided programming. This might well lead to a very confusing situation.[42]

6. Concluding Remarks

The directive attempts to combine a copyright protection which prevents unauthorised exploitation of the program by protecting certain modes of expression of ideas from being reproduced or changed, with the secrecy protection of the information content of the program. The inconsistencies caused by this attempt can only be solved by resorting to the very principles of the directive in order to establish criteria, with the help of which the contradictory provisions can be put into a working concept. Having identified certain problematic inconsistencies, or even contradictions, in the directive, lawyers, nevertheless, cannot ignore the object of their study because they dislike it for its mistakes. As a legal instrument the directive is part of the Community legal order. It obliges the Member States, which will implement it into national law. Therefore, even if the approach appears to be far from optimum, lawyers will have to interpret and apply the directive and the laws based on it. In order to facilitate this, some concluding remarks shall be added.

Since potentially all parts of a program can be used as interfaces one could interpret the restrictions to reverse translation in Article 6 as obsolete. Another way to ensure the free access to ideas and principles of the program according to Article 2(2) would be to interpret 'reproduction' in Article 4 as not covering temporary reproductions for the mere use of reverse analysis.[43] This has already been suggested for national copyright law.[44] Furthermore, the term "translation" in Article 4(b) would have to be understood as meaning not reverse translations but only translations into different languages for purposes of multiple reproduction. Such a meaning would anyway be more compatible with the generally accepted concept that not the translation of a work in itself, but only the multiple reproduction for the purposes of marketing infringes the copyright of the rightholder.[45]

Another possibility would be to adopt a restrictive approach to the application of Article 1(3) oriented on the caselaw of the German Federal Court. This would prevent many inconsistencies since it would narrow down the

---

[42] Meijboom (1990), *op. cit.* 433; Dreier (1991b), *op. cit.* 321.
[43] Similarly Dreier (1991b), *op. cit.* 321; dissenting: Bauer (1990), *op. cit.* 89.
[44] Holländer (1991a), *op. cit.* 421; see also Loewenheim (1990), *op. cit.* 597.
[45] Dreier (1991b), *op. cit.* 326.

applicability of copyright protection to only the top 10 per cent of current software production.[46]

These suggestions would bring the directive in line with generally accepted principles of international copyright law. Additionally such an interpretation would be compatible with the Bern Convention, to which the directive refers.[47] The fact that the interest of software houses in keeping their software secret is not catered for in such an interpretation of the directive is only the result of the choice of copyright law as a means of protection. If information content of a program is to be protected from access, a new form of program right must be created, as proposed and discussed above.[48] It is, however, doubtful whether this is really necessary, since the copying of competitors software will often infringe copyright as provided for by the directive, even if the access to the information necessary to copy cannot be barred. However, this is an old problem of copyright law, which can be easily dealt with under present legislation.

---

[46] As suggested by König (1990a), *op. cit.* 1127; see also Ernsthaler (1991), *op. cit.* 881; Bormann (1991), *op. cit.* 2641, 2646.
[47] Cornish (1990), *op. cit.* 129.
[48] König (1991a), *op. cit.* 1127.

7
John T Cross
Protecting Computer Databases under the United States Copyright Laws: Implications of the *Feist* Decision

1. Introduction

Facts, as such, are not protectable under copyright law.[1] Notwithstanding this basic tenet, courts in both the Commonwealth countries and the United States have found ways to protect *compilations* of information under the auspices of copyright.[2] Protecting such compilations certainly serves an important social policy. Without protection against copying, there is little economic incentive for someone to spend the time and effort to collect and organise information into a useful form. Because copyright law offers a well-developed and workable

---

[1] *Harper & Row Publishers, Inc.* v. *National Enterprises*, 471 U.S. 539, 556 (1985), 'No author may [copyright] his ideas or the facts he narrates'.; *Financial Information, Inc.* v. *Moody's Investors Serv.*, 808 F.2d 204, 207 (2d Cir. 1986), *cert. denied* 108 S.Ct 79 (1987); *MacMillan & Co. Ltd.* v. *Cooper*, 40 (1923) *TLR* 186; *Victoria Park Racing & Recreation Grounds Co. Ltd.* v. *Taylor*, 58 (1937) *CLR* 479; *Deeks* v. *Wells*, [1931] *Ontario Rept.* 818.

[2] See, e.g. *Ascot Jockey Club Ltd.* v. *Simons*, (1968) 64 *WLR* 411; *Ladbroke (Football) Ltd.* v. *Wm. Hill (Football) Ltd.* (1964) 1 *All ER* 465; *Interfirm Comparison (Austr.) Pty. Ltd.* v. *Law Society of New South Wales* (1975) 5 *ALR* 527; *Rockford Map Publishers Inc.* v. *Directory Service Co.*, 768 F.2d 145, 148 (7th Cir. 1985), *cert. denied* 106 S.Ct. 806 (1986).

This principle is reflected in the governing statutes. In Great Britain, both s.35 of the Copyright Act 1911 and s.48(1) of the Copyright Act 1956 include 'compilations' within the scope of protected subject matter. Similarly, in the United States Section 103 of the Copyright Act of 1976, Pub. L. No.94-553, *as amended* by the Berne Convention Implementation Act of 1988, Pub. L. No.100-568, *currently codified* at 17 USC §§ 101-810 [hereinafter the '1976 Copyright Act'] specifically allows copyright protection to extend to compilations of information, but only to the new material contributed by the author of the compilation.

regime of protection, the courts have naturally turned to copyright as a basis for protecting compilations of information.

The United States Supreme Court's recent decision in *Feist Publications Inc. v. Rural Telephone Service Company Inc*,[3] however, has cast serious doubt on whether copyright can be used to protect factual compilations in the United States. The Court in that case held that the constitutional requirement of originality in United States copyright law precluded an author from claiming copyright protection in certain compilations of facts. Although the *Feist* opinion is on its fact limited to telephone directories, the reasoning employed by the Court has profound implications for other types of information compilations.

This essay will explore the likely effects on *Feist* on a particular type of information compilation; namely, the computer database. Publicly-accessible databases have become a tremendously valuable asset in today's information-driven society. Yet, the very nature of some of these databases makes any attempt to protect them by copyright particularly vulnerable to a challenge based upon *Feist*. Although most databases probably exhibit sufficient originality to qualify for copyright protection, some types may no longer be protectable.

2. The Nature of Computer Databases

2.1. The Development of Databases

One of the most notable offshoots of the tremendous growth in computer technology has been the birth of an entirely new information industry. The modern computer is capable of both storing and manipulating vast amounts of information. Science and technology have devised ways to make productive use of the computer's capacity to deal with information. This phenomenon has naturally resulted in an extraordinary increase in the demand for information as a *product*. The traditional sources of information - libraries and file cabinets - no longer meet this demand. Today's information-driven society instead requires readily accessible compilations of information converted into a medium which a computer can understand. The result of this demand has been a tremendous increase in both the number and variety of electronic databases.

A computer database actually comprises two basic elements. The first is the raw information contained in the computer's memory. The second is the software - the 'search program' - which will search the information in accordance with the instructions of the user. A given search program may be capable of searching widely differing compilations of information.

These two elements of a database are normally, but not always, the fruits of two different individuals' labour. The search program is created by a computer

---

[3] 111 S.Ct. 1282. 11 L.Ed.2d 358 (1991).

programmer. The actual data which goes into a particular database is collected and entered into the computer's memory by a different person (the 'compiler'[4]).

This paper will deal *only* with the information element of a computer database. There is little doubt that, in the United States at least, the search program would be protectable under the copyright laws.[5] Although written for use in a machine, the work of the programmer constitutes a work of authorship. The information contained in a database, on the other hand, involves primarily a particular arrangement of a set of facts. As such, the information component of a database presents a much closer question under the copyright laws, especially in view of the *Feist* decision.

2.2. Types of Databases

Computer databases can take one of three basic forms, depending upon the ways in which the information is arranged and recalled. As an illustration, imagine a chef who desires to keep an inventory of all of the ingredients in the kitchen. The inventory could be organised in three different ways.

The first is the 'free-format' method.[6] Under this system, the chef would simply enter the names of all the ingredients into the database. When he or she desired to prepare a recipe, the chef could simply enter the names of all necessary ingredients. The computer program would then scan the entire list of ingredients, and tell the chef which were available.

The second and third methods involve considerably more organisation. Under an 'hierarchical' system, the chef would organise all of the ingredients by type; e.g. 'herbs', 'meat' and 'fruits'.[7] The chef's search would entail ascertaining the heading under which a particular ingredient would be listed, and then searching the ingredients listed under that heading. In many respects, an hierarchical database is analogous to the table of contents of a book.[8]

---

[4] This essay assumes that the compiler is human. In some situations, the compilation may be accomplished by a computer. These situations present complex questions of copyright authorship which are beyond the scope of this essay. In addition, many databases allow the user to add information of his own choosing to the computer's memory. The original compiler in this situation obviously cannot claim copyright in information added by the user.

[5] *Apple Computer Inc.* v. *Formula International Inc.*, 725 F.2d 521 (9th Cir. 1984); *Apple Computer Inc* v. *Franklin Computer Corp.* 714 F.2d 1240 (3d Cir. 1983), *cert. dismissed* 104 S.Ct 690 (1984).

[6] The three categories of databases, as well as the terms employed to describe them, come from Krajewski, 'Database Types', *Byte*, October 1984 at 137.

[7] Each of these categories could also be further divided into subcategories. the 'meat' heading, for example, could be subdivided into 'beef', 'pork' and 'lamb'.

[8] Krajewski also discusses a system which he labels the "network database". Krajewski, *supra* note 6, at 140. The network database is similar to the hierarchical

The third approach, the 'field management' system, requires that the information be classified in accordance with certain shared characteristics. In many ways, each of the fields serves as a separate 'list' of that part of the data which shares that characteristic. For example, our hypothetical chef might create a field corresponding to the date on which each item would spoil, in order to ensure that perishable items are used first. In order to search for the perishable items, the chef would define a search by certain shared characteristics within one or more of the fields. If the chef was interested in using up perishable meats, he or she could ask the computer to search the database for those 'meats' whose 'shelf life' would expire in the next few days.[9]

Of the three types of databases, the free-format and field-management systems are the most useful.[10] An hierarchical system classifies information based on characteristics defined by the compiler. Under a free-format or field-management system, however, the user is given more freedom to define her own relevant characteristics. The same information can therefore be used for a wide variety of purposes.[11] On the other hand, a free-format or field-management system is only practical when computer technology is available. Both systems require the search of a greater number of items than does an hierarchical system.

---

database, except for the fact that it allows the user to relate a given record to *any* other record in the system. For the purposes of this essay, the network database can be considered simply as a variation of the hierarchical.

[9] Of course, many of the fields used in a field-management system might also serve as headings in an hierarchical system. For example, our chef might desire to create a field corresponding to the food type of each ingredient, such as 'meats' or 'fruit'. Nevertheless, the field-management system gives the user considerably more flexibility. Unlike the hierarchical system, the field-management system enables the user to limit the search to those characteristics which fit the particular purpose at hand. An hierarchical system, for example, would probably require our chef to list all meats, not only those which were about to spoil.

[10] Many databases combine elements of two or more of the systems. The LEXIS and WESTLAW legal database systems, for example, allow both words and field searches. As will become apparent below, these 'hybrid' databases do not present any special problems under copyright law.

[11] Actually, pure free-format databases constitute a fairly small percentage of the *commercial* databases in use today. Most commercial databases are designed with specific groups of users in mind. Because it is relatively easy to anticipate the types of searches in which these users will engage, commercial databases are typically put together in a field-management or hierarchical format.

On the other hand, free-format databases are more prevalent among non-commercial databases. Because these databases are not designed for specific purposes, the free-format structure offers the greatest flexibility.

When large amounts of information are involved, only a computer can accomplish the search in a reasonable amount of time.[12]

Yet, it is the inherent flexibility of these systems that makes them vulnerable under the rationale of the *Feist* decision. In order to understand the full implications of that decision, it is necessary to take a brief excursion through the development of copyright law as it pertains to databases.

3. Copyright in Compilations of Information and the *Feist* Decision

3.1. A Copyright in Compilations.[13]

In theory, a compilation of information could qualify for copyright protection at two different levels.[14] First, the compilation itself could be protected. Copyright in the compilation would prevent anyone from using the compilation to prepare an identical or substantially similar compilation. Second, copyright protection could be extended to the individual facts which comprise the compilation. In the latter situation, the compiler's protection is much broader. If copyright extends to the individual pieces of information, an infringement would occur whenever someone copied even a small percentage of the information.

As noted at the outset of this essay, courts have managed to protect certain compilations of facts notwithstanding the basic tenet that the underlying facts themselves are not copyrightable.[15] The basis for this protection, however, has been the subject of some dispute. Over the course of the twentieth century, United States courts have developed two primary approaches to the question.

---

[12] The author's field of legal research again provides an excellent example. Prior to the advent of computers, legal authority was classified almost purely in an hierarchical fashion. Computer technology has fostered the development of systems like LEXIS and WESTLAW, which allow word and field searches.

[13] For an in-depth discussion of this issue, see Annotion, 'What Constitutes a "Compilation" Subject to Copyright Protection - Modern Cases', 88 *ALR Fed* 151 (1988).

[14] Actually, in the case of a computer database there is a *third* element that might qualify for protection; namely, the subset of information generated as a result of a given search. The *compiler*, however, is unlikely to be able to assert any copyright rights in this output. Assuming that the compiler did not write the underlying search program, he is not the 'author' of the output. There is indeed an interesting issue as to whether the *programmer* or *user* is the author of this output; see *Stern Electronics Inc.* v. *Kaufman*, 669 F.2d 852 (2d Cir. 1982); *Williams Electronics* v. *Arctic Int'l Inc*, 685 F.2d 870 (3d Cir. 1982). Because this essay focuses on the compiler, however, this issue lies beyond its scope.

[15] See *Supra* cases cited in note 2. See also E. P. Skone James, J Mummery, J. Rayner James, A. Latman & Silman, Copinger and Skone James on *Copyright* 46-47 (12th ed. 1980); Denicola, 'Copyright in Collections of facts: A Theory for the Protection of Nonfiction Literary Works', 81 *Colum. L. Rev.* 516 (1981).

Some have found the required authorship in the compiler's selection, arrangement, or co-ordination of the information.[16] Under this theory, copyright protection extends to the entire compilation, not to the individual pieces of information.

A view which focuses upon the compiler's organisational efforts will protect certain compilations of facts, such as books of maps[17] and stock market indices,[18] for which the compiler's organisational efforts play a major role. The theory has two shortcomings, however, which significantly restrict the scope of protection. First, the theory protects only the compilation as a whole. It does not protect the individual items of information that make up that compilation. Therefore, no cause of action would exist against someone who either took only a small part of the underlying data,[19] or who arranged the data in a different fashion.[20] Second, there are certain types of databases, such as phone books and sports statistics, for which the compiler's main effort is in the *accumulation* of the information rather than the arrangement. Conditioning copyright protection on the existence of substantial organisational effort means that these types of databases cannot be protected.

These shortcomings led other courts to develop an alternate theory of copyright to protect compilations of information. This 'sweat of the brow' theory rewards the compiler based upon the significant time and effort spent by the compiler in accumulating the data.[21] It recognises the inequity that would exist if a third party was allowed to appropriate information without having to reimburse the compiler for her time and effort in gathering that information. More importantly, the 'sweat of the brow' theory allows the compiler to prevent others from copying any of the pieces of information which comprise the compilation. The theory accordingly extends copyright protection to *all* types of databases.[22]

---

[16] *Schroeder* v. *William Morrow & Co*, 566 F.2d 3 (7th Cir. 1977); *Harfield* v. *Peterson*, 91 F.2d 998 (2d Cir. 1937).
[17] *Rockford Map Publishers Inc.* v. *Directory Service Co.*, 768 F.2d 145 (7th Cir. 1985), *cert. denied* 106 S.Ct. 806 (1986).
[18] *Dow Jones & Co* v. *Board of Trade*, 546 F. Supp. 113 (SDNY 1982).
[19] *McMahon* v. *Prentice-Hall Inc*, 486 F.Supp. 682 (ED Penn 1976).
[20] *Triangle Publication Inc* v. *Sports Eye Inc.*, 415 F Supp 682 (E.D. Penn 1976).
[21] *Hutchinson Tel Co.* v. *Frontier Directory Co.*, 770 F.2d 128, 131 (8th Cir. 1985); *Jeweler's Circular Publishing Co* v. *Keystone Publishing Co*, 281 F.83, 89, 95 (2d Cir.), *cert. denied* 42 S.Ct 464 (1922); *National Business Lists, Inc* v. *Dun & Bradstreet Inc*, 552 F.Supp. 89, 92-93 (ND Ill. 1982).
[22] The sweat of the brow theory has never met with universal acceptance. In *Financial Information Inc* v. *Moody's Investor's Service Inc*, 808 F.2d 204 (2d Cir. 1986), for example, the Second Circuit Court of Appeal rejected the theory as

3.2. Feist

The United States Supreme Court considered both of these theories in its *Feist* decision. The plaintiff in *Feist* was a telephone company which published a directory of its customers.[23] Like most directories, the plaintiff's listed the names of all telephone customers in alphabetical order, together with their city of residence and telephone number. The defendant had prepared a competing area-wide directory, which included both the plaintiff's customers and others. The defendant had compiled its directory using the information contained in the plaintiff's directory, without first obtaining the plaintiff's permission.[24] However, the defendant did not directly copy the plaintiff's entire directory.

The defendant instead removed some of the names that fell outside the region covered by its own directory, and re-alphabetised the remaining names with the additional names of people not listed in the plaintiff's directory.

The plaintiff sued in federal court alleging copyright infringement. The trial court and court of appeals held for the plaintiff; holding that compilations of information are copyrightable, and that the defendant's use of that information without the plaintiff's consent infringed that copyright.[25] The Supreme Court, however, reversed on the rationale that the plaintiff's directory did not qualify for copyright protection.

Justice O'Connor's opinion for the Court began by noting the tension between two fundamental premises of copyright. Facts are not copyrightable. Compilations of facts, on the other hand, may be copyrighted.[26] O'Connor argued that resolving the tension between these two principles turns on an understanding of why facts are not copyrightable.

The answer to the dilemma, O'Connor reasoned, lies in the fact that copyright protection is limited to *original* works of authorship.[27] In order to qualify as original, a work must not only be independently created by the author, but must

---

inconsistent with the fundamental rule that facts are not copyrightable. See also *Nimmer, Nimmer on Copyright* § 8.4.1.2, at 102-04 (1990).

[23] 111 S.Ct , 113 L.Ed.2d at 367. Plaintiff was required by law to publish this directory.

[24] The defendant had requested a license to use the information from the plaintiff, but had been refused. Unlike the laws of many countries, United States copyright law contains no general compulsory licensing provisions.

[25] The trial court's opinion is reported at 663 F. Supp. 214 (D. Kan 1987); the Court of Appeals at 916 F.2d 718 (1990).

[26] 111 S.Ct , 113 L.Ed.2d at 368.

[27] Prior to the 1976 Copyright Act, the requirement of originality did not appear in the copyright laws, but was a court-created doctrine. The courts reasoned that Congress did not intend to protect works that merely aped existing works. *See Burrow-Giles Litographic Co* v. *Sarony*, 4 S.Ct 279 (1884). Section 101 of the 1976 Copyright Act codified this common law requirement.

also possess a certain degree of creativity.[28] Facts are not protectable because they are not created by the author.[29] Compilations of those facts, on the other hand, may involve some independent creative effort; and accordingly may in theory qualify for copyright protection.[30]

A necessary corollary of this argument is that copyright protection in a compilation extends only to the author's creative efforts. Copyright protects expressions of facts, not the facts themselves. In the case of a compilation, an author expresses the facts of *selecting* which facts to compile and *arranging* those facts in a manner designed to reach the desired end. Therefore, the compiler may obtain copyright protection only for his or her selection and arrangement of facts. As long as an alleged infringer does not copy that selection or arrangement, she is free to use those underlying facts without infringing upon the rights of the author.[31]

Justice O'Connor then turned to the alternative 'sweat of the brow' theory which the lower courts had applied to sustain the plaintiff's copyright. Her opinion unequivocally dismisses that theory as inconsistent with not only the copyright laws, but also the provisions of the United States constitution governing copyrights.[32] Reviewing the genesis of copyright law in the United States, O'Connor found a clear Congressional intent to reject that theory in the discussions culminating in the current copyright statute.[33] Under current law, originality - not effort - is the touchstone of copyright protection. Copyright law

---

[28] 111 S.Ct. at 1288, citing *The Trade-Mark Cases*, 100 U.S. 82 (1879).
[29] 111 S.Ct , 113 L.Ed.2d at 370.
[30] *Ibid*.
[31] 111 S.Ct. at 1290.
[32] *US Constitution* art. I, § 8, cl. 8 allows Congress '[t]o promote the Progress of Science and useful Arts, by securing for limited Times to Authors and Inventors the exclusive Right to their respective Writings and Discoveries'.
Because the *Feist* decision was based at least in part upon the Constitution, Congress is powerless to reverse it. It is interesting to note that a strong movement was underfoot prior to *Feist* to afford protection to compilations of facts under the sweat of the brow theory. Most notably, a subcommittee of the American Bar Association had proposed amendments to the federal copyright laws that would specifically authorise copyright protection for compilations on that basis. The subcommittee argued that its 'industrious collection doctrine' was necessary in order to encourage the compilation of 'valuable collections' of what was otherwise public domain material; citing as examples CD-ROM and other databases. Committe No. 702, 1989 SP66-R/702-1, *Section of Patent, Trademark and Copyright Law, 1990-1991 Annual Report*. It appears unlikely after the *Feist* decision that the ABA's proposed amendment would pass constitutional muster.
[33] The current copyright statute in the United States is the 1976 Copyright Act, cited *supra* in note 2.

protects only the author's creativity in selecting or organising facts, and then only to the extent of such selection or organisation. Accordingly, the plaintiff's efforts in assembling the information for the telephone directory were not themselves sufficient to invoke the benefits of copyright with respect to the collected facts.

Finally, the Court addressed the issue of whether the plaintiff's efforts in selecting and arranging the information were sufficiently original to qualify for copyright protection. According to Justice O'Connor, the telephone directory in *Feist* involved only a modicum of creativity. First, as all customer names were included, there was no creativity whatsoever in the process of selection. Second, although the plaintiff had arranged the information, its arrangement simply involved placing the names in alphabetical order. Justice O'Connor held that this method of arranging information failed the originality requirement. Although noting that the copyright laws require only a minimum of creativity,[34] she reasoned that an alphabetic arrangement fell into 'a narrow category of works in which the creative spark is utterly lacking or so trivial as to be virtually non-existent'.[35] City and telephone directories had historically been published in alphabetical order. There was therefore nothing creative in the plaintiff's choice of that arrangement for its directory. Because of the lack of originality, the plaintiff could assert no rights under copyright law.

4. The Impact of *Feist* on Computer Databases

Although *Feist* itself dealt with a telephone directory, the rationale employed by the Court in rejecting the plaintiff's claim of copyright protection could quite easily threaten copyrights in certain computer databases. In some respects, computer databases are much like a telephone directory. Most of the compiler's time and effort will be expended upon collecting the information and transforming it to computer-readable form. In addition, because the real value of a database depends largely upon the *amount* of information it contains, the compiler will not exercise a great deal of selectivity in 'weeding out' information.[36] Finally, depending upon the type of database, the level of creativity involved in organising the data may fall short of even the minimal levels required by the Court in *Feist*.

The availability of copyright protection for databases after *Feist* will depend in large part upon the *type* of database involved. Each of the three types of

---

[34] 111 S.Ct., 113 L.Ed.2d at 377.
[35] *Ibid.*
[36] Further, as will be discussed below in the text discussing selection of the information, the scope of information which is *relevant* to a database may be quite large, depending upon the category of database in question.

databases discussed above involve different levels of selection and arrangement. It is therefore useful to discuss each of the three categories separately.

4.1. Hierarchical Databases

Of the three categories discussed above,[37] the hierarchical database is probably the most likely to qualify for protection. As stated above, a compilation must meet minimal standards of creativity in the selection or arrangement of facts in order to satisfy the originality requirement of copyright law. Virtually all hierarchical databases will easily meet this requirement because of the degree of arrangement involved in assembling the database. The compiler of an hierarchical database typically exercises substantial creativity in creating the multiple tiers of the hierarchy and in fitting each of the individual pieces of information within those tiers. Establishing the hierarchy requires the compiler to divide the relevant subject matter into discrete classes, and to tie those classes together in an hierarchical fashion which will be readily understandable by the user. This certainly surpasses the minimal levels of creativity to which Justice O'Connor referred in *Feist*.[38]

4.2. Field Management Databases

Although it is a closer case, the field-management database should also pass muster under *Feist*. Again, the process of *arranging* a field-management database will itself meet the originality requirement of *Feist*. The level of creativity will generally be less in a field-management system than in an hierarchical system. Nevertheless, the process of defining the relevant fields requires the compiler to exercise a great deal of independent judgement. These fields, after all, define the scope of searches which a user can conduct on that database.[39] The compiler will therefore exercise a great deal of care in choosing fields which are most likely to be useful to subsequent users.[40] Further, after selecting the relevant fields, the compiler must arrange the data in accordance

---

[37] See supra text accompanying notes 6-9.

[38] One possible exception, however, would be a one-tiered hierarchical database arranged solely in alphabetical, chronological, or numerical order. The arrangement of this database would be so lacking in creativity as to fail even the fairly lenient originality requirements of *Feist,* and would accordingly be unprotectable under United States copyright law.

[39] Take, for example, our hypothetical chef. In defining the fields to be used for his inventory, the chef must be conscious of what sorts of searches he may later desire to conduct. As in the earlier example, if he anticipates a need to use up perishable foodstuffs, he may elect to define a field which looks to the shelf life of the item.

[40] Limitations in the search program may also restrict the number of fields which the compiler may use. This requires the compiler to pick and choose carefully among the possible fields.

with those fields. Therefore, the level of creativity in a field-management database will be sufficient to attain copyright protection.

4.3. Free-format Databases

The free-format database presents a more perplexing problem. The compiler of a free-format database typically does not exercise any significant creativity in translating the underlying information into computer-accessible form. This does not mean that compilers of free-format databases are somehow lazy. Instead, because of the inherent nature of the free-format database, arrangement serves no real purpose.

A free-format database typically allows the user to retrieve the information simply by identifying one or more words, letters, or numbers that *appear* in the facts themselves. The user is in no way bound by any predetermined hierarchy or set of fields. Indeed, it is this lack of any logical superstructure that makes free-format databases so flexible. On the other hand, this lack of superstructure also reduces the need for the compiler to exercise any creativity in either selecting or arranging the data.

Consider first the issue of *arrangement*. The compiler of a free-format database typically will not arrange the information in any predetermined form. Instead the information will simply be transferred *in toto* to the medium of storage. Because the user gains access simply by identifying components of the facts themselves, arrangement of the information serves no purpose. The computer must always search each and every item of information in order to ascertain whether that item contains the desired component.[41] Therefore, the compiler of a free-format database typically has no incentive to arrange the information in any particular fashion.

Of course, the compiler's initial development of the database is 'creative', at least in the vernacular understanding of that term. It could accordingly be argued that storing a particular body of information in a format accessible by word searches is itself an arrangement, and that arrangement is sufficiently creative to qualify for copyright protection. But, this argument fails on two grounds. First, the simple act of entering raw information into a computer's memory is unlikely to satisfy the originality requirements of *Feist*. The compiler in these circumstances is merely transforming the information into a form commanded by the dictates of the underlying search program. This is no less

---

[41] Compare this to an hierarchical system. Again using our overworked chef, suppose our chef wants a list of all vegetables which he has on hand. This list can be recalled from an hierarchical database simply by proceeding through the hierarchy to the desired level. The search need not consider those individual items of information which fall under different parts of the hierarchy.

obvious an arrangement than the alphabetic listing of names at issue in *Feist*, and should therefore fail for lack of originality.

Second, even if the act of entering the information is a sufficiently creative 'arrangement', the creativity is not that of the compiler. Any creativity instead belongs to the programmer who devised the underlying search program. The compiler simply arranges the information into a format which the search program can use. Thus, because the *compiler* has exercised no creativity, the mere act of transforming the information into a computer accessible format will not earn him or her any copyright protection in the arrangement.[42]

The second possible grounds for obtaining copyright in a compilation under Feist is the degree of creativity in the process of *selection*. A compiler who exercises sufficient creativity in choosing the facts to include in the compilation may thereby earn copyright protection for the compilation. Relying upon selection as the basis for copyright protection of a free-format database, however, is problematic. A compiler admittedly may exercise a fair amount of judgement in determining what facts to include in the database. It is not clear, however, whether that selection may be protected under the copyright laws.

Copyright affords protection only to *expression*, not to the idea behind that expression. Ideas, like facts, are in the public domain and may freely be copied.[43] The problem lies in drawing a clear line between the idea and the expression. This problem is especially knotty in the case of a computer database.

Resolving this issue, of course, turns on how broadly one defines the 'idea' of a particular database. On the one hand, the 'idea' of a computer database could be the configuration of the database itself, *i.e.*, a compilation of information that fits within certain predefined parameters. On the other hand, one could argue that the 'idea' of a database is something broader than the parameters defining the database. The idea underlying a database might be the *purpose*, rather than the parameters, of that database.

Of these two definitions, the former is preferable. It is unlikely that a court would define the idea underlying the database by looking to the purpose of that database. The more commonplace cause of a play provides a useful analogy. The idea underlying a play is not the general desire to tell a story. It is instead the particular story line chosen by the playwright for that play.[44] Similarly, the idea underlying a database would be the specific choice to create a database

---

[42] C.f. *Signo Trading Int'l Ltd.* v. *Gordon*, 535 F.Supp. 362 (N.D. Cal. 1981) (translation does not involve originality).
[43] *Harper & Row,* 471 U.S. at 556.
[44] *Nichols* v. *Universal Pictures Corp.*, 45 F.2d 119 (2d Cir. 1930).

containing certain types of information, not the more amorphous desire to provide information to various types of users.[45]

Under the narrow definition, the process of selecting facts will not by itself secure copyright protection in the compilation. The compiler admittedly exercises a great deal of creativity in selecting the parameters which delineate the database. However, because those parameters define the idea, they may not be protected under copyright law. Therefore, the compiler may not prevent others from copying the 'idea' of a database containing certain types of information.[46]

In addition to selecting the parameters, of course, the compiler will also select individual items of information to include in that database. If the idea is the database itself, however, the process of selecting information involves no *independent* creativity. The parameters of the database itself define the types of information which will be included. Sorting through the universe of information to select the particular items to include is merely a mechanical process of determining which items fit within the preset parameters. That work is not creative in the manner envisioned by *Feist*. Further, although there may be a significant amount of work involved in weeding out the irrelevant information, *Feist* holds that this 'sweat of the brow' cannot by itself secure copyright protection for the compilation. The compiler of a free-format database accordingly may not claim copyright protection for a database on the basis of the time spent in selecting information to include in the database.

To illustrate, again consider our hypothetical chef. Suppose our chef decides to create a database including all ice cream flavours. This initial decision is

---

[45] If the broader definition were to be adopted, however, the free-format database might be protectable. The compiler's selection of facts to include would be treated not as the idea, but as a means of *expressing* that idea. Because that expression now involves some creativity, it might qualify the database for copyright protection even after *Feist*.

[46] Defining the idea of a computer database as the parameters of that database also raises the issue of whether the database might be denied copyright protection under the 'idea/expression identity' doctrine of United States law. Although copyright protection ordinarily extends to all original expressions of a given idea, there are some ideas that can be expressed in one or a very few ways. In such a case, United States courts will refuse copyright protection to the expression in order to prevent monopolisation of the underlying idea. *Baker* v. *Selden*, 101 U.S. 99 (1879) (accounting forms); *Morrissey* v. *Proctor & Gamble Co.*, 379 F.2d 675 (1st Cir. 1967) (rules of a game).
This exception, however, will not apply to most computer databases. There will ordinarily be many ways in which to set up a database containing the desired information. For example, the compiler must make the initial choice of determining which of the above-described database formats to use.

certainly creative. However, it is not protectable under copyright law inasmuch as it is an idea. Based upon this idea, the chef will next assemble the database by sorting through the vast body of available information and pulling out those items that relate to ice cream flavours. This sorting is not creative. It is merely a mechanical act defined by the underlying idea.[47] Providing copyright protection to the database on the basis of this sorting process would have the effect of protecting the underlying idea. Therefore, if the idea behind a free-format database is the parameters that define the extent of that database, the *Feist* decision suggests that a free-format database will no longer qualify for copyright protection.[48]

The Supreme Court's decision in *Feist* therefore casts serious doubts on the availability of copyright protection for the information stored in free-format databases. By definition, the compiler of a free-format database does not arrange the information in any meaningful manner. In addition, the compiler does not exercise any significant creativity in selecting information to include in the database. Absent some degree of creativity in either selecting or arranging the information, *Feist* indicates that copyright protection is unavailable. And without copyright, the compiler has no legal recourse against one who copies all or part of that database.[49]

5. Conclusion

The decision of the United States Supreme Court in *Feist Publications. Inc.* v. *Rural Telephone Service Co. Inc.* promises to have repercussions in the fledgling electronic information industry in the United States. By re-establishing originality as a touchstone of copyright law, the *Fiest* case may prevent certain computer databases from qualifying for copyright protection. The information compiled in a database is without doubt valuable. Its value, however, stems from the efforts of the compiler in accumulating that information. *Feist*

---

[47] The inherent flexibility in the types of searches which a user can conduct in a free-format database further reduces the need for the compiler to exercise selectivity. In order to avoid foreclosing any potential avenues of search, the compiler has an incentive to include as much information in the database as possible.

[48] This same rationale would also apply to hierarchical and field-management databases. Again, the selection of information for those databses is a mechanical process dictated by the decision to create the underlying database. As discussed above, however, hierarchical and field-management databases will qualify for copyright protection on the basis of the creativity involved in *arranging* the information in the database.

[49] Section 301 of the Copyright Act 1976 pre-empts all state laws which provide rights 'equivalent' to the rights granted under federal copyright law. Under s. 106(1) of that Act, the copyright owner has the exclusive right to 'reproduce' the work.

indicates that this 'sweat of the brow' is not a sufficient condition for copyright. The compiler must instead exercise some creativity in either selecting or organising the information.

Fiest, however, does not deny copyright protection to all databases. It is only the 'free-format' database - which involves little creativity in either the selection or arrangement of the component information - which presents a problem. The full implications of *Feist* on the free-format database will only become apparent over time.

8
Thomas Hoeren
Electronic Data Interchange: the Perspectives of Private International Law and Data Protection

1. Introduction

The increasing use of electronic data interchange (EDI) leads to many difficult problems in data protection law which have almost not been considered by court and academic literature up to now. Millions of sensitive personal data may be transferred daily from one country to another with the aid of EDI.[1] Data subjects have a right to be protected against these transborder data flows (TBDF) especially when their data are transferred to countries with inadequate data protection law.[2]

However, almost all data protection acts in the world have the taint of administrative law and are, consequently, only referring to national data transfers.[3] Additionally, the adaptation of data protection law to transborder data flows has widely been criticised as a 'bureaucratic nightmare, impossibly cumbersome, ineffective'.[4]

It is my aim to demonstrate how data protection law may be used as an effective weapon against national 'data havens' - without becoming a bureaucratic nightmare. Since it is not possible to refer to all data protection acts, I will restrict my remarks to an exemplary case:

> 'A German company has decided to co-operate with a British company. They made an agreement that they use EDI for all relevant data

---

[1] Cf. Briat, (1988) Personal Data and Free Flow of Information, in Hansen et al. (ed.), *Freedom of Data Flows and EEC Law,* Deventer, p.47.
[2] Cf. Millard, Transborder data flows: The European Perspective, Paper presented at the CLA conference on Distribution, Access and Communication, Amsterdam, 1st - 3rd June, 1988.
[3] See Bing, Reflections on a Data Protection Policy for 1992, 5 *YLCT* 1991, p. 175.
[4] Kirby, Data Flows and the Basic Rules of Data Privacy, 16 *Stanford Journal of International Law* 1980, pp. 27-66, at p. 29.

exchanges. In particular, personal data of employees are going to be exchanged between the companies. The contract includes provision for rights of the employees to access and rectification of their data. The employees of both companies consider this contract and the transfer of data to be unlawful; the question comes before a German court.'

2. EDI, Data Protection and the Question of Private International Law

First the question of what law is applicable in this case has to be discussed. Is this transborder data flow governed by German or British data protection law? Many theories have been discussed to solve this problem.[5] According to Rigaux[6], the law of the state in which the data subject usually lives has to be applied. Some authors[7] regard the place of data processing (whatever that means) to be relevant; in a similar way, the EEC proposal for a Council directive on data protection[8] provides in Article 4(1)(a) that the directive has to be applied to 'all files located in its territory'. Finally, the use of the domicile of the data users as a criterion for determining the relevant law has also been discussed.[9]

---

[5] See the profound doctoral thesis of Elleger, *Der Datenschutz im grenzuberschreitenden Datenverkehr. Eine rechtsvergleichende und kollisionsrechtliche Untersuchung*, Baden-Baden (Nomos) 1990, p. 584 et seq.

[6] Rigaux, La loi applicable a la protection des indivudues a l'egard du traitement de donnees a caractere personnel, *Revue critique de Droit International Prive* 1980, p. 443 et seq,; cf Koch, Rechtsvereinheirlichung und Kollisionsrecht, *Recht der Datenverarbeitung* 1991, p. 110 - 111

[7] Bergmann, *Grenzuberschreitender Datenschutz*, Baden-Baden (Nomos) 1985, p.239 et seq.; Fraysinnet/Kayser, La loi du 6 janvier 1978 relative a l'informatique, aux fichiers et aux libertes et le decret du 17 juillet 1978, in: *Revue Du Droit Public* 1979, p.686. Cf Rigaux, Le regime des donnees informatisees en droit international prive, *Journal Du Droit International* 1986, p.324.

[8] Proposal for a Council directive concerning the protection of individuals in relation to the processing of personal data of 27 July 1990, COM (90) 314 final - SYN 287. The text of the proposal is included in Chalton/Gaskill, *Encyclopedia of Data Protection*, London Sweet and Maxwell, 1991, No, 7-678. The proposal has been redrafted with regard to the amendments proposed by the European Parliament on 11 March 1992. The amendments are considered below. The second version of the Proposal will be published in Autumn 1992; unfortunately, the new proposal could not be dealt with in this article.

[9] Cf. Hondius, Data Law in Europe, 16 *Stanford Journal of International Law* (1980), p.109; A decade of International Data Protection, 30 *Netherlands International Law Review* (1983), p. 120; Clariana, TDF, Data Protection and International Law, (1981) *TDR 4*, P.33

In my opinion, the discussion has been too unbalanced and narrow-minded. A distinction needs to be made between at least two different questions:
- Which law is generally applicable in transborder data flow issues?
- Which law is governing the contract on EDI and international data traffic?

2.1. The general view

The first question is what law is generally applicable to transborder data flow issues. In Germany, this question is regulated by the new Data Protection Act of December 20, 1990 ('Gesetz zur Fortentwicklung der Datenverarbeitung und des Datenschutzes'/BDSG).[10] This Act does not contain a special provision on transborder data flows between private institutions.[11] However, the Act implies that all data users domiciled in Germany are obliged to observe its provisions (cf, Sect.27(1) and Sect.2(4)).[12] Hence the German law has to be applied if
- a data user, the person storing or transferring personal data;[13]
- has his or her domicile, usual residence or seat[14], in Germany.

This is the reason why the BDSG does not make any difference in the nationality of the data subject. Every data subject who is affected by data processing of a German file controller is able to use the rights under the BDSG - independent of his or her nationality.

In our example, the parties have agreed to exchange data mutually so the transfer of data from Germany to Britain is governed by German data protection law because the transferring company has its seat in Germany. In as much as the British company is transferring data from Britain to Germany, the transfer is governed by British law.

2.2. The Proper Law of a Contract on EDI

A different approach may be necessary to find the relevant law for a contract on EDI:

---

[10] *Bundesgesetzblatt* 1990 I, p. 2954. The Act entered into force on 1 June 1991; cf. article 6.
[11] Only the transborder data flow of state authorities is regulated; cf. sect. 17.
[12] See Ellger, Datenschutz, *op. cit.,* p. 604 et seq.
[13] In my view, a very difficult problem may result from online access. Via online access a British corporation may use personal data which are stored on a computer in Germany. In this case, it is unlikely that the German law will be applied although the direct transfer of data or the use of data by online access are similar procedures.
[14] See the decision of the Federal Supreme Court of 5 November 1980, BGHZ 78, p. 318, at p. 334; Grobfeld, *Praxis des Intenationalen Privat-und Wirtschaftsrechts*, Reinbek (Rowohlt) 1975, p. 44 *et seq.* - The German definition of the domicile of corporations is different from the definition in England and Wales; cf. *Ceena Sulphur Co. Ltd.* v. *Nicholson* (1976) 1 *Ex. D.* 428; *De Beers Consolidated* v. *Howe* (1906) A.C. 455; *Swedish Central Ry.* v. *Thompson* (1925) A.C. 495.

2.2.1. General Rules of the Lex Contractus

The question of the law applicable to contractual regulations on EDI is governed by Article 27 - 37 of the 'Einfuhrungsgesetz zum Burgerlichen Gesetzbuch (EGBGB)'. According to Article 27 EGBGB, the parties of a contract are free to choose the applicable law. If the parties have not made a selection (either explicitly or implicity), the law which is most closely connected with the contract must be considered (Article 28 (1) EGBGB). This depends on the characteristic duties of the contract, specially on the main non-pecuniary obligation.[15]

2.2.2. The Mandatory Nature of German Data Protection Law

These rules must, however, not be applied to contracts of EDI as far as personal data are concerned. According to Article34 of the EGBGB, mandatory regulations continue to apply notwithstanding the parties choice of a different law. The regulations of the BDSG are mandatory[16]: Sect.43 of the BDSG states that it is criminal to use data contrary to the BDSG. According to Sect.38 of the BDSG, the data protection authorities have to control the realisation of the provisions of the act; they are allowed to put heavy sanctions on the data users in the case of violations of the BDSG. Therefore, it is not possible to derogate from the regulations of the BDSG by contract. All disputes between the parties on the contract have, thus, to be settled by applying the law of the state in which the data user has taken his or her seat or residence (see above).

2.2.3. Application of the Mandatory British Data Protection Law?

The final question is whether the mandatory British data protection law has to be applied beside the German law. Some authors suppose that mandatory foreign regulations on data protection should be applied under certain circumstances.[17] The German courts, however, have unanimously held that foreign law should never be applied if a contract is governed by German law.[18] In my opinion, this

---

[15] Federal Supreme Court, Judgment of 6 February 1981, *Neue Juristische Wochenschrift* 1981, p. 1903; Oberlandesgericht Hamburg, Judgment of 15 December 1977, Recht der Internationalen Wirtschaft 1978, p. 615. This is similar to the English proper law doctrine; cf.Morris. *The Conflict of Laws*, 3rd ed. London (Sweet and Maxwell) 1984, p. 265 et seq.

[16] Ellger, Datenschutz, *op. cit.,* p. 602 *et seq.* and 635 *et seq.*

[17] Cf. Ellger, Datenschutz, op. cit., p. 643 et seq.; see Wengler, Anknupfung des zwingenden Rechts im Internationalen Privatrecht, 54 *Zeitschrift fur vergleichende Rechtswissenschaft* 1941, p. 197; Radtke, Schuldstatut und Eingriffsrecht, 84 *Zeitschrift fur vergleichende Rechtswissenschaft* 1985,p. 335.

[18] This rule is called the 'doctrine of territoriality' (Territorialitatsprinzip). Bundesgerichtshof, Judgement of 17 December 1959, BGHZ 31, p. 367 *Neue Juristische Wochenschrift* 1960, p. 1101; Bundesgerichtshof, Judgment of 16 April 1975, BGHZ 64, p. 189 *Neue Juristische Wochenschrift* 1975, p. 1220. For other doctrines see *Munchener Kommentar zum BGB/Martiny*, 2nd. ed. Munich (Beck)

consideration has to be supported for the following reasons: the sovereignty of a state is restricted to its territory; national law is therefore only mandatory within the borders of a state; it loses its mandatory nature after 'leaving' the orbit of statual power. Consequently, it is not the task of German courts to enforce foreign 'mandatory' law in a case where German law applies. This legal situation has not been changed by the European Contracts Convention[19], although Article 7(1) of the convention permits the court to give effect to the mandatory regulations of some third country, the German legislator has reserved its right under Article 22(1)(a) not to apply Article 7(1).[20]

2.3. Summary
The German Data Protection Act is applicable in all cases of transborder data flow initiated by a person with seat or residence in Germany. Foreign mandatory regulations have no effect in these cases. British law has to be applied where personal data are transferred from Britain to Germany. These rules are mandatory; a contractual choice of law is invalid (Article 34 EGBGB).

3. EDI and the New German Data Protection Act

3.1. Special Regulations
While Sweden, Denmark, Austria, Great Britain and France have included provisions on transborder data flow in their data protection acts, the German data protection law does not contain any special regulation on this subject in the private sector. This situation has not changed with the enactment of the amended Data Protection Act in June 1991. The legislator has still refused to create new provisions on TBDF although many voices in literature have criticised this statutory gap.[21]

3.2. Some Hints
However, there are some hints in the new BDSG which may help to solve the

---

1991, Art. 34 EGBGB, Note 25 et seq. with further references.

[19] For the text of the Convention see North (ed.) *Contract Conflicts*, London, Butterworths 1982 and Morris/North, *Cases and Materials on Private International Law* London (Butterworths) 1984, pp. 459 -465.

[20] Cf. Bundesrats-Drucksache 222/1/83, p. 9; see Martiny, Der Deutsche Vorbehalt gegen Art.7 Abs. 1 des EG-Schuldvertragsubereinkommens vom 18.6.1980 - Seine Folgen fur die Anwendungen auslandischen zwingenden Rechtes, *Praxis des Internationalen Privat - und Verfahrensrechts* 1987, p. 277 *et seq.*

[21] See Simitis/Dammann, *Commentary on the Bundesdatenschutzgesetz* 3rd ed. Baden-Baden (Nomos) 1981, 22 Note 51; Simitis, Grenzuberschreitender Datenaustausch - Notwendige Vorbemerkungen zu einer dringend erforderlichen Regelung, *Festschrift fur Murad Ferid zum 70. Geburtstag*, Munich (Beck) 1978, p. 354 - 375.

problem of TBDF and its legality under German data protection law:

3.2.1. *General Considerations on TBDF*

The German data protection law uses a very restrictive approach with regard to the processing of personal data: In general, all data processing, any data storage and any data transfer has been forbidden in the act. It allows the transfer of personal data in only two cases: either the data subject has given written consent to the transfer or the disclosure has expressly been authorised by specific statutory provisions (Sect.4(1)).[22] If a transfer of data is not based on consent or statute, it is held to be unlawful.

3.2.2. *Written Consent*

This gives rise to the difficult question of whether TBDF and EDI may be authorised by consent. In fact data users very rarely rely on the written permissions of data subjects. With regard to the amount of data transferred by means of EDI, it is too complicated to ask each data subject for consent. But even if a data user has got the consent, this consent may be void. Some authors[23] have regarded a general consent to any form of data processing to be *contra bonos mores* and invalid.

3.2.3. *EDI and Statutory Authorisation*

Therefore, the main question is whether TBDF and EDI may be authorised by statutory provisions. The BDSG contains very detailed and restrictive regulations on data transfer. According to Sects.28 and 29, the transfer of data is deemed to be lawful if the legitimate interests (schutzwurdige Interessen) of the data subject prevail.

But when do the legitimate interests of a data subject prevail in the case of TBDF and EDI? The German literature[24] unanimously distinguishes between two 'constellations' of TBDF. In the first personal data may be transferred to a country which has a data protection law comparable and equivalent to the German regulations. In this case the data subject has not lost his or her rights to access, rectification and erasure of data so that the data transfer does not effect his or her interests. The situation is different, however, if the data are transferred to a country which has no data protection law or imperfect regulations (compared to the German standard). The data subject has a right to be protected against data transfers in favour of 'data havens'. Therefore, the German law allows personal data only to be transferred to states with an 'equivalent' data

---

[22] This iron rule has been called the 'Magna Carta of the German data protection law'.
[23] Auernhammer, *BDSG* 2nd. ed. Munich (Beck) 1981, Sect. 4 Note 35; cf. Ellger, *op. cit.*, p. 412.
[24] Simitis/Dammann, *op.cit.*, 22 Rdn. 54,; Ordermann/Schomerus, *BDSG* 4th ed. Munich (Beck) 1988, 24 Anm. 5; Auernhammer, *op. cit.* 24 Rdn.9

protection law.

3.2.4. *The 'Equivalence'*

These considerations lead to the main problem of TBDF: What is meant 'equivalence'?[25] Which states are provided with a data protection law comparable to the German standard? Does the transborder data flow from Germany to Great Britain violate the legitimate interests of data subjects so that it is unlawful?

Up to now, Belgium, Greece, Italy, Spain and Switzerland have no data protection regulations at all.[26] Hence personal data must not be transferred from Germany to these states; such transfer is regarded as unlawful and may even be prosecuted as crime.

Unlike these 'data havens', the British legislator has enacted a detailed Data Protection Act (DPA) which shows many similarities with the German Act. For instance, they both cover automated personal data used in the public and private sectors. The problem of transborder data flow itself has been solved in Great Britain with a special provision (Sect.39) which is even more detailed than the German regulations. Both acts give data subjects:

- a right of access to records on themselves;
- a right to apply to the court for rectification and erasure;
- a right to apply to the courts for rectification of data and loss or unauthorised disclosure.

There are, however, some doubts as to the equivalence of the British Act since there are major differences between these two statutes:

- The DPA only protects automated data (Sect.1(2)) while the German Act also extends to personal data stored in manual records.
- The DPA does not contain special provisions regulating the storage and transfer of data, it only applies the Convention[27] of the Council of Europe with regard to some very general and vague data protection principles.
- The data protection registrar has never used his power under Sect.12 to restrict TBDF.[28] Additionally, he is not able to prohibit data traffic to

---

[25] For this difficult problem see Riegel, Gemeinschaftsrechtlicher Datenschutz. Entwurf einer EG-Datenschutzrichtlinie, *Computer und Recht* 1991, p. 181; Simitis, Datenschutz und Europaische Gemeinschaft, *Recht der Datenverarbeitung* 1990,p.11

[26] See table prepared by Christopher Millard in Chalton/Gaskill, *Encyclopedia of Data Protection*, London (Sweet and Maxwell) 1991, no. 7-630

[27] Convention for the protection of individuals with regard to automatic processing of personal data of 28 January 1981; the text of the convention may be found in Chalton/Gaskill, *Encyclopedia of Data Protection* , London (Sweet and Maxwell) 1991, no. 7-195. - Cf.Evans, European Data Protection Law, 29 *American Journal of Comparative Law* 1981, p.571 *et seq*

[28] Napier Vertragliche Losungen im grenzuberschreitenden Datenverkehr, *Recht der*

Spain which is merely bound by the European Convention, but has no data protection legislation.[29] This legal gap contrasts to the situation in Germany where a transfer of data to Spain is likely to be regarded as unlawful (see above)
- Sect.34 of the new German BDSG provides for a right of data subjects to be informed, free of charge, which of their personal data are used, for which purpose they are held and to whom they are regularly transferred (in the case of automated data). The British DPA only grants such rights if the data subject pays for the information (Sect.21(1)).[30]
- The DPA contains some exemptions which are unknown to German law, such as the provisions on payroll and accounts (Sect.32).

Consequently, it has to be decided whether despite these differences, the British Act is equivalent to the German provisions. Some authors criticise the British regulations as being too lax.[31] In my opinion, the problem cannot be solved by using sweeping statements. The British DPA has almost the same standard of protection with regard to automated data as has been established under the German Act. Both Acts grant the same protection against the transfer of personal data with the aid of EDI. The fact that the British Act does not include provisions on data stored in manual recordings is irrelevant in EDI cases.

The 'Spanish problem' mentioned above is, in my view, a more difficult issue. If personal data may be transferred to a state without any specific data protection law, the establishment of 'data havens' may be supported by transborder data flow and EDI. A German corporation is, for instance, not allowed to transfer data directly to Spain under German law. The English law may promote the idea of circumventing this regulation by transferring data first to England and then from England to Spain.

It is thus very doubtful whether the English data protection law is equivalent to the German law. A transfer of personal data from Germany to Britain by EDI may thus be unlawful under the German Data Protection Act.

3.3. The Computer Bureaux

The German Act contains another regulation with regard to TBDF focusing on computer bureaux, persons and corporations who provide services in respect of personal data.

Datenverarbeitung 1990, p. 214.

[29] Cf. Aldhouse, UK Data Protection - Where are we in 1991?, 5 *YLCT* 1991, p. 187 with reference to other problems of this section of the DPA.

[30] Cf. Walden/Edwards, Data Protection, in: Reed (ed.), *Computer Law*, London 1990, p. 216 - 217.

[31] National Council for Civil Liberties 1984, para. 2.1.; cf. Ellger, *op. cit.*, p. 388; Savage/Edwards, Transborder Data Flows: The European Convention and the United Kingdom Legislation, 35 *International and Comparative Law Quarterly* 1986, p. 710.

The German Data Protection Act only applies to the transfer of data if the transferee has to be regarded as a 'third person' (Dritter), e.g. a person different from and independent of the transferor (Sect.2 (3)).

The Act additionally provides that computer bureaux are in general not third persons in relation to their customers (Sect.2(9). Therefore, the disclosure of data to computer bureaux is generally lawful; furthermore, the new German Data Protection Act expressly provides that the customers, but not the computer bureaux, are liable for any violations of the act (Sect. 11(1)).

If the computer bureau is located abroad the situation is different. In this case, any disclosure of data is regarded as a transfer of data to a third person so that the bureau and the customer are responsible for the enforcement of the Act (Sect. 2(9)). This regulation has the effect that transborder data flow to a foreign computer bureau is only lawful under the restrictive conditions mentioned above.

3.4. The Proposal for a Council Directive on Data Protection

The actual legal situation may be summarised to the effect that a transfer of personal data from Germany to Great Britain is likely to be lawful, even in the case of a transfer to a British computer bureau. Therefore, the different standard of data protection within Europe is likely to become a big problem for TBDF and EDI.

The situation will yet change with the implementation of the future EC directive on data protection. The Commission has held in the preamble of its proposal for a data protection directive that the directive is necessary to promote an equivalent 'level of protection in relation to the processing of ... data .. in all the Member States'. Thus, an EC directive may be an effective way to create a uniform standard of data protection within Europe so that EDI will be lawful within all EC member states.

The German authorities have, however, made a very strange statement concerning the importance of the EC directive. For instance, at a conference in Munich on January 30, 1992 the Federal data protection commissioner, Dr. Alfred Einwag, stressed that the EC directive would only establish a minimum regime of data protection. In his opinion, the EC member states will still be allowed to create more restrictive data protection regulations. Therefore, Germany need not change its legislation because of the directive.

I do not agree to this way of thinking, Article 1 (2) of the EC proposal expressly states that the 'member states shall neither restrict nor prohibit the free flow of personal data between Member States' with regard to their national data protection law. Any regulation on data protection which goes beyond the scope of a EC directive will become an obstacle to the free flow of data within the Community.

Therefore, the German authorities would violate Article 8a of the EEC treaty and the idea of an European market without frontiers by postulating national regulations on TBDF different from the EC directive. The efforts of the EC Commission to establish a uniform level of data protection within Europe will force the German legislator to adopt the EC regulations and change the German Data Protection Act at least with regard to TBDF.

4. Contractual Regulations on Data Protection

The difficult legal problems mentioned above lead to the question of whether contractual arrangements may grant an equivalent data protection in TBDF cases. In our case, the parties have made some arrangements on TBDF and data protection in a special contract. Does this contract placate German data protection lawyers?

The question has been the subject of controversial discussion in Germany. Many authors claim that effective contractual obligations with regard to data protection may be sufficient to allow TBDF.[32] The former data protection commissioner of State Hessen, Spiros Simitis, has vigorously objected to this idea.[33]

The controversy has been caused by different views on the effectiveness of contractual rights. Simitis believes that the data subject will never be a beneficiary of a contract which has been closed between the data transferor and the transferee; the parties of this contract are free to change the contract and its data protection provisions at any time.This opinion may be true with regard to the English law which emphasises the Roman tradition of the 'privity of contract'.[34] The German law, however, allows contracts to be concluded on behalf of a third person (Sect.328 of the Burgerliches Gesetzbuch). Therefore, Simitis seems to have forgotten that access or erasure rights of a data subject may be embodied in a contractual agreement between data transferor and transferee.

However, the German courts have not yet solved all the problems to which

---

[32] Ordemann/Schomerus, *op. cit.*, Sect. 24 Note 5; Gallwas/ Schweinoch/ Schwappach, *Bunesdatenscheuzgesetz*, Stuttgart (Kollhammer) 1978, Sect 24 Note 84; Schwappach, Internationale Datenflusse im Bereich der Industrie, *Datenschutz und Datensicherung* 1978, p. 24; ibid., Grenzuberschreitender Datenverkehr und Datenschetz, *Wirtschaft und Vertwaltung* 1980, p. 32 et seq. Even the Data Protection Commissioner of Hamburg has supported this concept; see the Eighth Report of the Commissioner, November 1989, p. 130 f.; Tenth Report of the Commissioner, November 1991, p. 162.

[33] Simitis/Dammann, *op.cit.*, Sect. 22 Note 55.

[34] *Dunlop v. Selfridge.* [1915] A.C. 847; *Jackson v. Horizon Holidays Ltd*,[1975] 1 WLR 1468; cf. Napier, Vertragliche Losungen fur das Problem des gleichwertigen Datenschutzes im grenzuberschreitenden Datenverkehr, *Recht der Datenverarbeitung* 1990, p. 215; Ehmann "Vertragslosungen" auf der Basis der EG-Datenschutzrichtlinie, *Computer und Recht* 1991, p. 234.

this special form of contract may give rise. There are a lot of questions which remain ambiguous and unclear:

(1) Suppose the transferee refuses rectification of data to the data subject in breach of the contract. The data subject may then terminate the contract and claim compensation.[35] But what about the transferor? Is he or she allowed to terminate the contract, too? There are no precedents with regard to this problem. Some authors have held that a contract closed in favour of a third person may only be terminated if the third person consents (or if all contracting parties agree).[36] Other commentators suppose that the parties to a contract may terminate the contract without any consent of the third person.[37]

(2) The parties may reserve the right to change the contractual rights of the third person (cf. Sect.328(2)] of the BGB). This reservation may either be expressly included in the contract; or may be implied.[38] Thus, the parties of an contract on EDI may easily cancel the rights of a data subject. Some literature discusses whether this reservation must be accepted by the third person.[39]

(3) If the data subject asserts his or her contractual rights, the transferee may refuse to grant access or rectification of the data if the transferor has not fulfilled his or her contractual obligations towards the transferee (Sect.334 of the BGB). In our case, the employees will thus not be able to realise their rights in regard to the British company if the company has not received all relevant data from Germany. This problem may only be solved if there are contractual provisions which deal with this situation. However, there is some controversial discussion as to whether Sect.334 is mandatory or not .[40]

---

[35] Oberlandesgericht Munich, Rechtpfleger 1972 p. 32; Landgericht Bonn, *Neue Juristische Wochenschrift* 1970, 1084.

[36] Soerge/Hadding, *Burgerliches Gesetzbuch* 12th ed. Stuttgart (Kollhammer) 1990, Sect 328, Note 45; Dorner, *Dynamische Relativitat*, Munich (Beck) 1985, p. 304 *et seq.*

[37] *Munchener Kommentar zum Burgerlichen Gesetzbuch* /Grottwald, 2nd. ed. Munich (Beck) 1985, Sect. 335 Note 6; Erman/Westermann, *Kommentar zum Burgerlichen Gesetzbuch*, 8th ed. Munster (Ashendorff) 1990, Sect 335 Note 2.

[38] Bayerisches Oberstes Landgericht Mitteilungen der Rheinischen Notarkammer, 1989, p.111.

[39] Cf. Staudinger/Kaduk. *Kommentar zum Burgerlichen Gesetzbuch* 12th ed. Berlin (de Gruyter) 1979, Sect 328 Note 117; *Reichsgerichtsratekommentar zum BGB* /Ballhaus, 10th ed. Stuttgart (Kollhammer) 1967, Sect 328 Note 38 with further references.

[40] Cf. Landgericht Frankfurt, Judgment of 1 September 1982 (2/22 0 155/82), *Neue Juristische Wochenschrift* 1983, p. 53; Bundesgerichtshof, Judgment of 17 January

Consequently, a contract on TBDF has to be drafted to the effect that the data subjent gets inviolable and unchangeable rights equivalent to those under the German Data Protection Act otherwise the contract does not have the effect that transborder data flow is lawful.

The legal situation is likely to become more difficult with the future EC directive on data protection mentioned above. According to Article 24 of the proposal, the transfer of personal data to non-EC countries shall only be lawful if these countries ensure 'an adequate level of protection'. This regulation has been amended by the European Parliament[41] to the effect that the transfer of 'particular categories of specified data' (whatever that means) may 'be prohibited in order to prevent damage to data subjects interests from an inadequate level of protection'.[42]

Furthermore, the proposal presumes that contractual arrangements on TBDF and data protection are in general invalid if the third country has no adequate level of protection. The proposal exceptionally accepts TBDF contracts under special conditions (Article 25):

(1) The controller of the file has to give sufficient proof that an adequate level of protection will be provided.
(2) The Member State in which the file is located has to authorise such a transfer of data.
(3) The EEC Commission and all Member States have to be informed, and be given a ten-day period in which notice of opposition may be given.

On the one hand, this procedure is too bureaucratic and cumbersome. Supposing that the United States has a low standard of data protection compared to Europe, the transfer of any personal data from Europe to the United States will be subject to a complicated system of control and authorisation. This complex system will cover all transfers regardless of their importance and extent, and will even apply within to data transferred within a multinational corporation. Thus, it may threaten worldwide scientific and technical co-operation and will cause a lot of problems for multinational corporations.

On the other hand, the procedure endangers the protection of privacy. Article

---

1985 (VII ZR 63/84), BGHZ 93, p. 275 *Neue Juristische Wochenschrift* 1985, p. 1458 against Gernhuber, *Das Schuldverhaltnis*, Munich (Beck) 1989, 20 IV 3c.

[41] Amendments adopted by the European Parliament on 11 May 1992, reprinted in J. Dumotier (ed), *Recent Developments in Data Privacy Law*, Leuven (Leuven University Press) 1992, p. 159 ff.

[42] E.P. No. 78. This amendment demonstrates that the European Parliament has a more liberal view with regard to transborder data flow to non-EEC States. The way in which the Parliament has drafted its amendment indicates that TBDF shall be held to be lawful in general. It may only be prohibited if a Member state can prove an inadequate and dangerous level of protection in the third country.

25 includes a lot of ambiguous terms: What, for instance, is the meaning of 'adequate level of protection'? Does this term refer to the EC standard of protection or to the national data protection regulations of an EC Member State? How can a controller of a file guarantee this level of protection? By means of a contract? Which clauses should be included in the contract to ensure an adequate level of protection?

A period of ten days is too short in the case of modern telecommunications networks and the expanding use of EDI. If a corporation transfers a huge amount of personal data to non-EEC countries via satellites, the EC Commission and the Member States have to check very carefully whether these transfers comply with the European standard of data protection. It is absurd to give them only ten days in order to give notice of opposition.

If the requirements set up in Articles 24, and 25 are not realised, any transfer of personal data is held to be unlawful even if the person concerned has consented to its transfer. This is too rigid. Why should a person be protected against a transfer of data concerning him or her if such protection is unwanted? The European Convention on Human Rights and most national constitutions stress the individual right of self-determination. In my view this right is violated if the person concerned is not allowed to consent to transborder data flows. Fortunately, this problem has recently been considered by the European Parliament which amended Sect.24. The effect is that TBDF will always be lawful if it is carried out with express consent of the data subject. [43]

5. Conclusion

The existing legal framework has put heavy restrictions on the use of EDI for the purpose of transborder data flows. The example the of transfer of personal data from Germany to Britain has demonstrated that difficult problems of private international law and various aspects of data protection may prevent transborder data flows.

These problems have their origin in the fact that the conflict of laws and data protection have been regarded as national issues. There is still no European regulation in these areas are still missing. With regard to private international law, uniform European rules have only been established with regard to the contract law (see above).The European states have not been able to develop provisions equivalent to the national regulations on data protection. A European standard of protection cannot be created with the aid of the data protection principles embodied in the Convention of the Council of Europe, because these principles are too vague and empty.

---

[43] Cf. No. 78 and 127 of the ammendments adopted by the European Parliament on 11 March 1992: "The transfer of personal data to a third country may require the express consent of the data subject".

The importance of these problems will increase with the development of the Common European Market in 1993. The EEC Commission certainly has tried to deal with the TBDF issue and published their long-awaited proposal for a directive on data protection. These efforts have, however, been subject to worldwide criticism[44] especially because the EEC proposal has been prepared with undue haste and under the pressure of professional lobbyists. The German authorities[45] have already rejected the proposal; they think that the proposal might abrogate the constitutional principles of data protection, as:

(1) the idea of the German Constitutional Court[46] that all personal data should be protected in the same way so that special categories of sensitive data do not exist (cf. Article 17 of the EEC proposal);

(2) the idea of the German Constitutional Court that any controller of a file (both computer and non-computer files) shall respect the privacy of a data subject, even though the controller is working for a non-profit making body (cf. Article 3(2)(b) of the proposal, a credit - information organisation of the press (Article 19));

(3) the idea of the German Constitution court that the regulations on the processing and transfer of data should be made using clear and unambiguous terms as far as possible (cf. the term 'national security' in Article15(1)(a) of the proposal).

Consequently, there will be a lot of discussion in the future concerning the EEC directive on data protection and its implementation into German law.

---

[44] See for instance Knauth, Datenschutz und grenzuberschreitender Datenverkehr in der Kreditwirtschaft, *Wertpapier-Mitteilungen* 1990, p. 213; Ellger, Datenschutz und europaischer Binnenmarkt, *Recht der Datenverarbeitung* 1991, p.134-135.

[45] Cf. Walz, Europaische Gemeinschaft - Informationeller Großraum und Harmonisierung der Datenschutzes, Paper presented at the IIR conference 'Datenschutz in der Industrie' in Munich, 30 January 1992.

[46] Federal Constitutional Court. Judgment of 15 December 1983, NVerfGE 65, 1 *Neue Juristische Wochenschrift* 1984, 419; Judgment of 9 March 1988, *Neue Juristische Wochenschrift* 1988, 2031; cf. Federal Supreme Court, Judgment of 15 December 1983, *Neue Juristische Wochenschrift* 1984, 1889; Federal Labour Court Judgment of June 6 1984, *Neue Juristische Wochenschrift* 1984, 2910.

Part IV
EVIDENTIAL MATTERS

9
P.A. Collier and B.J. Spaul
A Forensic Methodology for Countering Computer Crime

1. Introduction

According to a Council of Europe Committee of Ministers report on Computer Related Crime[1] 'computer-related crime is a real and, at least in respect of certain offences, expanding phenomenon.' The impact of computer abuse is illustrated by a recent report carried out by the London Business School[2], which put British annual losses from computer fraud at over £407 million. The survey supports the findings of other UK surveys like the Audit Commission,[3] which reported an increase in both the number of incidents and losses and observed that 'opportunities for misuse continue to increase in line with technological advance.' These results together with similar reports from the US[4] suggest that computer crime is a threat, which it would be unwise for businesses to ignore. Such findings, plus increased publicity on hackers and viruses[5], gave rise to business pressure for legislation, which led to the passing of the Computer Misuse Act in 1990.

This legislation may not solve the problem. As Stanley[6] stated these are the major problems in investigating computer crime:
     (1) competency of the investigators;
     (2) definition/terminology difficulties;
     (3) evidentiary problems; and
     (4) jurisdiction/law deficiencies;
and legislation only deals with the last of these. This statement is supported by recent history on the success of the authorities in prosecuting computer crime.

---

[1] *Recommendation No.R (89) 9 of the Committee of Ministers to Member States on Computer Related Crime*, Council of Europe.
[2] Reported in *Management Accounting*, March 1990, 63(3): 24-26.
[3] *Survey of Computer Related Fraud and Abuse*, 1990, London: HMSO.
[4] See Hoffer J A and Straub D W Jr. The 9 to 5 Underground: Are you policing computer crimes? *Sloan Management Review* 1989.
[5] See Bowcott D and Hamilton S (1990) *Beating the System*, London: Bloomsbury.
[6] Stanley, P.M., Computer crime investigation and investigators *Computer and Security* 1986 (5) 309-313.

For example, the latest Department of Trade and Industry figures, as reported in *PC Business World* 13 February 1990, reveal that of 270 computer crimes notified in the last five years only six have been prosecuted. This problem is not confined to the UK, in Germany in 1987 2777 cases classified by the police as computer crimes resulted in only 170 convictions and in France, since the passing of their computer misuse legislation, only 10 of the 70 substantiated complaints to the police have been successfully prosecuted in the courts (Council of Europe Committee of Ministers Report 1989).

Any system of controls can be classified as either proactive or reactive. In relation to computer crime proactive controls are responsible for preventing criminal acts by reducing opportunities, this type of control is emphasised in computing and accounting literature. However, these controls alone have proved insufficient to stop the increase in computer misuse and reactive controls, such as the effective detection and prosecution of computer criminals, must supplement them. This paper discusses how the laws against computer crime can be enforced. A crucial element in achieving this will be the development of a forensic methodology for application to computer crimes and abuses.

2. Definition of Forensics

The word forensic is defined in the Oxford English Dictionary as an adjective meaning '... used in, or connected with a court of law', and the term forensic science as a 'science that deals with the relation and application of scientific facts to legal problems.' Traditionally forensic science has centred on the physical and applied sciences such as medicine, engineering, chemistry, ballistics, etc. However, more recently social sciences, such as psychology and accounting, have been added to the forensic science armoury. These social science extensions of forensic science have a dominant requirement for interpretative and judgmental skills, rather than the detection of physical evidence. This paper advocates an extension of forensic science to cover crimes committed using computers. The extension is termed computer forensics and would cover the collection of forensic evidence from computers for use in a court of law. This requirement establishes a standard of work for the forensic systems analyst or investigator. Public scrutiny in a court of law places unique burdens on forensic scientists. For the computer forensic expert the problems are exacerbated by the obvious difficulties of explaining the complexity of criminal computer based activities to a jury of twelve members of the public, and uncertainties in the UK on what constitutes admissible computer generated evidence.[7]

---

[7] See Walden, I (1989) *EDI and the Law*, New York: Addison Wesley.

3. Role of Computer Forensics

Computer forensics is new in that it gives a label to existing but very limited activities amongst the police and consultancy firms. The different areas in which computer forensics could play a constructive role include:

(1) Civil matters - there is an increasing need for expertise in the investigation and assessment of the integrity of computer systems in civil cases. The estimation of the size and nature of losses from negligence, invasions of privacy, industrial espionage and social nuisance (e.g. the release of viruses) are increasingly required in civil cases.

(2) Criminal matters - recently white collar crime has become increasingly computerised as criminals recognise the potential for crime given by the anonymity of computer systems and the development of electronic funds transfer systems and electronic data interchange systems.

(3) Insurance - the preparation and assessment of insurance claims arising as a result of system failure or penetration, on behalf of both insurers and the insured may well require the assistance of a forensic systems analyst.

(4) Government - the forensic systems analyst can assist governments with regulatory compliance by ensuring that the appropriate legislation is being applied in private organisations, where applicable.

4. Reactions to the Threat of Computer Misuse

As has been stated, firms have a vested interest in improving proactive controls and making computer crimes harder to commit. Senior management must accept that computer crime poses a real threat and impost cost effective measures for its prevention. The exact controls used vary between organisations but a strengthening of personal procedures, physical access restrictions, tightened password procedures, better supervision of computer staff and securing data transmissions are typical defensive measures.

Some governments reacted to computer misuse by focusing on detection, prosecution and deterrent sentences. The UK has belatedly, in comparison to the US, Canada and much of Europe,[8] recognised computer crime as a separate offence. The growth in computer crime also requires that society ensures that those who prevent, detect or otherwise counter computer crime are properly trained. This need has been recognised in the Netherlands[9] where the Dutch police have established an experimental squad of specialised computer crime detectives at a cost of some £5 million to improve conviction rates. At a minimum, training should cover:

---

[8] Hollinger, R C and Lanze-Kaduce L , The Process of criminalisation: The case of computer crime laws *Criminology* 1988 26(1): 101-126.
[9] See *Computer Weekly* 25 October 1990.

(1) The police - according to Cornwall[10] out of 144,000 police officers only four or five officers concentrate on computer crime at any one time. An unacceptable situation given the importance of securing evidence as soon as a crime is detected.
(2) The Crown Prosecution Service - prosecuting barristers specialising in computer crime are essential if the current prosecution success rate is to be improved.
(3) Senior Management in public and private sector organisations - countering computer fraud requires that management in all organisations be aware of the threat and the importance of a systematic approach to its prevention, detection and prosecution.
(4) Security officers in public and private sector organisations. Despite countermeasures, computer crimes will occur in firms. An important deterrent is the 'on the spot' expert.

5. The Computer Forensic Methodology

Currently assistance with prosecuting crimes which involve computers is available from two sources: consultants; and the police. The appropriate agency to give assistance will depend on the investigation process, which can be viewed from two standpoints:
(1) internal investigations - carried out by the possible victim organisation or their agents, perhaps as a preliminary to involving public agencies, or until sufficient evidence is collected to pursue a civil case;
(2) external police investigations - either from the outset, utilising a specialist team of experts, who deliberately distance themselves from employees of the victim organisation, or following on from an internal investigation.

The skills implicit in a computer forensic approach to a computer crime investigation will probably be provided by a multi-disciplinary team of a similar constitution regardless of whether an internal or external investigation is taking place. However the *modus operandi* of the two types of team would necessarily be quite different.

The members of a forensic team conducting an investigation will have the following skills:
(1) investigative - to supervise the conduct of the investigation and interview suspects and witnesses;
(2) legal - a knowledge of the laws which can be applied against computer related offences and the laws of evidence;
(3) court room presentation - acting as a witness or expert witness; and

---

[10] Hacking away at computer law reform, *New Law Journal* 1988 (30): 702-770.

(4) computing - to uncover how the crime was committed, assist in reconstructing computer evidence and tracing proceeds of the crime.

Although computer forensic skills are currently provided by those with police, legal and computing skills, if the growth of computer crime continues, it is possible that computer forensics specialists with the complete range of skills listed above will emerge from consultancy firms or be provided by the police.

Having outlined the areas of expertise it would be useful to examine each of the skill areas identified in greater detail.

6. Investigative Skills

Computer forensics skills should include the conduct of an investigation into computer crime or abuse. Nasuti[11] suggested that computer crime investigations should be based around a formal action plan prepared for this eventuality. In particular the plan should cover:

(1) objectives - guidelines on defining the scope of the inquiry. Management must specify the goals, which could include recovery of past losses, discovering how the crime was committed, identifying controls to prevent a recurrence but not prosecuting the perpetrator, identifying the perpetrator and collecting sufficient evidence to support a dismissal or identifying the perpetrator and pressing criminal charges;

(2) notification - standard internal procedures should exist for notifying senior management and relevant outside bodies. The maintenance of secrecy is important in computer crime cases as computers facilitate either the destruction of evidence or malicious damage to the installation by the alerted perpetrator. At a minimum those notified should include the board of directors, the heads of internal audit and of finance; and

(3) membership of an investigating team.

Computer forensic skills will be involved in deciding upon an action plan irrespective of whether the investigation is internal or involves the police. The likely major steps to be followed include:

(a) determine the exact nature of the computer crime or abuse and whether it is ongoing or complete;

(b) identify how the crime was committed and the hardware and software involved;

(c) determine whether the crime was a solo effort or relied upon collusion and whether the perpetrator(s) came from within or from outside the organisation;

(d) determine sources of evidence and their admissibility;

(e) identify possible witnesses and suspects;

---

[11] Investigating computer crime *Journal of Accounting and EDP* 1986, 8(3): 13-19.

(f) examine personnel records of suspects for 'red flag' indicators (Albrecht *et al.* 1984) such as not taking holidays, a possible grudge against the organisation, extravagant lifestyle and falsified references.

(g) interview witnesses and suspects; and

(h) analyse and re-analyse the evidence gathered on a continuing basis.

As well as skills in managing the investigation, computer forensics requires the ability to interview suspects, analyse evidence and quantify losses. Although managers may have the skills to interview job applicants or counsel staff, interviews in the course of a computer crime investigation will require special abilities and may well best be left to the police. The following guidelines apply:

(1) the interview should be carried out by two or three people (more would intimidate the interviewee), notes should be taken and the interview tape recorded. At the end of the interview the tape should be copied and handed over to the company solicitors or police in return for a timed and dated receipt to remove accusations of the recording having been tampered with.

(2) The objective of the interview is to, as stated by Comer[12], 'create such empathy and confidence that admissions and confessions are almost obligatory'. Achieving this requires a three stage approach. The first stage involves building empathy and demonstrating that the truth will inevitably out. Following this the interviewer builds up the stress by showing that the interviewee will inevitably be found guilty and that therefore a confession is the only sensible option. Once guilt is admitted the interviewer in the final stage obtains detail of the crime.

Investigative skills also require an ability to analyse and re-evaluate the evidence collected and the results of interviews. In essence, the process is akin to solving a puzzle with the important difference that it may never be solved. At the least, the method of the crime must be determined so that controls can be strengthened. Finally, investigative skills cover the documentation of the investigation in a form suitable for management and perhaps the prosecuting authorities.

Finally the investigative team will need to quantify the losses, both direct and consequential, consider the wider financial implications of the matters under investigation and instigate procedures to trace monies lost.

7. Legal Skills

Until August 1990 and the Computer Misuse Act, there was no such thing in the UK as a computer crime (except the Data Protection Act 1984) and therefore the prosecution of offences involving computers had to be based on the offences

---

[12] *Corporate Fraud* (1985) USA: McGraw-Hill.

available under the existing body of law. The Act has simplified the position and criminalised the following three actions:
   (1) unauthorised access to computer material (s.1);
   (2) unauthorised access with the intent to commit or facilitate the commission of further offences (s.2);
   (3) unauthorised modification of computer material (s.3).
To prove that an offence has been committed the following must be demonstrated:
   (a) the computer performed a function as a consequence of either access being attempted or actual access (sections 1 and 2);
   (b) the access was unauthorised (sections 1 and 2);
   (c) the person attempting access knew that it was unauthorised (sections 1 and 2);
   (d) the access was a preliminary to committing or facilitating a serious offence (s.2);
   (e) the modification to computer material was or would have been caused (s.3);
   (f) the modification was unauthorised (s.3);
   (g) the person attempting the modification knew it was unauthorised (s.3); and
   (h) the intention of the modification was to impair the computer's operation (s.3);

It is no easy matter to establish these points. At a minimum there must be an access control system with a secure log, which records all accesses, but even then it is necessary to link the terminal being used with the perpetrator of the offence. This would only be easy if a person authorised to certain access attempted to exceed these limits while signed on under his or her own password. Otherwise the person using the terminal would need to be caught in the act. Even in the first situation the user could throw doubt on the evidence on the ground that the user:
   (a) left the machine logged on and the unauthorised access was by a third party taking advantage of the situation; or
   (b) was the victim of a compromised password.

The demonstration of intent in the s.2 offence may be even more problematic. In the event of hacking, the multiple password attempts recorded in the access control log will provide some evidence but further evidence will probably depend on the nature of the system being accessed. The proof of unauthorised modification is straightforward provided that there are regular back ups, secure transaction logs and clear rules on the types of transactions employees are authorised to carry out.

The Act has simplified the prosecution of persons responsible for attempting to or actually penetrating a computer system and those introducing viruses or other rogue software. The offence is punishable by a fine and/or term of imprisonment.

The Act belatedly brings English law into line with the situation in the US, Canada and much of Europe. For example, in the US virtually all states (excepting District of Columbia, Maine, Vermont and West Virginia) have followed the lead of Florida and Arizona in 1978[13] and have enacted specific laws against computer abuse often following a model computer law available from the Data Processing Management Association. In 1984 and 1986 Congress enacted two pieces of computer crime legislation (US Public Laws 98-473 and 99-474) and in January 1988 state laws were strengthened by a federal Computer Crime Act. Similarly in Canada, ss.301.2 of the Criminal Code states that a mischief is committed by persons who wilfully: destroy or alter data; render data meaningless, useless or ineffective; obstruct, interrupt or interfere with any person in the lawful use of data; or denies access to data to any person who is entitled to access thereto. In France, Article 462-2 of the Law 88-19 provides an offence of fraudulent access to a machine. West German legislation made it illegal to gain unauthorised access to secure computers and the Swedish Data Act 1973 is probably the earliest creation of the offence of gaining unauthorised access to a computer. Currently, according to the Law Commission,[14] of major industrial countries only Belgium and Japan rely upon existing laws to counter computer crime and abuse. The Computer Misuse Act 1990 also covers the Law Commission's recommendation (Law Commission Report number 180 1989) for surmounting the jurisdiction problem, which arises in situations such as where a terminal in New York can be used to access computers in the UK, by merely requiring in section 4 that there must be at least one significant link with the domestic jurisdiction for the legislation to apply.

Currently relevant offences, which extend and might be used in conjunction with the Computer Misuse Act 1990, in the context of computer forensics are:

(1) Theft Act 1968 s.1(1) and s.17(1), which define the offence of false accounting as the alteration, concealment, destruction or falsifying of accounts. However the Act would not cover the theft of information since as Lord Upjohn observed in *Boardmann* v. *Phipps*[15] "In general, information is not property at all" - therefore it cannot be stolen. This prevents prosecution under the Act in data theft situations where access is made to computer files purely to obtain information.

---

[13] See Tapper, C (1990) *Computer Law*. London: Longmans.
[14] See *Computer Misuse* (Law Com. No. 186 Cm 819). London: HMSO.
[15] [1966] 3 *WLR* 1009, [1966] 3 *All ER* 721.

(2) Theft Act 1968 s.15(4) which covers deception. Its applicability to computer crime is limited in that it is the human mind (and not the computer), which must be deceived.

(3) Forgery and Counterfeiting Act 1981 s.1, which is relevant in situations where a person makes a false instrument with the intention that it shall be used to induce somebody to accept it as genuine. In *R* v. *Gold and Schifreen*[16], the Act's applicability to computer crime was reduced by the requirement that something of permanence must come into existence. However, it may be relevant where access to the computer is obtained *via* a forged device, for example a fake electronic identity device, or possibly if the computer were manipulated to raise documentation which authorised the movement of goods or money. However, it is probable that the alteration of data within a computer, which subsequently leads to documents being issued which cause a deception, would not be covered as the computer and not the person has been deceived and made the false instrument. In probability the use of this Act will be unnecessary given the new misuse legislation.

(4) Criminal Damage Act 1971 s.1(1), which covers the unlawful destruction or damage of another's property or reckless behaviour leading to such damage or destruction. This is suitable for prosecuting malicious acts against either the computer or the files as well as for topical computer abuses like viruses and logic, Trojan horses and logic bombs as described in Burger (1988). This act was used in *Cox* v. *Riley*[17] when the defendant deliberately erased a computer program from a plastic circuit card of a computerised saw so as to make it inoperable and again in *R* v. *Whiteley*[18] resulted in the successful prosecution in the Crown Court of virus attacks on university computers. Notwithstanding these decisions, there must be considerable doubt concerning the extent to which the erasure of data or programs stored as electrical impulses can be argued to be damage to tangible property as required by s.10 of the Act. This very unsatisfactory position lead the Law Commission in their 1989 report to reject the extension of s.10 to include data and programs in favour of a new offence, which was enacted in the Computer Misuse Act.

(5) Criminal Law Act 1977 retained the common law offence of conspiracy to defraud. Although the scope is wide, as was confirmed in *Scott* v. *Metropolitan Police Commissioner*,[19] it cannot be committed by a person acting alone.

---

[16] [1988] 2 *WLR* 984.
[17] [1986] 83 *Cr.App.R.* 54.
[18] [1991] 93 *Cr. App. R.* 25
[19] [1975] *AC* 819.

As well as a knowledge of possible offences, which may be committed by a criminal using a computer, computer forensics also requires a knowledge of the law of evidence. Evidence in English law is categorised as either being direct or indirect (hearsay) and under common law only direct evidence is admissible. Criminal evidence rules related to the admissibility of documents stored on computer are contained in the Police and Criminal Evidence Act 1984 and the Criminal Justice Act 1988. The Criminal Justice Act 1988, s.24 provides that documents arising from trade, business, professional, occupational or official activities which record information supplied by a person who has personal knowledge of the matters, are admissible if the maker of the statement cannot reasonably be expected to remember the matters contained in the record as would often be the case in computer environments. Further, as was held in *R v. Minors*[20] a computer produced statement must also meet the requirements of the Police and Criminal Evidence Act 1984, s..69 which states that:

(1) no reasonable grounds for believing that the statement was inaccurate due to the improper operation of the computer; and

(2) the computer was operating properly, or if not that any irregularities would not affect the statement's accuracy.

The evidence must be certified. The certificate must specify the document, describe how it was produced including details of the equipment, state that s.69 requirements are met and be signed by a person responsible for the operation of the computer. The court is empowered to require oral evidence to support submissions but is unlikely to do so unless the accuracy of the matters certified is disputed.

These provisions give the defence considerable scope for shedding doubt on the computer derived evidence.

Another area of contention is authentication of the evidence (a print-out may be authentic in that it was produced by the computer even if it proves to be inaccurate or unreliable). There are no English cases which deal directly with the authentication of evidence derived from a computer. The closest case is *R. v. Maqsud Ali*[21], which centred on a tape recording in an obscure Punjabi dialect. A translation prepared for jurors (a parallel may be drawn to the transcription of magnetic into printed output) was acceptable provided the voice was properly identified and the accuracy of the recording was proved. However the judge gave the caveat that 'Such evidence should always be regarded with some caution and assessed in the light of the circumstances of each case'. The US position in the Federal Rules of Evidence is more relaxed. The requirement in rule 901(a) is 'evidence sufficient to support a finding that the matter in question

---

[20] [1989] 1 *WLR* 441.
[21] [1966] 1 *QB* 688.

is what the proponent claims' and interpretations, as in *US* v. *Velda*[22], suggest that 'a level of authentication greater than that regularly practised by the company in its own business activities go beyond the rule ...'. A more rigorous approach it is argued is tantamount to a presumption that computer records are *prima facie* inaccurate.

In the practical sphere, where a computer has been used in the commission of a crime, steps should be instigated to protect and preserve the evidence. In 1988 *R* v. *McMahon*[23] collapsed because of a failure by the police to secure the computer disks, which held key evidence, in a satisfactory manner. The possibility of malicious or self-destruct features may also be considered and files on the system should be saved prior to investigating the system to guard against this. Further, access to the computer should be carefully controlled not only at a physical level but also by suspending all current passwords and reissuing new passwords to trusted staff.

Finally, computer forensics should involve co-ordinating efforts to recover funds stolen. Such activity is not primarily a police function, although they will obviously provide assistance, and therefore a defrauded firm will usually consult accountancy and legal specialists. In solving a computer crime the police will often attempt to trace the funds and if the funds are in the UK the police can apply for court orders to assist tracing them. Once found if the monies are in a bank account abroad, the authorities may have the right to freeze the account but this step is not available under UK law although a High Court Judge may, following an application from the prosecutor, issue a Restraint Order as a prelude to obtaining a Confiscation Order from a Crown Court on conviction. This should enable some of the funds to be recovered. If the funds are abroad victim companies will have to pursue recovery through local legal processes.

8. Court Room Presentation Skills

Cases involving computer fraud and abuse often combine a need to absorb large volumes of data presented as evidence and to comprehend conflicting evidence, which is couched in the technical jargon of the computing and accounting disciplines. This can prove confusing to jurors and witnesses and reduces the likelihood of justice being dispensed in a rational and methodical fashion. To avoid hiding the issue rather than clarifying it when presenting volumes of technical data, computer forensic skills must include an ability to present evidence in an understandable form. This will involve the computer forensics practitioner in making appropriate use of information technology facilities like:

(1) visual aids displayed on screen;

---

[22] [1982] 673 F.2nd 86 (5th Circuit) 371, 387, 388.
[23] 1988, *New Law Journal* 30th September, 702-703.

(2) the storage, retrieval and display of processed financial data; and

(3) the storage retrieval and display of document images.

However the use of information technology creates a number of problems:

(1) Proper notice must be given on the intention to use the graphic output so that defence evidence may be similarly presented.

(2) The limited space and time in court and obvious cost factors mean that realistically defence and prosecution must share one system of projection. This raises the problem of access, security, confidentiality and compatibility.

(3) The actual control of the projection system is a matter, which is far from clearly covered at present in the courts. At present, in the UK it is almost unheard of for the defence to use this type of facility, the reasons may be costs, lack of appropriate skills, or simply tradition.

(4) Not all courtrooms are suitable for the display of computer graphics, though when new courts are built now, this factor is often considered in their design.

Further there is a need for certain safeguards and standards of practise for example, access to all case documents, diagrams and charts on disc by the defence (unless the material is properly privileged). Nevertheless the use of information technology for display purposes can help a computer forensic practitioner in:

(1) Producing schedules combining figures from more than one document. This can be done 'on-line' using a spreadsheet or database package, so as to aid jurors in their understanding of how various figures have been arrived at.

(2) Displaying more than one document or schedule at a time so comparisons can be made highlighting the relevant figures. The reduction in the volume of paperwork also reduces the problem of storage and security of documents used in court.

The ITAC Working Party Final Report highlighted the possibilities given by technology as follows:

There can be no doubt that technology has a role to play, not only in serious and in other fraud cases, but in the wider criminal jurisdiction ... The beneficial effects of the proper use of modern techniques in an area such as the criminal trial are, we suggest, clearly seen. If the challenges we have identified can be met the benefits that will result are likely to contribute to a marked advance in the continuing efforts to secure quicker and more effective trials in the future.'[24]

---

[24] *The ITAC Working Party FInal Report on Technology in Serious Fraud Trials* 1989.

Computer forensic practitioners could play a leading role in this process.

9. Computing Skills

A fundamental principle of forensic science is the Principle of Interchange which was propounded by Edmund Locard in 1910.[25] The principle asserts that when a person commits a crime something is always left at the scene of the crime that was not present when the person arrived. In computer forensics the computer is the scene of the crime and computing skills will be needed to collect evidence left by the person committing the crime. The evidence will enable the investigator to identify that a crime or abuse is being committed, discover how the crime or abuse is being committed, reconstruct evidence in situations where the programmer has tampered with files and extract evidence from computer files.

The investigator needs a combination of the EDP audit skills and the system specific knowledge of a computer manager. The route to identifying that a computer fraud or abuse is taking place and linking the crime with an individual will depend upon individual circumstances but the following abilities may be pertinent:

(1) Scrutiny and testing of the operations and teleprocessing logs. The former contains relevant information such as runs made, interruptions to processing (technical frauds often involve the use of recovery procedures, file recreations and restarts from check-points as a means of covering tracks and removing audit trails), transfers of programs to and from production libraries and the use of utilities such as 'zap'. While analysis of the teleprocessing log may reveal strange behaviour by authorised personnel or attempts from outside to gain access.

(2) Examination of computer programs and comparison of source and object versions of programs to identify unauthorised coding. Packages, which aid the former operation by printing flowcharts of the program logic flow, are available;

(3) Use of concurrent auditing techniques, which can test logic of programs in operation and highlight exceptional items. Examples include integrated test facilities, snapshots of transacts, extended records and system control audit review files;

(4) Covert observation techniques like logging all accesses to a given CPU or waiting for an access from a given source and examining in detail the nature of the activities undertaken;

(5) Knowledge of modes of privilege access controls and concurrency controls and an awareness of how these controls can be rendered ineffective or circumvented;

---

[25] See, Kind, S. and Overman, M., (1972), *Science Against Crime*, London: Aldus.

(6) Methods of tracing system accesses with the assistance of telecommunication service providers and the police. Powers under the Interception of Communications Act 1985 permit this with the permission of the victim. This right, which existed only for indictable offences, was extended to unauthorised access offences by s.14 of the Computer Misuse Act 1990; and

(7) Application of computer assisted audit techniques and other audit software utilities. Expertise in recovery techniques is needed to facilitate the reconstruction of evidence. The appropriate technique will be dependent upon the nature of transaction logging and back-up procedures used by the organisation. At a minimum, there will be an input log which holds details of transactions processed for a set period. This record will often be supplemented by movement journals containing for a defined period information like: before images of the master file prior to update; after images of the master file post update; or change parameters of changed records unique identifiers and pointers. In many situations vital evidence may be recovered merely by restoring items flagged for deletion on the database.

The greatest problems in reconstruction arise when a considerable period of time elapses between the crime being committed and reconstruction activity commencing, as the retention period of all logs is limited. The admissibility of such evidence in UK courts is somewhat unclear at the moment, but these computer forensic procedures will assist prosecutions.

10. Conclusion

The paper argues that the moves by the police and consultancy firms to successfully enforce the new legislation against the increased threat of computer crime and abuse requires the bringing together of investigative, legal, courtroom and computing skills in an extension of forensic science. The term suggested for this new discipline is computer forensics. It remains to be seen whether a recognised discipline, applicable to computer crimes and abuses, emerges in the next few years. The authors believe that unless this is the case there will be a series of failed major prosecutions before the subject is seen to present unique problems, which require special treatment.

10
Michael Hirst
Computers, Hearsay and the English Law of Evidence

1. Introduction

This paper is concerned with some of the issues that may arise under English law where a party to a civil or criminal action seeks to rely upon evidence stored upon or derived from computers. There are certain statutory provisions which apply specifically and exclusively to such evidence, but it will be seen that most of the difficulties and controversies which have arisen to date have been concerned with the relationship between computer evidence and the rule against hearsay. This old common law rule was developed in circumstances far removed from those which are likely to prevail where computer evidence is involved, and it was no doubt inevitable that difficulties would arise when new technology and ancient legal doctrines collided. It was perhaps also foreseeable that those difficulties would be exacerbated by judicial misunderstanding and by poorly drafted or misconceived attempts at legislative intervention. Could it, however, have been foreseen that some of the gravest errors would result from fundamental misunderstanding of the old legal doctrine, rather than a failure to understand the workings of the new technology?

2. Computers and Computer Evidence

There is no single or universal definition of computers or computer evidence for the purposes of English law. This may be due, in part, to the difficulties which have been encountered in other jurisdictions where attempts have been made to provide such a definition. A provision widely adopted by American states[1] defines computers as:

> *'electronic devices that perform logical, arithmetical and memory functions by the manipulation of electronic or magnetic impulses.'*

This definition manages to include digital watches and automated traffic signals, whilst excluding modern optical computers which use light rather than

---

[1] See B.J. George, 'Contemporary Legislation Governing Computer Crimes' (1985) 21 *Criminal Law Bulletin* 389.

electricity,[2] but is at least superior to the only English attempt at legislative definition. Section 5(6) of the Civil Evidence Act 1968 provides that, for the purposes of that Act, *"computer' means any device for storing and processing information ...'*. This definition would seem capable, if interpreted literally, of embracing filing cabinets and many other basic appliances. In *R v Shepherd*,[3] the Court of Appeal were invited to apply it by analogy to criminal proceedings over which the Act was not directly applicable, but doubted whether it would be correct to do so, and ultimately managed to avoid deciding that question.

More recent legislation, such as the Computer Misuse Act 1990, therefore avoids any attempt at a definition, although it is possible that the Criminal Justice Act 1988 has embraced the Civil Evidence Act definition by accident.[4] For most purposes, the question of whether a given device is a computer has been left to be decided on a case by case basis. Like elephants, computers may be easier to recognise than to define.

3. The Common Law Approach to Evidence

The English law of evidence is notorious for its complexity and excessive technicality. In particular, it shares with many other common law jurisdictions a commitment to exclusionary rules which generally have no counterparts in civilian systems, where the dominant principle is that of the 'free appreciation of evidence'. In other words, English lawyers have to be concerned, not just with the quality of evidence in terms of its relevance and capacity to convince a court or tribunal of the facts with which it deals, but also with its classification and formal admissibility. Evidence may sometimes be ruled inadmissible, even where it is clearly relevant, or indeed decisive, from a logical or 'common sense' perspective.

The development of the exclusionary rules can be attributed, in some part at least, to the adversarial nature of the common law trial. The traditional role of the English court or judge is not that of enquiry into the facts which are in dispute, but that of adjudication between the merits of arguments and evidence put before it by the opposing parties. Since the court is therefore primarily an umpire rather than an investigator, it is not altogether surprising to find that the

---

[2] See M. Wasik, *Crime and the Computer* at p.4.
[3] Also reported as *Shephard*,(1991) 93 *Cr.App.R.* 139. The point does not seem to have been argued in the subsequent appeal to the House of Lords ([1993] 1 *All E.R.* 225: see footnote 21, below).
[4] Schedule 2 to the 1988 Act provides that expressions used in that Act and in the Civil Evidence Act 1968 are to be construed in accordance with section 10 of that Act. Section 10 in turn states that the term 'computer' has the meaning assigned by section 5 of that Act.

judges have developed strict rules to govern the conduct of the contests over which they preside.

The rules of evidence have also been influenced by the predominantly oral character of the English trial. Although documents have always been admissible as exhibits, the general rule remains that any facts in dispute should be proved by the oral evidence of witnesses, testifying on oath before the court, and testifying on the basis of their own first-hand knowledge. This, the notorious 'hearsay' rule, will ordinarily preclude the courts from relying on the truth of factual assertions contained in documents, even where the documents in question appear to be reliable. In an English trial, cross-examination of a witness by the opposing party or by that party's lawyer (and in some cases by the judge) is seen as the best possible way of exposing falsity or error. A statement in a document, whether an entry in a diary, a letter or a computer printout, cannot be subject to quite the same kind of scrutiny, and its veracity cannot necessarily be tested at all.

There are, of course, certain exceptions to the exclusionary rules. In the absence of such exceptions, there would be relatively little scope for the use of computer evidence in English trials. Unfortunately, however, the scope of the various exceptions depends on rules of evidence which are often no less technical than the exclusionary rules themselves.

The influence of the jury system, and of the use of unqualified lay magistrates, must also be noted. Many of the exclusionary rules of evidence betray a lack of confidence in the intellectual abilities of jurors and magistrates. Thus, hearsay evidence is generally excluded, in criminal cases at least, because it is considered that the 'untrained' minds of lay magistrates or jurors would find it difficult to assess its real weight or significance. Civil cases in the High Court or the county courts are generally tried by professional judges sitting without juries, and it is significant that, in those courts, the hearsay rule no longer applies with its old severity.

4. Civil and Criminal Evidence Contrasted

There have always been significant differences between the rules of evidence in civil cases and those which govern criminal cases, but it was once possible to regard the hearsay rule as equally applicable to each. In 1968, however, the Civil Evidence Act introduced major reforms which made it possible for hearsay to be admitted in the civil courts in many circumstances where it would remain inadmissible at common law.

These reforms were not, on the whole, matched by comparable changes to the hearsay rule in criminal cases. In 1972, the Criminal Law Revision Committee proposed such changes as part of a wide-ranging review of the laws of criminal evidence; but the Committee's proposals on this and other areas were greeted with protests from almost every quarter. It was said, amongst other things, that juries and lay magistrates would not be capable of handling hearsay evidence in the same way as professional judges, and the whole report was put to one side.

Despite this initial rejection, many of the Committee's proposals have since been dusted off and enacted in subsequent legislation. The Police and Criminal Evidence Act 1984 and the Criminal Justice Act 1988 accordingly share some common ground with the Civil Evidence Act, particularly where documentary evidence is concerned, but they still fall short of the 1972 proposals, and largely confirm that the civil and criminal jurisdictions have now gone their separate ways insofar as the admissibility of evidence is concerned.

5. Civil Proceedings in Magistrates' Courts

The assertion that there are two distinct systems nevertheless requires some qualification. In a sense, there are three systems, because the Civil Evidence Act 1968 has never been extended to the magistrates' courts, which exercise a limited but significant civil jurisdiction. In respect of that civil jurisdiction, the reforms of 1984 and 1988, which govern those courts in the exercise of their much larger criminal jurisdiction, are equally inapplicable. The result is that the severity of the hearsay rule in such cases is mitigated only by the somewhat narrower provisions of the Evidence Act 1938: a situation which seems largely to have passed unnoticed until the government chose the magistrates' courts as the instrument for the judicial enforcement of community charge or 'poll tax' liability. The local authorities to whom this short-lived tax was payable depended on computers to record details of payments or non-payments, and the admissibility of such records under the 1938 Act proved to be a matter of great uncertainty, which was resolved only after special provisions were inserted into the enforcement regulations, expressly providing for the use of local authority records and computer evidence.[5]

6. The Hearsay Rule at Common Law

The rule against hearsay has been described as 'simple in principle, if not in application'.[6] The principle is that the courts should not be invited to rely upon the truth of a factual assertion, unless that assertion comes from a witness who is testifying in court, on the basis of first-hand knowledge. It is, in other words, a rule against second-hand evidence. At its simplest, it prevents a party from trying to prove what happened by calling a witness who can do no more than tell the court what X or Y stated had happened.

---

[5] These are the Community Charge (Miscellaneous Provisions) Regulations 1992 (see footnotes 26-28, below).
[6] Phipson, now edited by, John Huxley Buzzard, Richard May and M.N. Howard 1990, *Phipson on Evidence*, 14th Ed., London: Sweet and Maxwell, at para. 21.02.

It makes no difference, at common law, whether the witness was told this orally or read it in a document prepared by X or Y. If witnesses lack first-hand knowledge, their testimony cannot be accepted; and nor can the document containing the statement be accepted as evidence in its own right. The court would want, instead, to hear from the authors of the document, assuming that they do have first-hand knowledge. They can then be tested in cross-examination. The document cannot be so tested, and is accordingly regarded as an inadequate substitute for live testimony.

There have always been certain exceptions to this rule, and some of these may be relevant to evidence which could be stored on computers. Thus, hearsay evidence in the form of public documents - documents containing information of public interest, and which are available for public inspection with or without payment - are admissible at common law.[7] Computer discs or tapes may apparently be classed as documents for this purpose,[8] although it should be noted that modern statutory definitions of documents, which expressly include discs and tapes etc, are applicable only by analogy. They are not directly applicable at common law. A computer printout, on the other hand, would very clearly qualify as a document, even under the narrowest of definitions.

Unfortunately, the common law exceptions fall well short of permitting the use of documentary hearsay wherever it can be shown to be reliable and important. This was demonstrated in the notorious case of *Myers v Director of Public Prosecutions*,[9] where the House of Lords held that documentary records compiled by a motor manufacturer were inadmissible for the purpose of showing what serial numbers had originally been attached to the chassis, engines and cylinder blocks of certain vehicles they had produced. Had those records been admissible, they would have proved beyond doubt that Myers had been engaged in the selling of stolen cars, which he had disguised with registration documents, chassis plates and engine numbers taken from wrecked vehicles of similar design. The cars concerned still bore the indelible, stamped-in, cylinder-block numbers with which they had been first provided, and this could be demonstrated by comparison with the manufacturers' records. On common sense grounds, the evidence was not just relevant, but decisive. Nevertheless it was hearsay: the court was being asked to rely on the accuracy of the records, and since no relevant exception to the hearsay rule was applicable on those facts, the records were ruled inadmissible. It seems that the common law has passed beyond the age at which it could give birth to new exceptions to the established rules. Any new exceptions to the hearsay rule must now be statutory.

---

[7] *R v Halpin* [1975] *Q.B.* 907.
[8] See *Derby v Weldon* [1991] 1 *W.L.R.* 652.
[9] [1965] *A.C.* 1001.

Myers was not a case about computer records; but the principle applied was clearly one that would have been equally applicable to records entered and stored on computers. This has more recently been confirmed by the High Court's ruling in *R v Coventry Justices, ex parte Bullard*,[10] where it was held that non-payment of the community charge, or 'poll-tax', could not (at common law) be proved in magistrates' courts by production of computer printouts, nor by the oral testimony of 'witnesses' whose only knowledge of that supposed non-payment was derived from their study of those same printouts.[11]

7. Computers, Hearsay and Original Evidence

The relevant statutory exceptions to the hearsay rule are explained below; but it would be wrong to assume that computer evidence can only ever be admitted by way of some such exception. Not all computer evidence is hearsay; some can be classified as original or even 'real' evidence, and can then be admitted on largely the same basis as a photograph or a tape recording of an incident. It depends on the way in which the computer has been operating, and in some cases on the availability of supporting oral testimony relating to the input of data.

7.1. Automatic Recordings or Displays

A computer printout or display showing information automatically recorded by the computer itself, or by machines or sensors linked to it, is no more hearsay than is a film or audio tape recording of an incident. The hearsay rule guards against the supposed unreliability of information originating from or transmitted through human sources. Machines or instruments such as computers may be capable of error or inaccuracy, but do not suffer from the lapses of memory or wilful mendacity that characterises some human testimony. There is accordingly no reason why automatically recorded data should be treated in the same way as hearsay.

The original nature of such evidence was overlooked by the Court of Appeal in *R v Pettigrew*,[12] with the result that automatically recorded details of serial numbers on bank notes printed by the Bank of England were quite wrongly held to be inadmissible at a criminal trial. The judges simply assumed the evidence to be hearsay, and strove in vain to find some exception to the hearsay rule that could justify the reception of that evidence. On that reasoning, it would have been difficult to admit data measured on simple meters or gauges, and many subsequent prosecutions were adversely affected by imaginary difficulties of that kind.

---

[10] [1992] *T.L.R.* 74.

[11] No attempt was made by the local authority to invoke the provisions of the Evidence Act 1938, which might have been relevant. See 8.4 below.

[12] (1980) 71 *Cr.App.R.* 39.

Pettigrew was a seriously defective precedent, and it is fortunate that the Court of Appeal were prepared to acknowledge their mistake when academic writers pointed it out to them.[13] The first such acknowledgement came in *R v Wood*[14] and this paved the way for the final rejection of *Pettigrew* in the cases of *Castle v Cross*[15] and *R v Spiby*.[16] In *Castle v Cross*, it was held that a printout from a breath analysis machine could be treated as 'real' evidence of a motorist's failure to provide a proper specimen after arrest on suspicion of a drink-driving offence. In *Spiby*, the Court of Appeal similarly categorised a printout produced by a hotel computer, showing details of telephone calls made by hotel guests. The details had been automatically recorded so that the hotel could charge for them, and they provided evidence of the appellant's criminal contacts.

What then of the risk of computer malfunction? Should there not be proof that the computer was working properly? This is a quite separate issue from that of hearsay, and is dealt with under section 69 of the Police and Criminal Evidence Act 1984 (or, in civil cases, under section 5 of the Civil Evidence Act 1968); but as we shall see, the criminal courts for many years insisted (notably in *Spiby* itself) that the safeguards within section 69 were applicable only where the evidence was admissible as hearsay.[17]

7.2. Computers as Calculators

When used as calculators or processors, computers clearly add to or develop the information originally supplied to them; but this does not necessarily mean that there will be any problem with the hearsay rule. In *R v Wood*, a consignment of valuable metals had been stolen, and certain metals, alleged to have come from the stolen consignment, were found on the appellant's premises. Tests were performed on these metals to determine their precise chemical composition, and data obtained from these tests was then analysed with the aid of a computer, which was used to perform a number of complex mathematical calculations. The scientists involved were able to compare the results of the analysis with the results of similar tests carried out on the original metals at the time of manufacture, and it was found that they were identical; but was this admissible evidence? If it was hearsay, it would not have been admissible under the legislation then in force.[18]

---

[13] See J.C. Smith's seminal article: [1981] *Criminal Law Review* at p.787.
[14] (1982) 76 *Cr.App.R.* 39.
[15] [1985] 1 *All E.R.* 87.
[16] (1990) 91 *Cr.App.R.* 186.
[17] An interpretation eventually repudiated by the House of Lords in *R v Shepherd* [1993] 1 *All E.R.* 225 (see further, below).
[18] This was the Criminal Evidence Act 1965 (now repealed).

The Court of Appeal held that computer evidence of this kind posed no problem, as long as the accuracy of the data on which the calculations were performed could itself be proved by admissible evidence, or perhaps admitted by the other party. In its function as a calculator, the computer was held to be analogous to a weighing machine, or even a piece of litmus paper used to test the acidity of a solution. Hearsay problems will arise only where there is no separate admissible evidence as to the accuracy of the data recorded or processed.

7.3. Computer Evidence as Hearsay

Computerised bank records provide a good illustration of the ambit of the hearsay rule in relation to computers generally. A computer printout relating to a customer's account will typically contain elements of hearsay and elements of original evidence.

One should begin by asking what the printout is being used to prove. If it is being used to prove what sums have been credited or debited to the account over a given period, it will be original evidence, rather than hearsay, because the computer itself determines what sums are credited and debited. If, in other words, a transaction is accidentally omitted from the computer records, it will not be credited at all until the record is amended. If, on the other hand, the computer record is tendered as evidence that a certain transaction took place (e.g. to show that the account holder withdrew £500 on July 2nd), then it is being offered as evidence of that other fact. It will accordingly be hearsay, unless it is an automatic record of a transaction performed without any direct human input. Standing orders etc. may have been paid automatically in this way, and an automatic record may have been made of withdrawals from automated cash dispensers, but any record of a cash deposit or chequebook withdrawal will have been entered by human agency. If the computer record is to be relied upon here, recourse must be had to some statutory exception to the hearsay rule.

8. Exceptions to the Hearsay Rule

8.1. Civil Evidence Act 1968, Section 5

Section 1 of the Civil Evidence Act 1968, which governs civil proceedings before the High Court, the county courts and some tribunals (but not, as yet, the magistrates' courts) provides that a statement, other than one made by a person while giving oral evidence in the proceedings, may only be admitted as evidence of any fact stated therein to the extent that it is admissible under that Act or some other legislation. Section 5(1) of the Act then provides that:

> *'A statement contained in a document produced by a computer shall, subject to rules of court, be admissible as evidence of any fact stated*

therein of which direct oral evidence would be admissible, if it is shown that the conditions mentioned in subsection (2) are satisfied ...'

The conditions referred to are painfully complex and verbose, particularly insofar as they make special provision for cases in which two or more computers are used in combination. They manage, at the same time, both to include unnecessary restrictions on the admissibility of reliable evidence, and to omit any safeguards against the use of computer evidence derived from potentially inaccurate human input. Thus, if the computer is used for a special purpose, rather than for its usual purpose, its printouts etc. cannot be relied upon, however clear it may be that the data used and operations performed are reliable. If, on the other hand, it can be shown that the computer was properly operated and that the data concerned was of a kind regularly supplied to it in the course of its operations, then the printout etc. would appear to be admissible, regardless of the fact that the input data may have been highly unreliable and inadmissible under any other provision of the Act. It should also be noted that nothing in the wording of sections 2 or 5 appears to restrict the application of those provisions to hearsay evidence alone. It is true that this Part of the Act bears the heading, 'Hearsay Evidence', but this heading cannot be treated as an operative part of the statute, and cannot therefore be used to modify the otherwise clear meaning of its provisions. In other words, computer evidence that does not satisfy the section 5 requirements would appear to be inadmissible, whether hearsay or not.

8.2. Documentary Hearsay in Criminal Cases

In criminal cases, there is no single statutory provision, comparable to section 5 of the Civil Evidence Act, upon which the admissibility of computerised hearsay evidence can be said to depend. There are, instead, a number of overlapping common law rules and statutory provisions, some specifically concerned with one particular kind of document (e.g. bankers' records) and others concerned with a wide range of documents. None of these are specifically concerned with computer-generated documents; but such documents, if they clear these initial hurdles, must then satisfy the specific requirements imposed by section 69 of the Police and Criminal Evidence Act 1984, if statements contained therein are to become admissible at criminal trials. Space precludes comprehensive coverage of the various exceptions. A brief analysis of the more important examples must suffice.

Sections 23 and 24 of the Criminal Justice Act 1988 are the most important provisions of general application and, of these, section 24, which deals with business and official documents, is clearly the more likely vehicle for the introduction of computer evidence. This provision replaces section 68 of the Police and Criminal Evidence Act 1984, which was itself a short-lived replacement for section 1 of the Criminal Evidence Act 1965. The 1965 Act was passed, in haste, to deal with the inadequacies of the common law, as revealed by the House of Lords in *Myers*. The 1988 provision can therefore be seen as Parliament's third attempt to exorcise the *Myers* ghost.

Section 24(1) of the Act provides that, subject to section 69 of the 1984 Act and to special rules governing confessions,

> *'A statement in a document shall be admissible in criminal proceedings as evidence of any fact of which direct oral evidence would be admissible, if the following conditions are satisfied:-*
>
> *(i) the document was created or received by a person in the course of a trade, business, profession or other occupation, or as the holder of a paid or unpaid office; and*
>
> *(ii) the information in the document was supplied by a person, whether or not the maker of the statement, who had, or may reasonably be supposed to have had, personal knowledge of the matters dealt with.'*

Subsection (2) provides that:

> *'Subsection (1) applies whether the information contained in the document was supplied directly or indirectly but, if it was supplied indirectly, only if each person through whom it was supplied received it:-*
>
> *(a) in the course of a trade, business, profession or other occupation; or*
>
> *(b) as the holder of a paid or unpaid office.'*

A document tendered in evidence under section 24 will only be admissible to prove a fact if direct oral evidence of that fact would have been admissible. A document which contains prejudicial references to a defendant's previous convictions may thus need to be edited so as to exclude any such references; and a document which contains information relating to the defence of the realm or the identity of police informers may be excluded on grounds of public policy, notwithstanding its compliance with the other requirements of section 24.

A further restriction is placed on documents containing statements prepared in connection with a criminal investigation or in connection with criminal litigation. Under subsection (4), such statements may only be proved by means of the document where the maker is dead, abroad, missing, too ill to testify or too scared to testify or if he or she cannot reasonably be expected to have any recollection of the matters concerned. Police records and files, which might otherwise have become generally admissible under section 24, thus remain subject to significant constraints.

How does one prove that a statement in a document satisfies the tests of admissibility prescribed under section 24? This can be done in various ways (e.g. by means of oral evidence from persons familiar with the origins of and background to the document), but not by means of any statement or recital in the document itself. As the Court of Appeal pointed out in *R v Case*,[19] one cannot use a document which has yet to be proved admissible as admissible evidence of that same document's admissibility!

A final point to consider in relation to section 24 is that the court or trial judge ultimately has a discretion under sections 25-26 of the Act as to whether such evidence may be used once it has been proved to be admissible. If it is considered that the interests of justice would not be served by admission of a statement in such a document, then the court 'may direct that the statement shall not be admitted'. This discretion may be exercised so as to exclude defence evidence as well as prosecution evidence, a significant departure from the general rule in criminal cases. In practice, it is inevitable that prosecution evidence is more likely to be excluded in this way. The courts may, in particular, be wary of accepting documentary prosecution evidence (computer-generated or otherwise) if it would be difficult for the defence to subject this to effective challenge or scrutiny.[20]

Since many criminal prosecutions involve investigations into the banking transactions of defendants, reference must also be made to section 3 of the Bankers' Books evidence Act 1879 (as amended). This provides that copies of entries in bankers' books are admissible as evidence of the original books, and of the matters, transactions and accounts therein recorded. The 'books', for these purposes, now include all records used in the general business of the bank, including those kept on magnetic tape or electronic data-retrieval systems.[21] The Act also provides that the original records need not be produced in court, 'unless by order of the judge, made for special cause'. There is accordingly no need to inconvenience the bank itself by forcing it to part with its discs or tapes: authenticated printouts will suffice.

8.3. Police and Criminal Evidence Act 1984, Section 69

Under this provision, no statement contained in a document produced by a computer may be admissible as evidence in criminal proceedings unless it is shown:

(a) that there are no reasonable grounds for believing that the statement is inaccurate because of improper use of the computer;

(b) that at all material times the computer was operating properly, or, if not, that any respect in which it was not operating properly or was out

---

[19] [1991] *Crim.L.R.* 192.

[20] They will not however regard it as unfair if the accused is effectively forced to testify in order to challenge the documentary evidence: see *R v Price* [1991] *Crim.L.R.* 707.

[21] See section 9 of the Act, as amended by the Banking Act 1979.

> *of operation was not such as to affect the production of the document or the accuracy of its contents; and*
> *(c) that any relevant conditions specified in rules of court under subsection (2) ... are satisfied.*

No rules have yet been made under subsection (2). The requirements of subsection (1)(a)-(b) can usually be discharged quite easily, either by oral evidence from persons familiar with the operation of the computer, or by production of a certificate from a person occupying a responsible position in relation to the operation of the computer, in accordance with paragraph 8 of schedule 3 to the Act. Compliance with these requirements will sometimes be a mere formality, and a certificate may sometimes state matters merely 'to the best of the knowledge and belief' of the person responsible. If, however, there is any real issue as to the accuracy of the computer or the correctness of the operating procedure, paragraph 9 of schedule 3 enables the court to require oral evidence on that issue.

The relationship between section 69 and the supplementary provisions contained in schedule 3 was recently examined by the House of Lords in *R v Shepherd*.[22] Their Lordships held that, whereas parties seeking to tender computer evidence in criminal proceedings must always comply with section 69, regardless of whether it is hearsay evidence or not, it does not follow that they must rely on the schedule 3 procedure in order to do so. Schedule 3 provides that a certificate from a person with responsibility for the operation of the computer *may* be used to satisfy the requirements of section 69; but if oral evidence is relied upon instead, this need not necessarily come from a person who would have been competent to sign such a certificate.

In *Shepherd*, the appellant had been convicted of stealing food and clothing from a branch of Marks & Spencer, largely on the basis of evidence given by a store detective, who testified that the computerised till records in the store showed no trace of any transaction that might have provided a legitimate explanation for the goods being found in the appellant's possession outside the store. The detective was not a computer expert, and held no position of responsibility in relation to the fairly simple central computer which recorded transactions at the various cash tills in the store; but she was thoroughly familiar with its operation, and testified that the till records showed no sign of malfunction during the period in question.

Upholding the appellant's conviction, Lord Griffiths recognised that there might be cases in which the burden of proving the absence of computer malfunctions or improper use would indeed require expert evidence,[23] and that

---

[22] [1993] 1 *All E.R.* 225.
[23] An example of which might be *R v Cochrane* [1993] *Crim. L.R.* 48.

the nature of the evidence required must vary from case to case. In this case, the store detective's non-expert evidence was sufficient.

This is clearly the right approach to the problem. Had the jury been left unconvinced by the store detective's evidence, they would no doubt have acquitted; but the overall strength of the evidence against the appellant was such that an acquittal would have been little short of perverse. It must be remembered that, whilst the standard of proof required for conviction under English law is always that of proof beyond reasonable doubt, the sufficiency of evidence relating to the operation of a computer may depend to a large extent on its relationship to other evidence in the case. Had the appellant produced receipts which appeared to contradict the till records, then the jury might have taken a huge amount of convincing before they would accept that the till records were correct. They might have remained unconvinced even by a battery of responsible computer experts; but the appellant had no receipts, no Marks & Spencer bags and no plausible explanation for her possession of the goods. It would have been surprising if the till rolls had shown anything different, because they were entirely consistent with the rest of the prosecution evidence.

Section 69 provides an interesting contrast with section 5 of the Civil Evidence Act. Whereas section 5 makes computer evidence admissible wherever it complies with its own requirements, section 69 is basically a negative provision. Admissibility must be traced to some existing rule of common law or some other statutory provision, and section 69 need not even be considered unless this initial hurdle has been passed. If, on the other hand, a statement in a document produced by a computer passes the ordinary tests of admissibility, it may still fall at the section 69 hurdle, for want of proof that the computer has been operated properly.

Shepherd resolved a number of other controversies. The Court of Appeal, despite numerous protests from academic commentators, had persistently held that section 69 was applicable only in cases where the contents of the computer document were some form of admissible hearsay.[24] There was nothing in the wording or rationale of section 69 to justify such a view, and the House of Lords emphatically rejected it.

At the same time, their lordships confirmed the correctness of the decision in *Sophocleous v Ringer*.[25] The Divisional Court in that case held that section 69 has no application to cases where oral evidence is given by persons who have merely made use of computers when preparing that evidence. It is confined, instead, to cases in which a computer printout, or some other document derived from a computer, is adduced as evidence in its own right. In *Sophocleous v*

---

[24] See *R v Minors* [1989] 1 *W.L.R.* 441; *R v Spiby* (1990) 91 *Cr.App.R.* 186.
[25] [1988] *R.T.R.* 52.

Ringer, a Home Office analyst was accordingly permitted to refresh her memory from the printout of a computer she had used, without bringing section 69 into operation.

This decision had also been criticised by many commentators, but it was not obviously inconsistent with the wording of section 69, and could be defended on the ground that the witness could herself be cross-examined as to any matters, including matters relating to her operation of the computer, which might have been thought to affect the reliability of her evidence. Section 69 provides a check on the use of the printouts themselves, which cannot of course be cross-examined in this way.[26]

8.4. Evidence Act 1938, Section 1

The 1938 Act was once of general application in civil cases; but it now applies only in magistrates' courts. Like its more modern counterparts, it permits the use of documentary evidence in certain circumstances, notably where the maker had personal knowledge of the facts dealt with, or where the document forms part of a continuous record compiled by him or her in the course of duty and the information concerned was supplied by persons who may be supposed to have first-hand knowledge of those facts. The maker must ordinarily be called to testify in support of the document, unless he or she is dead, ill, abroad, missing etc.; but the court may waive this requirement if it appears that undue expense or delay would otherwise be caused.

With the passing of the Civil Evidence Act 1968, the 1938 legislation apparently ceased to concern the authors of evidence textbooks, and readers of those books might well have been left with the impression that it had been wholly repealed. It was not until the problems of poll-tax collection reached the magistrates' courts that interest in the Act suddenly revived. Could the Act be relied upon for the purposes of introducing computer printouts of tax defaulters? This question was never fully answered. The only reported case to reach the High Court was *Coventry Justices, ex parte Bullard*,[27] and this was disposed of on the basis of common law principles, because the local authority surprisingly made no attempt to rely on the 1938 legislation.

The position is now largely governed by special provisions rushed through for the specific purpose of enabling computerised records to be used. These are the Community Charges and Non-Domestic Rating (Miscellaneous Provisions) Regulations 1992.[28] These provisions are not without their own problems. They have been criticised as one-sided, on the basis that the local authority alone

---

[26] For a defence of *Sophocleous v Ringer*, see Andrews & Hirst, 1992, *Criminal Evidence* London: Sweet and Maxwell (2nd ed. at para.11.51)
[27] [1992] *T.L.R.* 74.
[28] SI 1992 / 474.

is thereby entitled to rely on computer printouts in order to prove its case.[29] Nor should it be assumed that the problem will disappear with the Poll Tax itself. Identical regulations have been drafted to deal with the collection of the new Council Tax.[30] If these Regulations are not amended, defendants in Council Tax cases will have to rely upon the limited and untested provisions of the 1938 Act, should they wish to introduce documentary evidence or computer evidence of their own.

9. The Primary Evidence Rule

After all the problems caused by the hearsay rule, it may be of some comfort to learn that the 'primary evidence rule' - the common law rule that ordinarily precluded the use in evidence of anything other than the original version of a document - now poses little difficulty where computer evidence is concerned.

The primary evidence rule is often described as the last surviving remnant of the now defunct 'best evidence rule', although some legal historians argue that it is historically a distinct rule, and of even greater antiquity. The rationale behind it is obvious: oral evidence or copies cannot generally prove the contents of a document as reliably as the original document itself. A hand-written or typed copy may contain errors or falsifications, and even modern photocopies may fail to reveal alterations which would be detectable on the original. Where, however, information is stored on magnetic tape, film or computer discs, it may sometimes be impossible to tell whether this document is an original or a copy. A computer may also produce several printouts from the same disc. Are the printouts 'originals' or copies? It seems not to matter, because the courts have now declared that the primary evidence rule 'is limited and confined to written documents in the strict sense of the term' and has no relevance to modern storage mediums.[31] This suggests that a printout, whether or not regarded as 'original' would be acceptable. There might still be argument as to the status of a photocopy of such a printout; but in practice such a copy, if authenticated, would almost certainly be acceptable under one or more of a number of statutory provisions permitting 'secondary' evidence of documents.[32]

10. Conclusions

On the whole, the problems which tend to arise in connection with the use or proposed use of computer evidence in English law are not caused by failure to provide specifically for the use of such evidence. They may arise through the law's failure to make adequate provision for the use of documentary hearsay

---

[29] See generally Alan Murdie, (1992) 142 *New Law Journal* 1551.
[30] Council Tax (Administration and Enforcement) Regulations 1992; (SI 1992 / 613).
[31] *Kajala v Noble* (1982) 75 *Cr.App.R.* 149.
[32] See for example section 27 of the Criminal Justice Act 1988.

generally, and may in some cases arise through specific but misguided attempts to legislate for the use of computer evidence. Section 5 of the Civil Evidence Act 1968 provides the principal example of such misguided legislation, with its absurdly wide definition of a computer and its failure to provide for any quality control over the accuracy of a computer's input. Other problems have been caused by perverse judicial interpretation of what might otherwise have been perfectly satisfactory legislation. Section 69 of the Police and Criminal Evidence Act, as originally misinterpreted by the Court of Appeal, provides an example.

A more radical criticism of the English approach might question the very existence of the exclusionary rules. Many unsatisfactory decisions are reached by English courts - the criminal courts in particular - because one of the exclusionary rules has led to important evidence being ruled inadmissible.[33] The computer evidence cases merely reflect this more general problem.

---

[33] For a shocking example, see *R v Blastland* [1986] *A.C.* 41, where the jury at a murder trial were prevented from hearing that another man had confessed to the crime, and had known of it before it became a matter of public knowledge. See also *R v Kearley* [1992] 2 *All E.R.* 345.

11
Andreas Galtung
Evidential Issues in an Electronic Data Interchange Context : According to Norwegian Law[1]

1. Introduction

From a legal point of view, evidential issues can be divided into two major topics. The first is the question of admissibility: that is, whether EDI-related data can ever be admissible before a court. The second concerns the burden of proof: 'who is to bear the burden of proof in case of doubt?'. Both these topics are interrelated.

To review the evidential problems it is necessary to look at their more technical aspects. The question here is whether EDI generated information can provide proof which requires an examination of the authentication level of an electronic signature. Furthermore, when do we have a proof and when just an indication? In several jurisdictions this is an important question since the distinction between proofs and indications may be crucial to assessing the evidential value of the information.

A key question in this context is, of course, in what kind of disputes are evidential issues likely to occur. As a point of departure one can say that there are two kinds of disputes where problems may surface.

(1) The first kind would be those that directly involve specific EDI transactions of data. Let us presume that two parties have agreed to exchange their trading information by means of EDI. This works well until the day one of the parties claims that he or she never sent a certain message received by the other party, or that the message had a different content. Another question would be what kind of proofs are available to show that a message is sent or received at all? In this kind of dispute, the use of electronic signatures and other security measures go a long way

---

[1] This paper is mainly based on chapter 5 in my book: *Paperless systems and EDI, a survey of Norwegian Law*. CompLex 4/91. Tano. Oslo 1991.

towards proving what has actually taken place. The evidential question here is of a very forensic character; for instance, an examination of the level of authentication for different kinds of signatures may be required.

(2) The other issue concerns the use of EDI-generated data as indirect evidence. For instance, where a company using EDI is brought before the courts for tax evasion, the EDI-generated data could provide useful evidence of transactions that may have taken place. But the data itself is, of course, not directly related to the alleged tax evasion; hence it would be correct to say that the evidential issue is of a more indirect character.

2. The Question of Identification and Authentication

2.1. General Issues

The need for a signature is rarely required in Norwegian law - however signatures are widely used to confirm and identify data on written documents.[2]

The most frequent form is the traditional hand-written signature showing the name of the signer, although stamps, fingerprints etc. are also used. These ways of signing have been widely accepted for centuries, and are used in all kinds of trade.

The electronic signature is beginning to be accepted in many areas, for instance with respect to the use of ATMs (automated teller machines). It is important to bear in mind that many different methods of electronic signatures are in use and these methods have different qualities. It is also necessary to bear in mind that much business is conducted without the use of signatures or other visible proof at all.

2.1.1. *Identification*

The signature is used to identify the signer and, furthermore, to authenticate that the message given in a document is correct. The traditional hand-written signature is said to have a high level of identification. In the science of graphology it is maintained that one can identify a false signature even though the graphologists never conclude by stating that they are absolutely sure that a handwritten signature is either true or false.[3] This form of signing is considered to be relatively secure.

A thumb print used on paper would be even more secure since no thumb prints are exactly identical.

---

[2] *Op. cit.* pp. 13-29.

[3] In Norwegian forensics, when hand-written signatures are assessed, graphologists have four levels of concluding whether a signature is true or false, these are: possibility, probability, strong probability, certainty.

A loose rubber stamp meant to give the same effect is, of course, less secure because it is not physically attached to the holder, and furthermore it does not carry any of the signer's personal characteristics.

As far as electronic signatures are concerned, there are many different methods. The most common ones are passwords or PIN-codes. They are, of course, quite secure as long as one can be sure that the holder of the code has managed to choose one that is not too easy to break, and managed to keep it secret. However, unlike the handwritten signature these forms of signature have no physical and personal link to the holder. By using a chip card in addition to a code the security increases somewhat but there is still nothing that links the code directly to the authorised signer.

The use of fingerprints (or other biological identifying elements, like eyes, hair, etc.) provides a *personal link* between signer and the signature. In short, the signature can from the signer's point of view be described and distinguished as something one *knows*, something one *has* or something one *is*. Table 11.1 provides a survey of some of the different methods. These methods can of course be used in combination; for instance, an electronic banking card is a combination of a *have* and *know* signature.

As we see, the signature with the lowest ID level must be the typed one since it does not have any direct link between the signer and the signature.

Method	Link	ID-Level
Typed Signature	Has	Very Low
Handwritten Signature	Is	High
Fingerprint	Is	Very High
Electronic card/key	Has	Low
PIN-code/password	Know	High

Table 11.1: *A survey of identification methods*

The ID level is highly dependent on the security measures taken. A card can be stolen and used by an unauthorised person, and a PIN code or a password can be stolen or cracked. The ease with which this can be done depends, of course, on the security measures taken, including the number of digits used in the PIN code.

2.1.2. Authentication
The question is which method provides the best form of authentication. *Authentication is an assurance that a message sent or information given really is the information intended to be transmitted.* The identification techniques shown above are used to authenticate information. The question, however, is

whether there are any differences between them in regard to the actual information given. We have seen that the risks of a signature being used by an unauthorised person vary from type to type.

In the case of password or secret key system, a well known problem is that it is fairly easy to acquire cheap software (for an amount of only approximately 200 ECU) enabling the user to crack and debug passwords or secret keys used in a system. Systems for identifying and checking such programs are being developed. One system uses the combination of an electronic key detached from the system where it is supposed to function. This key must be in the possession of the authorised password holder. The key is in itself a microprocessor and when it is connected to a computer system, the user must use a password before the key can operate. When the key operates this is done in interaction with the computer system, which then randomly chooses a password or PIN code given to the user. If the user at first tries to operate the key by giving a wrong password, this will make the computer choose a wrong password. It is estimated that this kind of system has a very high level of security.

For authentication, a guarantee that the information is correct is also needed. This implies that one cannot deal with the authentication question without assessing the way the information is communicated. In doing so, one especially has to take account of the possibilities to get evidence that information actually has been sent and/or received. There is also the possibility of information having been altered during the communication process. It is necessary to assess this in order to determine what substantial reasons there are for the courts to assign a higher or lower evidential value to EDI-generated material. For instance, in disputes related to the offer and acceptance stage of a contractual conclusion, the question is related to what is actually offered or accepted. The optimal solution would be the *no risk at all system*, which of course, does not exist.

The most common method used to communicate trade data is, and has been for a long time, paper documents signed by hand for the purpose of authentication, and these paper documents are communicated through the traditional mail service.

Although paper is a quite secure method, it is possible to forge the content. It is therefore not uncommon to use registered mail as proof of information actually being sent. But what does this prove? It gives a certain proof of something - being sent and it can give some proof of something being received, but otherwise nothing much. A registered postal sending does not prove anything about the content of the actual information being sent.

Much business has been and still is conducted by *telex*. But telexes do not offer a very secure identification link between the sender and the information sent, nor are there any registration possibilities recording the reception of the information.

Since the mid 1980s, the *telefax* has to a large extent replaced the telex systems for the exchange of business data. Telefaxes have made it possible to transmit documents electronically across the world provided that the receiver is connected to a telephone line and has a telefax machine. Although telefax messages often are signed (handwritten signatures) documents, the copies received have a limited forensic value as far as the signature is concerned. This is due to the low quality of the transmissions and the fact that it is a *copy* of the signature. The transmitted document might also only contain a copy of the signature.

The crucial question from an evidential point of view is if the *electronic data interchange* provides a better mode than the existing methods, and not whether it meets the requirements of a non-existent optimal solution. It is often maintained that it is easy to tamper with electronic documents without leaving any trace. This may be so, but it depends on the security measures taken. Those who interchange trade data, will have taken different measures. First of all they have a high level of computer security within their firms. Furthermore, it helps having a third party (an EDI system provider) who provides the information exchange, and stores the trade-information log.

One could say that a parallel to this is the way trade in the securities markets are registered. In Norway this registration is taken care of by the Norwegian Registry of Securities. This is, of course, a very different kind of institution. First of all it is public; secondly, they have a legal monopoly for their operations. But it is obvious that the information passing through the Securities Registrar has a very high evidential value. It is furthermore obvious that the level of security has not been reduced because of the transition to a computerised securities exchange.

It has also been suggested that big firms doing business *via* EDI should build an internal record keeping system.[4] Benjamin Wright describes the internal record keeper as a special department within the sender or receiver enterprise maintaining controls which prevent it from corrupting records. Such an internal body should, of course, make use of the best security techniques available. In addition to this Wright suggests that the internal body could be controlled by an independent watchdog like, for instance, an external accountant. Finally Wright concludes that; *there is no reason why an internal record keeper could not be just as reliable as an external record keeper.* Wright is obviously correct on this point, but it would depend on the measures taken, and the integrity of the

---

[4] See Benjamin Wright, Authenticating EDI: the location of a trusted recordkeeper, *The Journal of Computer and Communications Law*, January-February 1990.

internal department and whether a court would share his or her view in case of a dispute.

In the light of what has been said above, there is no reason why EDI-generated information should not be considered to have a higher evidential value than the more traditional paper-based systems.

Several measures should be agreed upon in the interchange agreements. It is evident that the so called UNCID rules will have a substantial influence on how the interchange is conducted. The UNCID rules (see Appendix for text) are recommendations on good conduct for the interchange of trade data by teletransmission.

As far as legislation is concerned the admissibility and the value of computer generated data as evidence, have been considered very differently in different legal systems. As far as the rules of the burden of proof is concerned, the main principles seem very much alike - one must, however, remember that the question of burden of proof and the question of admissibility are closely interrelated.

2.2. The Admissibility Question

The important question here is to what extent computerised data can be presented as evidence before the courts, or whether we can identify the situations where computer generated evidence is considered to be illegal, and therefore inadmissible.

2.2.1. *Civil Procedure*

In Norwegian and Nordic jurisprudence, the point of departure is that all evidence is admissible. The Norwegian legislation does not have, like several common law countries, separate evidence acts, but Chapter 14 regulates some evidential problems. The basic principle can be derived from s.183[5] of the Civil Procedures Act (CPA) which states:

> *'When nothing else is provided by law, it is up to the court to determine after an assessment of the whole procedure and the line of argument, what facts are to be used as a basis for the judicial decision.'*

As we see, this section states the free evidence rule. This gives the court a very liberal discretion to determine the kind of evidence that can be put before a court, and, furthermore, what value it should be assigned.

Some other provisions should also be considered in regard to EDI and paperless systems. Chapter 19 of the CPA contains several special provisions regarding written evidence. S.249 regulates the matter where a party pleads written evidence and states:

---

[5] The author is responsible for all translations from this Act.

> *'If a party pleads written evidence, which is in the possession of that party, it should be presented to the court.'*

This section states that what is pleaded, should be shown. The interesting question here is if the term *writing* only refers to what is written down on paper. The section does, of course, not solve this issue, nor does the legislative history, as the statute was enacted in 1915. One can therefore maintain that *written* evidence means *writing* on paper and nothing else. As far as this provision is concerned, one should not stress the matter too hard, since evidence derived from EDI also will be printed out on paper.

The second paragraph of this section together with section 252(1) may, however, at least from a theoretical point of view, cause some more problems. According to s.249(2):

> *'If the evidence is pleaded in the documents of the case, the evidence should be put forward in the original or in the form of confirmed transcript.'*

S.252, governs which evidence presented during litigation, contains the following provision:

> *'Written evidence must, if possible, be presented in original or by means of a confirmed transcript.'*

In Norwegian law this is the closest we come to the best evidence rule, although it is very different from that of the common law countries. It must, however, be pointed out that, as we see from the section, confirmed transcripts are also accepted as evidence. Nevertheless, it is necessary to fit these provisions in an EDI context.

The first question is how one interprets *original* in an EDI context or in a context of computerised data in general. The reason for this question, is that the original computerised data cannot be distinguished from an original as is the case with more traditional written documents and items in general. In order to give this provision a meaningful interpretation in an EDI context, it should be understood to require documentation which is authenticated in the best way possible. The crucial question is of course how the courts will consider such a situation. The provisions cited above are formulated in very flexible way, i.e. in s.252 it is emphasised that *written evidence must, if possible be put forward in original*. This implies that an original is not an absolute requirement.

It is furthermore evident that what the courts would see in case of a dispute, would be printouts on paper, which means that we in all practical matters will be talking of *copies* where the crucial question will be to what extent the court can rely on such copies. In case the court should have doubts as to whether or not such a document is genuine or not, s.261(1) of the Civil Procedures Act would have to be taken into account. This section will be discussed below.

Another section of special interest is section 189 which gives the court the power to exclude certain kinds of evidence brought before a court. This section states:

> *The Court can refuse an offer of evidence to be given or to be proceeded upon before the courts:*
> *(1) When it does not concern the case;*
> *(2) When it concerns occasions, that are obvious, confessed or already proved;*
> *(3) When it is obvious that it does not have any evidential value;*
> *(4) When the court finds it is submitted in another way than offered;*
> *(5) When the evidential procedure substantially would prolong the case, and the part deliberately or by gross negligence has refrained from submitting the evidence at an earlier stage of the proceedings;*
> *(6) When the evidence would lead to break in the proceedings, disproportionate to the value of the evidence;*
> *Under the proceedings the court can relinquish an evidence offered, which has not been given as soon as it was possible to submit it, if the submission is delayed for the sole purpose of prolonging the case or to surprise the counterpart or if the other party demands it and the case otherwise would be substantially delayed. A decision permitting new evidence can not be appealed. A decision permitting new evidence can not be appealed. During the proceedings a decision not to present evidence submitted is decided by a procedural decision.'*

In relation to this section it is interesting to consider s.3 which gives the court the power to refuse the submission of evidence with no value. In this context the key question is, in what way EDI-generated data will be viewed. Since so far there have not been any disputes over EDI, one would have to look at the legal practice around computer generated data in general.

As mentioned earlier (see introduction) it would be useful to distinguish between direct and indirect use of computer generated data. The first type concerns the use of computer generated data used as evidence to identify something within the area where the system is supposed to work. An example here would be to use information generated from the use of ATMs[6] as evidence of the actual transaction. Another case would be to use the information generated by the use of ATM's to be given as evidence in a case concerning something else than the actual transaction(s). As an example, one could suggest a case where ATM transaction tracks were used as evidence in a case were it was necessary to prove a person's whereabouts during a certain period of time. One could call this an indirect use of computer generated data as evidence.

---

[6] Automated Teller Machines.

Due to the free evidence rule there have never really been any problems in accepting computer generated data as evidence in the first type of case. In disputes where a party would want to submit evidence for indirect use it might be necessary to assess the evidence in relation to s.189(3) cited above.

The question then is whether the court would refuse a party to submit computer generated evidence because the data do not have any evidential value. One can not give a general answer to this. It will depend on what the type of evidence the different kinds of data is supposed to yield. For example, if ATM-generated tracks are used to give evidence to a person's whereabouts, one would have to take into account that such data do not prove anything else than that someone in possession of the card and with knowledge of the necessary PIN code probably has been on the spots shown by the transaction. Although it is not a perfect evidence it does at least give some indication that the holder of the ATM card has been on the spots shown in the transaction tracks.

In Norwegian and Nordic jurisprudence such aspects concerning the different types of data will affect the way the courts would assess such evidence if submitted, but not the question of admissibility. A general conclusion would therefore be that there are in Norwegian law no general legal obstacles to submit computer generated data as evidence both for direct and indirect use. There are, however, two things to consider in this context. First, there may be regulations concerning secrecy that may prevent different kinds of computer generated data to be submitted and admitted as evidence. Second, there are some discussions of admissibility and the protection of privacy. It is a fact that the use of computer generated data for new objectives may be considered as a violation of privacy. Some examples of this will be given below.

2.2.2. *An Example of a Special Rule Concerning Admissibility*

Section 91 of the Sales Act 1988 states in its first sentence that purchase agreements can be concluded orally or in writing, and that such an agreement can be proved by any means available including witnesses. This means that a court must accept any form of evidence and consider the evidence thoroughly. Section 91 furthermore regulates the situation where a written agreement decides that any form of alteration or cancellation of the agreement must be done in writing. What is interesting to see in this context, is that s.93 entitled *telegram and telex* states that telegram and telex can be used without any hindrance of ss.91 and 92.[7] One could of course ask that since the section only mentions telegram and telex whether it excludes EDI. Probably not. The reason why EDI is not mentioned is that it still is relatively new and thereby not as common as the telex/telegram. It is, however, strange that the law has not included telefax,

---

[7] Section 92 regulates the question where a foreign jurisdiction has a written requirement.

since the telefax revolution was a fact by the time the law was enacted by parliament in 1988.

2.2.3. *Criminal Procedure*

As far as the admissibility question is concerned with the respect to criminal procedure, the free evidence rule applies in general. This rule was stated in the previous Criminal Procedures Act of 1887. In the current Criminal Procedures Act of 1981, a corresponding provision does not exist. The committee did discuss whether the Act should include a provision similar to that of the 1887 Act. It was, however, seen as unnecessary, and the free evidence rule now exists as a legal principle.

As is the case for civil procedure, the free evidence rule relates both to the *types* of evidence admitted and the *value* of the evidence item. This means that we do not have any formal rules in our Criminal Procedures Act excluding certain kinds of items as evidence. This does not, of course, imply that all kinds of evidence are legal. The point is that in case of illegal evidence, the illegality is related to the way the evidence is obtained, and not substance.

Since there still no cases dealing with EDI-generated data as evidence, one would in criminal cases have to look at computer generated data in general.

Useful examples here are instances concerning theft from basis *via* ATMs. The generated tracks have been used here as evidence for the different transactions. Another matter, is of course, in what way the courts would look upon cases where computer generated data are used for more indirect evidence. By indirect evidence is meant a situation in which the computer-related data are used as evidence for another purpose than that which the data were actually produced or. One could easily see how ATM transactions could be used as evidence for a person's whereabouts, or for a person's purchases of various kinds, where the interest is the kind of goods, and not the actual funds transfer. There have so far been no cases where ATM generated data have been an issue in this context. There has, however, recently been a case dealing with the matter within the area of automated traffic control.[8] The facts of the case were as follows:

There was a burglary in the Stavanger area where lots of goods were stolen from a private home. There were suspects, but no evidence. A bit later, a man received a fine for speeding which he refused to pay since his car was stolen at the time of the alleged speeding. The photographs generated from the automated traffic controls were of a very high quality, and the person behind the wheel of the car appeared to be one of the suspects. When the police took a closer look at

---

[8] Decision by the Norwegian Supreme Court November 1990. Also see Nils Langtvedt: *Bruk av trafikkfotobevis i straffesaker som ikke gjelder trafikkforhold.* Lov & Data nr. 22. Juni 1990.

the photography, they also found that it showed goods from the burglary mentioned above. The person in the picture was indicted. In the proceedings, the question as to whether or not the photograph should be disregarded as evidence was considered. The conclusion of the court was that it could be admitted.

The arguments during the proceedings were on the one hand that this was the only evidence existing in the case and it was beyond doubt that the evidence as such was of very high quality. On the other hand, the data were gathered for a very different purpose. During debates, parliament had concluded that the information gathered for traffic control should not be used for other purposes. The district court of Stavanger nonetheless decided that the evidence was admissible. This decision was upheld by the Supreme Court in November 1980.

The reason for the hesitancy to use this kind of material as evidence, is the fear of the *big brother.society*. If one were to accept the use of the material in this case it might be one step towards a large scale surveillance system.

In light of the case just mentioned, it appears however that the courts will take a very liberal view as far as admissibility is concerned. It seems difficult to find any limits at all concerning the use of computer generated data in criminal law suits.

An important question in this matter is, of course, if similar kinds of cases are likely to occur within the area of EDI. By similar, I mean cases where something other than the specific transaction is the focus of the case. An example would be a case where a company is indicted for some sort of environmental crime. In such a case an EDI transaction data could be used as evidence of the production process. More likely would be the use of the EDI transaction data to investigate economic crimes and cases concerning tax evasion. In these kinds of cases the EDI-generated data would be of great value in a judicial process, and the fact that the data would be generated from EDI is not likely to be an obstacle as far as the admissibility question is concerned.

3. The Burden of Proof

The burden of proof is used to qualify the party upon which the obligation to establish something is proved is placed. The term also relates to a degree of certainty by which the thing must be proved.

The main principle is that the party who alleges something, carries the burden. This principle is valid in both civil and criminal matters (although it takes more to reach a conviction in criminal disputes). It is, however, not expressed as a general rule in either of the procedural acts.

The principle is, however, stated in s.261(2) of the Civil Procedures Act, which governs the use of public documents. S.261(1) is a rule of presumption, which states that public documents are presumed to be genuine. However, if there should be doubt whether the document is genuine, that matter is regulated by s.261(2) which states:

> 'If there is special reason to doubt whether the document is genuine or not falsified, the one who pleads the document has the burden of proof.'

If one puts this section in an EDI context, one can ask if it would be interpreted in such a way that EDI-generated data derived from public entities would benefit from the rule in such a way, that one would demonstrate a stronger presumption for these data being correct. This may be so. But it may be so even without drawing on s.261, since a public EDI system in general would have a better standing with the courts.

Furthermore, it must be stated that since we have the free evidence rule, even the principle of the burden of proof becomes very vague. The principle implies that as a general rule, an alleging party would have to prove something with more than 50% certainty, and that in case of doubt, it will be the alleging party who has to bear the burden, and eventually loose the case if such an amount of certainty can not be reached.

This risk of doubt can be seen in two different ways.[9] If one uses as a point of departure an example where the issue is whether an incident has taken place or not (or an order is placed), the first model operates with a point of balance where the probability that the transaction has taken place is more or less than 50% and thereby proved regardless of how small the actual difference is. For a court, this model implies that one would have to decide whether a transaction has taken place or not. In the other model one does accept that there is a *zone of doubt*, which goes from an uncertain amount of *underweight* to an uncertain amount of *overweight*. It is in this second model one has to reflect over the rules of burden of proof. The rules prescribing which standard of proof has to be obtained, may be prescribed as rules moving the point of balance.

3.1. Two Different Models for the Burden of Proof

Model 1: *Reflecting that any overweight is decisive*

```
                              V
0%_____50%_____100%
```

Model 2: *Reflecting an area of uncertainty around the point of 50%*

```
                              V
0%_____    _____100%
```

As mentioned above, as a point of departure, it is the alleging party who bears the burden of proof. If one translates this principle to an EDI dispute, it would

---

[9] The figure is shown in W.E. von Eyben. *Bevis*. GAD København 1986.

mean that a party alleging technical failure in the system of the other party would bear the burden.

One can in this context mention that in some areas of the consumer oriented electronic funds transfer systems there are examples where the burden of proof is being reversed (in favour of the consumer), either by law or by contract.

An example of this from Norway would be the recommended standard contract issued by the Norwegian Banking Association, which has in clause 5.3 reversed the burden of proof in matters of technical failure.

In Denmark this has been done by law, in the Danish Act of Payment Cards. A reverse burden of proof in certain matters is also being incorporated in the preamble of the Consumer Law Group of the European Community. Having rules for reversed burden of proof does, in my view, make good sense when it favours the consumer in consumer oriented affairs, since their knowledge of technical matters in most cases would be of a very limited kind compared to the one possessed by the financial institutions.

One can, of course, discuss whether or not one should develop more specific rules for the assessment of EDI-generated proof or computer generated data in general. In this context, the technology, itself is the most important matter. It is of substantial importance that the parties involved establish satisfactory routines for proving actions achieved by EDI. To a large extent, this work needs to be carried out from a technical point of view.

If one should have legislation at this point, it would be rules guiding the courts in assessing the actual data. The UNCID rules (see appendix to this chapter) could here serve as a helpful remedy. One could, for instance, imagine a system stating that it is up to the parties to show that they, in their use of EDI, have complied with the UNCID rules for logging and storage of data, and that the parties not complying with the rules would have to bear the burden of proof in the actual case.

As mentioned earlier, it is very important to determine when we are dealing with proofs and when just with indications. Of course, indications have lesser value in an evidential context, but clearly they play an important role in the establishing of facts in judicial proceedings.

4. The UNCID Rules in the Context of Evidence

The UNCID rules contain some provisions that will have a very practical impact from an evidential point of view, not in the sense that matters of admissibility and the burden of proof are regulated, but in the sense that they suggest procedures for the users on how the user transactions should be conducted, and what kind of information and transactions should generate. For users who follow these procedures, substantial evidence for different kinds of actions taken within the context of use of EDI will be provided. It seems rather obvious that it will be easier for a court to accept and assess the evidence if the material is derived by following the procedures recommended by international bodies such as those behind the UNCID rules. One could say that the following articles of the UNCID rules are relevant: Articles 6-8 and Article 10. These articles are titled as below:

> Article 6 Message and transfers
> Article 7 Acknowledgement of a transfer
> Article 8 Confirmation of content
> Article 10 Storage of data

Most important in this respect is probably art.10 on the storage of data. This article states in its paragraph (a) that *each party should ensure that a trade log is maintained of all transfers as they were sent and received, without any modification.* It should, in my view, here be pointed out that the recommendations should have been much stronger in their expression when giving such an advice. It is furthermore obvious that if one were to consider any special legislation with regard to EDI, one of the more important issues would be for the legislation to require for a mandatory system log.

5. Some Final Remarks and some Special Attention to the Use of Security Measures with Respect to Evidence

In a sense one could argue that the most important legal question in regard to EDI and paperless systems, is the question of evidence. The problem of the electronic signature is a question of evidence in a forensic sense, meaning what kind of signature provides the best evidence. It seems, however, rather obvious that with all the security measures taken in the EDI environment complying with the UNCID rules, the degree of security, and the value of evidence provided, can be much higher compared to the traditional forms of communicating data. It is furthermore obvious that the solution to many problems can and should be incorporated in an interchange agreements. In the standard interchange agreement drafted by the British EDI Association[10] it first of all stated that the agreement should take the UNCID rules into account. Several provisions in the interchange agreement are relevant in an evidential context. Like the UNCID rules, the interchange agreement has chapters concerning the storage of a trade data log and concerning data security. In the provisions concerning the *data security*, it states in clause 3, that each party should take reasonable care to ensure that messages are secure, and to prevent unauthorised access to its system.

---

[10] EDI Association Standard Electronic Data Interchange Agreement. 1st Edition, March 1989.

The use of the WORM technology may have a better standing in the event of a dispute. Furthermore, if one uses a trusted third party provider for the record keeping, the fact that one is dealing with an independent third party will give the evidential material a better standing before the courts.

One can, however, always come to the point where there is doubt. At this stage it all becomes a question of placing the burden of proof. By doing so, one will of course have to lean on the general rules for the *burden and standard of proof*.

As far as the admissibility question is concerned, the issue in the near future will be whether or not information collected for one purpose should be admissible as evidence for another purpose. But as the TEDIS report concludes, this seems to be more of a problem in common law countries than in the civil law countries, although it seems that even they to some extent have solved the problem, hence s.5 of the UK Civil Evidence Act 1968.

I will, however, ask whether or not the increasing use of EDI and other paperless systems call for a revision of all of our procedural acts. As shown above, several sections in the Civil Procedures Act concern the use of documents as evidence. One could, of course, ask whether or not the Act should include a new chapter concerning computer generated evidence. Since there are no formal obstacles concerning the acceptance of EDI-generated data. I do not think it in principle would be necessary to amend the Civil Procedures Act. The overall question, however, is how a party can convince a court that the EDI or computerised evidence is the best. The UNCID rules will certainly help, but a better way would be by referring to the best security routines possible. In case of a dispute, an example of what elements a party should present for the court could therefore be the following (the list may not be exhaustive):

- Installation test of hardware;
- Show how the software operates and who the operators are;
- Show how the software is tested;
- Show the kind of controls that are made of incoming data;
- Recording of data processing and the logging of data;
- Show what kind, and how, data can be deleted;
- Specify who has access to the system;
- Show what kind of access control and other technical and organisational security measures have been taken;
- Show what kind of routines operate for the identification and correcting of errors;
- Show the kind of backup facilities the systems provide;
- Show the security measures applied on the actual data communication (ie, different means of encryption, etc).

What elements would be most important in this list, depend, of course, on the nature of the dispute. But a party that can refer to these points concerning security measures, and provide the court with satisfactory answers, will in my opinion have a strong case. Whether a party is able to go through such a list depends, of course, on the professionality of the party. In a dispute where a third party EDI provider is involved, it must be taken for granted that it would be expected from the provider that he or she should be able to account for all the elements listed above.

Several of the elements in this list correspond with the UNCID rules, or - at least - with the *intention* of the UNCID rules. But, as I have already said, these rules are vague in their form, and are furthermore not meant to be anything but recommendations.

Many of the elements in the list above should, however, be considered in an interchange agreement, but be specified in greater detail than what is done in many of the standard agreements provided by different associations.

As a final remark, I would say that, among all the legal issues in regard to EDI and the paperless systems, the issue of evidence is probably the most important and the one of greatest concern. From what we have seen above, the legal obstacles to use EDI-generated data as evidence seem to be relatively minor as far as the Nordic countries are concerned.

This means that the question of evidence is a matter of convincing the courts that the evidence that can be derived and provided from EDI systems are just as good as any traditional evidence, if not better. One can therefore say that the question of evidence to a large extent is a question of organisation, where the matter of security is the most important.

Appendix

Uniform Rules of Conduct for Interchange of Trade Data by Teletransmission (UNCID)

Article 1 - *Objective*

These rules aim at facilitating the interchange of trade data effected by teletransmission, through the establishment of agreed rules of conduct between parties engaged in such transmission. Except as otherwise provided in these rules, they do not apply to the substance of trade data transfers.

Article 2 - *Definitions*

For the purpose of these rules the following expressions used therein shall have the meaning set out below:

(a) *Trade transaction*: A specific contract for the purchase and sale or supply of goods and/or services and/or other performances between the parties concerned, identified as the transaction to which *a trade data message* refers;

(b) *Trade data message*: Trade data exchanged between parties concerned with the conclusion or performance of a *trade transaction*;

(c) *Trade data transfer (hereinafter referred to as 'transfer'*: One or more trade data messages sent together as one unit of dispatch which includes heading and terminating data:

(d) *Trade data interchange application protocol (TDI-AP)*: An accepted method for interchange of *trade data messages*, based on international standards for the presentation and structuring of *trade data transfers* conveyed by teletransmission;

(e) *Trade data log*: A collection of *trade data transfers* that provides a complete historical record of the trade data interchanged.

Article 3 - *Application*

These rules are intended to apply to trade data interchange between parties using a TDI-AP. They may also, as appropriate, be applied when other methods of trade data interchange by teletransmission are used.

Article 4 - *Interchange standards*

The trade data elements, message structure and similar rules and communication standards used in the interchange should be those specified in the TDI-AP concerned.

Article 5 - *Care*

a) Parties applying a TDI-AP should ensure that their transfers are correct and complete in form, and secure, according to the TDI-AP concerned and should take care to ensure their capability to receive such transfers.

b) Intermediaries in transfers should be instructed to ensure that there is no unauthorised change in transfers required to be retransmitted and that the data content of such transfers is not disclosed to any unauthorised person.

Article 6 - *Messages and transfers*

a) A trade data message may relate to one or more trade transactions and should contain the appropriate identifier for each transaction and means of verifying that the message is complete and correct according to the TDI-AP concerned.

b) A transfer should identify the sender and the recipient; it should include means of verifying, either through the technique used in the transfer itself or by some other manner provided by the TDI-AP concerned, the formal completeness and authenticity of the transfer.

Article 7 - *Acknowledgement of a transfer*

a) The sender of a transfer may stipulate that the recipient should acknowledge receipt thereof. Acknowledgement may be made through the teletransmission technique used or by other means provided through the TDI-AP concerned. A recipient is not authorised to act on such transfer until he has complied with the request of the sender.

b) If the sender has not received the stipulated acknowledgement within a reasonable or stipulated time, he should take action to obtain it. If, despite such action, an acknowledgement is not received within a further period of reasonable time, the sender should advise the recipient accordingly by using the same means as in the first transfer or other means if necessary and, if he does so, he is authorised to assume that the original transfer has not been received.

c) If a transfer received appears not to be in good order, correct and complete in form, the recipient should inform the sender thereof as soon as possible.

d) If the recipient of a transfer understands that it is not intended for him, he should take reasonable action as soon as possible to inform the sender and should delete the information contained in such transfer from his system, apart from the trade data log.

Article 8 - *Confirmation of content*

a) The sender of a transfer may request the recipient to advise him whether the content of one or more identified messages in the transfer appears to be correct in substance, without prejudice to any subsequent consideration or action that the content may warrant. A recipient is not authorised to act on such transfer until he has complied with the request of the sender.

b) If the sender has not received the requested advice within a reasonable time, he should take action to obtain it. If, despite such action, an advice is not received within a further period of reasonable time, the sender should advise the recipient accordingly and, if he does so, he is authorised to assume that the transfer has not been accepted as correct in substance.

Article 9 - *Protection of trade data*

a) The parties may agree to apply special protection, where permissible, by encryption or by other means, to some or all data exchanged between them.

b) The recipient of a transfer so protected should assure that at least the same level of protection is applied for any further transfer.

Article 10 - *Storage of data*

a) Each party should ensure that a complete trade data log is maintained of all transfers as they were sent and received, without any modification.

b) Such trade data log may be maintained in computer media provided that, if so required, the data can be retrieved and presented in readable form.

c) The trade data log referred to in paragraph (a) of this article should be stored unchanged either for the period of time required by national law in the country of the party maintaining such trade data log or for such longer period as may be agreed between the parties or, in the absence of any requirement of national law or agreement between the parties, for three years.

d) Each party shall be responsible for making such arrangements as may be necessary for the data referred to in paragraph (b) of this article to be prepared as a correct record of the transfers as sent and received by that party in accordance with paragraph (a) of this article.

e) Each party must see to it that the person responsible for the data processing system of the party concerned, or such third party as may be agreed by the parties or required by law, shall, where so required, certify that the trade data log and any reproduction made from it is correct.

Article 11 - *Interpretation*

Queries regarding the correct meaning of the rules should be referred to the International Chamber of Commercice, Paris.

Part V
ARTIFICIAL INTELLIGENCE APPLICATIONS TO LAW

12

R.J. Hartley, S. Morris and John Williams
The Use of an of an Expert System Shell to Present the Mental Health Act to Social Workers[1]

1. Introduction

The application of expert systems to areas of law is well established at least at the level of research projects if less so at the operational level. However the majority of these applications are in areas of commercial and financial law whilst the application of expert systems to social welfare law is much less common. In this paper we discuss the development of an expert system in the area of mental health law. In the following section of the paper the law of Mental Health is briefly outlined and its suitability as an area for expert system development discussed. An explanation of the circumstances showing the potential of such a system for social workers is considered in the next section. This is followed by a description of the system developed. Finally, lessons from our experiences are considered. There is a temptation in the writing of a paper to present a sanitised version of reality. We have sought to resist this temptation and presented a discussion of our experiences as fully as possible. It seems important to take this approach since there is no single agreed approach to the development of expert systems. Accordingly, the recording of both positive and negative experiences and lessons is of value to future workers.

2. The Mental Health Act as an Expert System

The Mental Health Act 1983 replaces the Mental Health Act 1959. It is complemented by a Department of Health and Social Security *Memorandum* and

---

[1] This project was funded by the University College of Wales, Dyfed County Council, The Central Council for Education and Training of Social Workers and the PICKUP initiative. Further funding is required to keep the project alive but this has been difficult to obtain - many potential funding bodies consider that the interdisciplinary nature of the project causes it to fall outside their remit.

a *Code of Practice* issued under s. 118 of the Act. A number of important changes were made by the 1983 Act largely as a result of a number of reviews undertaken by the Government and others of the working of the earlier legislation. The Act seeks to provide safeguards for those who are mentally ill against unwarranted intrusions into their basic civil liberties. Safeguards in the Act include the role of the Approved Social Worker, review of detention, the Mental Health Review Tribunals and the consent to treatment provisions. However, it also seeks to protect society from 'inappropriate behaviour' and the mentally ill from harming themselves and others. These objectives will often be in conflict and actions under the Act call for a sensitive handling and a full awareness of the legal issues involved. There is much debate as to whether the Act is too intrusive and stresses too much the need to protect at the expense of the civil liberties of the individual patient, but this is not an appropriate forum to discuss such matters. Suffice it to say that the Act has serious consequences for those who are subject to its provisions; professionals called upon to implement its provisions require a detailed knowledge of its provisions.

Provision is made for a person (known as the 'patient') to be compulsorily detained in hospital for specified periods and purposes if the statutory criteria are satisfied. As an alternative to detention in hospital the patient may be subject to guardianship whereby he or she continues to live in the community but subject to some restrictions. The key professional under the Act is the Approved Social Worker (ASW). S. 114 requires each local social services authority to appoint 'a sufficient number of approved social workers for the purpose of discharging the functions conferred upon them' by the Act. Under the Act the ASW has a central role in the compulsory admission of patients to hospital or into guardianship. Applications for admission into hospital or into guardianship may be made either by an ASW or by somebody called the nearest relative. S. 26 identifies the nearest relative. This section is complex and is one of the areas where an expert system can help to simplify a complicated mechanical process. A hierarchy or relatives must be considered which is made more complex by rules on half-blood relationships, illegitimacy, age and cohabitation. Most applications are made by the ASW, although even then he or she is obliged to either inform (admission for assessment) or consult (admission for treatment) the nearest relative. The Act is quite rare in that it imposes a personal responsibility on the ASW to make an application if he or she is of the opinion that 'it is necessary or proper' (s 13(1)). Thus the responsibility is not an agency one but rather that of the individual ASW. Again this underlines the importance of ASWs knowing the law and procedure surrounding the admission process.

In deciding whether or not to make an application the ASW must have regard to the following principles laid down in the *Code*:

'people being assessed for possible admissions under the Act or to whom

the Act applies should:
> *receive respect for and consideration of their individual qualities and diverse backgrounds ...;*
> *have their needs taken fully into account ...*
> *be delivered any necessary treatment or care in the least controlled and segregated facilities practicable;*
> *be treated or cared for in such a way that promotes, to the greatest practicable degree, their self-determination and personal responsibility consistent with their needs and wishes;*
> *be discharged from any order under the Act to which they are subject immediately it is no longer necessary.*[2]

This emphasises the complexity of the decision that the ASW has to make. It is essential that he or she takes into consideration a wide range of information, opinions and alternatives before deciding whether or not to admit.

Another important element of the admissions process is the need for the ASW to obtain written recommendations from two registered medical practitioners that the statutory conditions for admission have been met. In the case of an emergency admission under s.4 of the Act only one such recommendation is required. There are detailed rules in the Act which specify the timing and the format of these recommendations. Although the recommendations will be important in the ASWs decision whether to admit the patient, they will not be the determining factor. It is the decision of the ASW that matters and he or she may, in appropriate circumstances, feel justified in acting contrary to the opinion of the registered medical practitioners. This is a point often forgotten by medical practitioners and also by ASWs. It is important the both professional groups have a sound understanding of their respective roles under the Act in order to avoid confusion and the erosion of any safeguards which may exist for the patient.

The limited discussion of the Act should indicate that it is of appropriate complexity for an expert system solution. Sadly the problem area with which the system was intended to deal is all too obviously a recurring problem and so a further requirement for an expert system is met.

There is considerable agreement regarding situations which are suitable for the application of expert systems technology. These have emerged from the growing body of experience in developing expert systems and have been enunciated in various recent textbooks on the subject, for example Edwards[3] and Ford[4] and in the legal context Capper and Susskind.[5] These can be summarised

---

[2] Para 1.3 *Code*

[3] Edwards, J.S. (1991) *Building Knowledge-based Systems Towards a Methodology* London: Pitman, pp. 37-39.

[4] Ford, N (1991) *Expert Systems and Artificial Intelligence,* London: The Library

as a self bounded domain of knowledge which is capable of being split into a number of modules and which is sufficiently complex to justify the effort involved in creating the system. The problem being tackled should recur sufficiently frequently to warrant the creation of a system and there should be some payoff for the development of the system. This case appears to meet many of those conditions. In particular the law of mental health is an unusually self contained area of legal knowledge. It requires little reference to other law except for children under the age of 16 when the Children Act 1989 applies. One further piece of legislation which may be appropriate is the National Health Service and Community Care 1990 which seeks to shift the emphasis away from institutional care towards community care. Some recent examples of the working of community care (see for example the case of Ben Silcock who entered the lions' den at London Zoo) have called into question the working of the Mental Health Act within the community and the Government is considering limited reform.

A human expert was readily available for this project in the shape of one of the authors of this paper who has published a book on the legal domain(Williams)[6] and who is regularly involved in running training courses for social workers on legal topics including the Mental Health Act. The existence of Williams' book together with that of Jones[7] and the text of the Act and the *Code of Practice* meant that as well as the human expert there was ready access to written sources of knowledge relevant to the application.

Whilst they are clearly professionals in their own right, it is reasonable to view ASWs as para-professionals as far as legal training is concerned. Thus they make an interesting case for the use of expert systems where the system can be used to enhance the legal knowledge of the social worker and provide the necessary legal framework within which he or she must operate. Furthermore there is an obvious need for legal expertise regarding mental health law to be available over a wide geographical area.

It is usual to suggest that an expert system should only be developed if there is a high expectation that there will be some pay-off from its development and regular use. In the case of mental health law there is no obvious pay-off in the narrow commercial sense in which these matters are judged. Nevertheless it is apparent that anything that can help social workers with the very difficult decisions which they have to take and ensure that patients receive the best possible treatment has its own pay-off.

Association, pp, 229-232.
[5] Capper P. & Susskind R. (1988) *Latent Damage Law* London: Butterworth.
[6] Williams, J. (1990) *The Law of Mental Health* London: Fourmat.
[7] Jones, R.M. ed (1988) *Mental Health Act Manual* London: Sweet & Maxwell.

3. Legal Training for Dyfed Social Workers

The provision of legal training for social workers in Dyfed has long been a concern of the Department of Law at the University of Wales, Aberystwyth. Numerous courses have been offered to social workers from the Dyfed Social Services Authority and many have been related to mental health law. A recurrent problem with these courses, regardless of topic covered, has been the difficulty caused by the geography of West Wales. Dyfed is a large rural county covering some 2,200 square miles. It stretches from the shores of the Dovey estuary in the North to the Gower peninsula in the South and from St. David's Head in the West to the Black mountains in the East. Not only is the area large but communications are restricted by a poor infrastructure of public transport and roads. Social workers must spend considerable time travelling to training courses, which are, as far as the Mental Health Act is concerned, a statutory requirement. Furthermore, there is considerable effort expended in travelling to visit clients who may be based in remote villages or hillside farming communities. Training and practice resources are less efficiently utilised than in an urban environment. It follows that any contribution to social worker training which involves a lessening of the travel involved would be a welcome development.

These factors led to discussions between Dyfed Social Services Department and the University about utilising novel approaches to training to supplement traditional techniques. Computer based training had many attractions, in particular the fact that both the social workers and the University staff had access to IBM compatible microcomputers. A social worker is much more likely to have access to a micro than to a video machine or other sophisticated training technology.

It has been argued that computer aided learning has not lived up to expectations and that intelligent tutoring systems are needed.[8] This led us to consider the possible use of knowledge based systems as a training tool. Simple experimentation led to the view that it would be possible to produce a training system which would may have a role as a guidance tool. It should be emphasised that as a training tool, it is envisaged that the system would be used as one *part* of a comprehensive training programme which would include more conventional training methods such as lectures and seminars. We believe that the benefit of the system can also be as a practice tool outside the confines of formal training where it can be used to reinforce material learnt within the classroom. Social workers can be provided with a number of case study problems to resolve and the system would be used as an aid in the solution of these problems. It is hoped

---

[8] Jones, R. P. (1989), 'Computers Assisting Learning in Legal Education', *The Law Teacher* 23: 2, pp. 246-264

that this approach would provide a link between the classroom based training and the operational use of the system as a guidance tool to social workers.

4. The System

The system has been divided into the following modules which relate to the different parts of the Act:-

Module 1:
> Definitions (mental disorder, approved social worker, nearest relative etc.)

Module 2:
> Civil admission
> - for assessment
> - for treatment
> - guardianship
> - duration
> - absence without leave

Module 3:
> Patients in criminal proceedings

Module 4:
> Consent to treatment (common law plus provisions under MHA 1983)

Module 5
> Mental Health Review Tribunals
> - jurisdiction
> - membership
> - procedure
> - powers

Module 6:
> Property and financial affairs of patients
> - Enduring Power of Attorney
> - Court of Protection

At the present time we have developed the module relating to civil admission to hospital for treatment. Figure 12.1 indicates both the essential structure of the completed module and the manner in which a backward chaining rule based system operates. The patient can be admitted to hospital IF all the conditions have been met. Of course each of the antecedent clauses has related rules which need to be tested to determine whether or not that clause has been met. For any individual case, the system asks questions, representing these more specific rules, designed to ascertain whether or not these conditions have been satisfied.

Figure 12.1

	An example of a Crystal rule
THEN	patient can be admitted to hospital
IF	patient is not a special person in terms of the Act
AND	evidence on the patient's behaviour has been gathered
AND	prima facie evidence of grounds for admission exist
AND	other relevant evidence has been sought
AND	patient has been interviewed in a suitable manner
AND	ascertained nearest relative
AND	consult relative
AND	wishes of nearest relative considered
AND	patient has been seen within last 14 days
AND	social worker is satisfied application should be made
AND	bed available in nearest named hospital
AND	application for admission has been made
AND	client conveyed to hospital

Whilst this figure indicates the essential structure, it underestimates the size of the system considerably. Currently the completed module contains more than 250 rules. These rules are grouped into various sections concerning the procedures for admission to hospital. Thus there are various preliminary questions designed to ensure that the potential patient falls within the provisions of the Mental Health Act. Children under the age of 16 and diplomats are exempt from certain provisions of the Act. For example, one rule states:

IF patient is a diplomat THEN patient is exempt from the provisions of the Act.

The next section ensures that the social worker has consulted with appropriate people specified in the Act. These include medical practitioners, relatives and neighbours as appropriate. Further sections guide the social worker through the process of ensuring that a hospital place is available and that all duties required under the Act have been properly performed.

Clarification of questions and explanation of terms is available to the user wherever possible using the text of the relevant parts of the Act. For example, it is normally necessary for a patient to be examined by two general practitioners both of whom must produce a statement which complies with s.3(2) of the Act. The system asks whether or not such statements have been obtained by the social worker and offers the option to see an explanation of s.3(2) before a response is given. This section of the Act includes terms such as 'mental illness' and 'mental impairment' and these may be further explained at the request of the user.

Many expert systems must deal with uncertainty due to the very nature of the problems with which human experts deal. For example, a doctor making a diagnosis may do so by expressing the view that the problem is highly likely to be X but it may just be Y. AI researchers have developed a variety of techniques for handling uncertainty in expert systems with the result that KBS are able to offer diagnoses, advice etc. with a degree of certainty attached. For example, a doctor might say ' I am 75% certain that you are suffering from......'. Many of these methods are controversial because it can be argued that they have no sound theoretical basis. The counter argument is that they appear to work in particular situations and in any event mirror the way in which a human expert operates. However, the controversy can be neatly avoided in the case of legal expert systems because legal experts handle uncertainty by means of words such as 'probably' or 'it seems highly likely that in this case...'. Thus we have followed the lead of Keen[9] in his system for clarifying employment law and dealt with uncertainty by means of such language. It seems more appropriate to produce a system which handles uncertainty in the manner in which it would be handled by legal professionals rather than one which uses available techniques for uncertainty handling.

The 'knowledge' incorporated into the system has been taken from the Act together with texts which interpret the Act (Jones 1987,[10] Williams 1990[11]). When necessary, further clarification has been provided by John Williams, the author of one of the texts relating to the Act. The next stage in the development of the system is its exposure to more social workers so that we can add to the legal knowledge within the system some knowledge about how social workers actually apply the Act. The intention being that the system will incorporate not only legal knowledge but also social work 'best practice'. When this stage has

---

[9] Keen, M. (1990) Expert System in clarifying employment law in Bramer, M. (ed) *Building Expert Systems* Chichester: John Wiley.
[10] Jones, (1988), *op. cit.*
[11] Williams, J. (1990), *op. cit.*

been completed the system will incorporate legal knowledge both from the Act and an expert in the subject and from social workers experienced in the application of the Act. To date there have been few problems in knowledge elicitation from the print and human sources. Knowledge elicitation from multiple sources has caused problems in the development of some expert systems and has led to the development of techniques for the resolution of conflict between experts.[12] As the system has been exposed to social workers, it has become apparent that they attach different priorities and have a different perspective. This is likely to lead to some changes in the structure of the system. It has not yet led to disagreements which could not be resolved.

It should be emphasised that there is no intention to replace professionals particularly in such sensitive areas as social work, rather the system is intended as a tool to guide social workers. As a guidance tool, this system offers a method of ensuring that cases are dealt with consistently across a number of social workers operating over a wide geographical area and over a time. An expert system will not suffer from an off day and it will guide social workers through the accurate operation of the Mental Health Act. The legal advice can be readily available wherever the social worker has access to an IBM compatible micro. Whilst it has been envisaged that this would be at the office there would be nothing to stop the system being installed on a portable micro for the social worker to take on the road. It has not escaped our attention that there may be a role for this system in a wider context than a social services department and it may have a role to play in organisations such as Citizens Advice Bureaux and even public libraries. In these environments guidance on the Act could be made available to the general public some of whom might have a real need to check whether the provisions of the Act are being correctly followed as far as a relative or friend is concerned. However, these might be contentious issues and we have chosen not to address them at this stage.

To enable the system to be used as a training tool rather than an advice giving system, we have a version of the system which operates somewhat differently. In a guidance system, if the social worker takes a course of action which does not comply with the Act then the system would offer this advice and the session would be terminated. In the training system, the fact that a particular clause of the Act has not been complied with is noted and the system continues to the next question. The learner continues the consultation until all the provisions have been dealt with and at this stage the user is presented with a list of those sections of the Act not complied with. By this means the social worker can be given a series of case studies to work through as a part of a training

---

[12] See McGraw, K.L. & Seale M.R. (1988) 'Knowledge elicitation with multiple experts: considerations and techniques'. *Artificial Intelligence Review* 2. pp. 31-44.

programme and is then provided with feedback which indicates those provisions of the Act which the social worker has sought to use inaccurately and which need further study.

5. Lessons

There are a number of lessons to be gained from our experiences. The first is that it is perfectly possible to develop an expert system without programming skills or indeed a deep knowledge of artificial intelligence concepts. The use of a shell which provides a knowledge representation structure and an inference mechanism enables the system developer to concentrate on the accurate representation of the application and on designing the user interface within the limitations of the facilities provided by the shell. Crystal proved to be a good development tool. It is easy to learn and is supported by good documentation. It is not surprising that it has been used as a development tool for numerous legal expert system projects. The main problem that we experienced was the limited amount of space available for providing legal explanations. One way of resolving this problem has been demonstrated by Widdowson et. al.[13] who has linked Crystal to a piece of shareware hypertext software and used the latter for the provision of additional legal explanations. The shortcoming of this approach is that the interface of the hypertext software is less sophisticated than Crystal an in the interests of creating a 'seamless' system the quality of the interface had to be traded down to the lower quality product.

Whilst the use of a shell such as Crystal makes the development of a knowledge based system a much simpler task, it must be emphasised that the development of KBS is a time consuming task. In this case it has involved the use of printed sources and experts in two disciplines whose viewpoints have to be reconciled. Gaining the involvement of some experts is not without its difficulties. Some social workers were reluctant to make time available to use the system and comment upon it. Pressure of work and professional commitments prevented some people from being able to attend pre-arranged sessions at which the system was tested. Although we recognise the burden of work which confronts social workers, we felt that a lot of work has to be done to win over their 'hearts and minds' to the idea of an expert system.

Having demonstrated that the use of a shell enables an expert system to be developed without any deep knowledge of programming we would also suggest that presence of such knowledge might well have produced a more sophisticated system. We certainly did not utilise all the facilities offered by Crystal. It is arguable that an experienced programmer would have been inclined to so do.

---

[13] Widdowson, R, Prichard, F and Robinson, W (1992), 'Brussels Revisited: The European Conflicts Guide', *3rd National Conference on Law, Computers and Artificial Intelligence*, Aberystwyth, 1992.

Crystal's limited ability to provide legal explanation or the text of the law through the Help facility was referred to earlier was referred to earlier. An alternative solution, adopted by Capper and Susskind was to program their own Help screens.[14] Not only are non-programmers less likely to be limited in their exploitation of the facilities offered by a piece of software they are more likely to be constrained to working within those facilities rather than programming alternative solutions.

It has been interesting to observe the completely different approaches to the law and its application provided by on the one hand a lawyer and on the other social workers. The treatment of diplomats provides a good example. The reasoning of the lawyer was that since diplomats are largely exempt from the provisions of the law it made sense to ascertain at the outset whether or not the individual under consideration was a diplomat. If that was the case then there was no point in seeking to apply the Act. The approach of the social workers was immediately to suggest that in practical terms this was an irrelevance since the people with whom they dealt were never diplomats thus asking the question was simply wasting time. It is reasonable to point out that the system has been developed with rural Dyfed in mind. This is not an area noted for its high concentration of embassies, high commissions etc. and hence diplomatic personnel. It is perfectly possible that social workers in London may feel that the question should be asked at the outset.

This raises the issue of customisation. Initially it had been our view that it ought to be possible to collaborate with the local social services department and as a result of that collaboration produce a tool which is useful across a wide area. Now it seems more realistic to accept that a certain amount of customisation is probably necessary to enhance the utility of the system. The social workers pointed out that as well as the system providing the guidance that they need to obtain the written medical recommendation from two registered medical practitioners, it would be very helpful if the system was able to provide them with the names and addresses and telephone numbers of such doctors in their area. This could be achieved either within Crystal or by using the fact that Crystal provides interfaces to other software including dBase 4.

Social workers are under intense pressure. The reality of their working day is vividly illustrated by Davies and Goldson in their description of a typical day in a social services department.[15] Thus, it soon became clear to us that it would not be possible to maintain the system in the large modules which have been described for the operational system since their consultation took an unacceptably long time. Faced with these large modules the response of a social

---

[14] See Capper & Susskind *op. cit.* p. 51.
[15] Davies, L and Goldson J., (1991), 'Snowed Under', *Social Work Today* 22(46) 12-13.

worker would be to ignore the system. Thus at the time of writing we are considering ways of breaking the system into a series of smaller modules to meet the requirements of social workers. Fortunately the facilities offered by Crystal mean that this is easily achieved without losing the earlier work. This will enable the busy practising social worker to consult smaller sections of the Act to seek guidance in the handling of a particular case.

It appears to be possible to utilise the Crystal expert system shell to develop tools which can be used as either guidance systems or as a part of training programmes. The flexible nature of the development tools means that it is possible to develop a training tool which takes the social worker on a training course through the relevant sections of the Act in a structured way which reveals all the relevant features of the Act. It is also possible to develop a guidance system for practising social workers in which the same knowledge base is packaged into different and smaller modules so that subsets of the knowledge can be available to the practising social worker in a manner which will maximise the chances that they will use the system.

The literature of KBS implies that there is a clear distinction between the roles of knowledge engineer and subject expert. However, in our experience the roles have become blurred while the subject expert frequently discussing the manner in which the system has been developed and structured and the system developers learning a considerable amount about the provisions of the Mental Health Act.

13
Trevor Bench-Capon and Frans Coenen
The Maintenance of Legal Knowledge Based Systems

1. Introduction

Researchers in knowledge based systems and law are often asked why, given the success claimed for their research prototypes, there is not a greater take up of such systems in practice. This is an important question, and one which merits an answer. The question can, of course, be directed also at knowledge based systems in other domains, but we believe that there are considerations peculiar to the legal domain which mean that the question can be usefully addressed with reference to that domain. The answer is not that there is no potential demand for legal knowledge based systems: nor is that demand confined to lawyers lacking the financial clout to support the development of such systems. The most significant impact is likely not to be on lawyers at all, but on those whose jobs are governed by law (or law-like regulations). As evidence for this claim we may consider the following quotation written by Paul Duffin, a prominent member of the UK Central Communications and Telecommunications Agency (CCTA):

> *The UK Civil Service is the largest single user of conventional IT equipment and services in the UK ... The CCTA has a specific responsibility to research and then encourage the use of appropriate IT to assist in the administrative mechanisms of Government. KBS represents one such technology which CCTA has identified as being of particular benefit ... In terms of government administration, KBS may be the single most significant development to emerge since the computer itself, for it offers a means of streamlining and improving decision-making to an unprecedented degree.*'[1]

The activities that he saw being particularly influenced by such systems go to the heart of administration:

> *'Much of the government 'mainline business' involves the administration of regulations or the following of set procedures or, frequently, both.*

---

[1] Duffin, P.H. (ed), (1988), *Knowledge Based Systems: Applications in Administrative Government*, Chichester: Ellis Horwood, p, 7

These areas of application are amenable to computerised assistance using ES [Expert Systems] techniques, as has been demonstrated.[2]

If we widen our notion of a 'legal' KBS to include not only the 'laws of the land' but also the internal procedures and guidelines used by companies to direct the activities of their employees, Duffin's remark about the Civil Service of the UK becomes relevant to any large organisation which performs a good deal of administration - that is, any large organisation whatsoever. All administrators must make decisions within the policies and guidelines of their employers, and this activity is an informal analogue of legal decision making, and susceptible to the application of similar KBS techniques. As an example of this law-like activity, banks have policies on lending, and issue guidelines to their staff to realise these policies. A system which supported a loan scheme would be able to employ much the same techniques as a truly legal system, such as a system to support the adjudication of claims to welfare benefits.

Thus legal KBS are wanted as practical systems, and it is this very potential for use that has attracted many researchers to the area. So is the problem that they are infeasible? Much research has been devoted to showing that this is not the problem either: the British Nationality Act project[3] has shown how legislation can be represented in an executable form, and further related work, such as[4] has explored the relation of such a formalism to a practically useful system. Many other examples of successful, in the sense of feasible, systems exist. And indeed there are practical examples of such systems in use, perhaps most notably the Retirement Pension Forecast and Advice System (RPFA)[5] and the VATIA system.[6] Of course, there remains a gap between the demonstration of a feasible research prototype and a demonstration that such systems could be of real practical utility in an operational situation. A demonstration of the latter can, however, be achieved only by a rather greater number of live systems coming into use.

---

[2] *Ibid.*, page 12

[3] Sergot, J.J., Sadri, F., Kowalski, R.A., Kriwaczek, F., Hammond, P. and Cory, H.Y. (1986), *The British Nationality act as a logic program* in *Communications of the ACM* 29(5), pp. 370-386.

[4] Bench-Capon, T.J.M. (1988) 'Applying Legal Expert Systems Techniques: Practical Considerations', in Duffin, P.H. (1988 a) *KBS in Government 88,* (1988,a) Pinner: Blenheim Online. pp. 205-214.

[5] Spirgel-Sinclair, S. and Trevena, G. (1988) *The Retirement Pension Forecast and Advice System,* in Duffin, P.H. (1988) *op. cit.* pp. 34-40.

[6] Susskind, R. and Tindall, C. (1988) VATIA: Ernst and Whinney's VAT expert system, *Proceedings of the Fourth International Expert Systems Conference,* London, 1988.

Thus while it can be said both that there is a great potential demand for such systems, and that it has been shown that it is possible, and, in a few cases, profitable to build such systems, our original question remains: why are such techniques not part of the routine armoury of large organisations? Why is it that those with the power to commission such systems do not have sufficient confidence in the viability of the KBS solution?

Part of the answer lies in organisational issues. The traditional consultative model of an expert system is simply not appropriate to support many of the tasks which need to be addressed. The RPFA, mentioned above, does not follow this model, and the need to take the task seriously and to tailor the support provided to the particular task is well documented in[7] where the same legislation is shown to give rise to very different systems when these systems are directed to different tasks founded on that legislation.

These issues, however, mean that it is that much more time consuming and difficult to build such a system, not that it is impossible. It is our belief that the greatest barrier to the routine use of KBS techniques for practical legal applications lies not so much in the problems of building the systems, since this process is becoming better understood and methodologies for knowledge engineering are becoming established, as in the problems associated with the maintenance of such systems. Building a KBS requires a substantial investment, and such an investment will only be forthcoming if the expected benefits outweigh the envisaged costs. The calculation depends critically on the expected life of the system. Now while, to take a simple example, a system to diagnose faults in a machine can be expected to last until the machine becomes obsolete without much need for change (except to correct errors in the program), this is not at all the case with a system in the domain of law. One thing that is certain about law (except in some freak domains such as Nervous Shock[8]) is that it will change over time. This is especially true of those kind of regulation-oriented domains where we expect KBS techniques to be most useful. This means that the life expectancy of the system is wholly unpredictable unless there is some clear strategy to enable the system to cope with these changes. It would be the purest folly to invest in a legal KBS unless there was some assurance that it would be maintainable, and this is an issue which has received far too little attention. For a clear discussion of these issues, and a description of the

---

[7] Bench-Capon, T.J.M. (ed.) (1991) *Knowledge Based Systems for Legal Applications*, London: Academic Press.

[8] Smith, J.C. and Deedman, C. (1987) 'The application of expert systems technology to case-based law', *Proceedings of the First International Conference of Artificial Intelligence and Law*, Boston, 1987, Baltimore: ACM Press. pp. 84-93.

inadequate way in which they are addressed by current approaches.[9] So our answer to the original question about practical take up is that there can be no confidence in the applicability of KBS until a convincing answer to the maintainability of such systems can be given. It is our intention in this paper to make an attempt to provide the beginnings of such an answer.

2. Changes in Regulation Based KBS

The way in which the knowledge relevant to a Regulation Based KBS changes is different from many of the areas to which KBS techniques are applied. In this area of fault diagnosis, for example, where the subject of the domain is some machine designed and constructed by humans and the malfunctions that may occur, and the remedies that may cure them, the knowledge that a system must use is relatively stable. The system may require debugging, but this is often a matter of extending the knowledge that needs to be included without invalidating what already exists. While the machine remains in use, the core of the system needs little attention. This happy state of affairs does not exist in a regulation based domain. For regulations are repealed and amended as well as added to, and a decision in a landmark case may necessitate revision of existing interpretations of the law. This is a significant difference, posing significant problems. The situation is analogous to the well known problem of truth maintenance in KBS: so long as information is simply increased there is no problem, but when an additional piece of information requires existing beliefs to be revised, the matter is no longer simple, as the variety of truth maintenance systems and non-monotonic logics found in the AI literature demonstrates. Thus while the incremental refinement of the knowledge base as a solution to maintenance, often cited as a strength of classic expert systems, whereby rules are 'simply' added to the knowledge base, may be a feasible strategy for some domains, such a strategy is certainly inappropriate to regulation based KBS, where the existing knowledge may become useless overnight. In practice this incremental approach is not without its problems in other domains also, as the ever growing team maintaining XCON will testify.

Problems arising out of the changes in regulations are well known in conventional data processing: changes in tax law, for example, must be announced well in advance of coming into effect so as to allow time for the considerable task of altering the programs which have to apply these laws in payroll and other applications. However the problems associated with KBSs are greater than with a conventional system. In the conventional system the limited

---

[9] Bratley, P., Freemont, J., Mackaay, E. and Poulin, D. (1991) 'Coping with change' in *Proceedings of the 3rd International Conference on AI and Law,* Oxford 1991, Baltimore: ACM Press, pp.62-68.

range of tasks which such a system can perform tends to restrict the knowledge represented. Thus a payroll system will need to have recorded within it such things as the rates at which tax is paid and the thresholds at which these rates come into effect, but it will not record the sort of expertise and knowledge of precedent that we would expect from a tax lawyer. The kinds of thing which are recorded tend to change at regular intervals, are signalled well in advance, and change in relatively predictable ways. The regulation based KBS, in contrast, will typically be expected to incorporate some elements of expertise as well, and this will change in an irregular and unpredictable manner as decisions are made, or as external circumstances change. This means both that the detecting of such changes, and the decision of the appropriate response and incorporating them into the knowledge base may be problematic.

3. Maintenance Assistance for Knowledge Engineers (MAKE)

The MAKE project, a collaboration between the University of Liverpool, ICL and British Coal, is investigating the issues connected with maintenance of regulation based KBS. The specimen application being considered concerns claims for compensation for work related injuries made by employees of British Coal (BC). Such an application is fairly representative of the sorts of application claimed in the introduction to offer the greatest potential for the exploitation of KBS.

The BC application bears out the expectation that there is a considerable need for maintenance. Regarding the law itself, each year, there are between 10 and 20 court judgements in British Coal cases and another 5 relating to other employers, but with significance for British Coal. There are up to 20 new relevant Statutory Instruments, and 10 technical instructions issued. In addition the policy of British Coal is modified from time to time, and some 10-15 such policy decisions are made in a typical year. All of these alterations need to be assimilated by the clerks dealing with the claims. Other changes in the expertise of these employees arise out of changes in medical views, for example the acceptance that a particular substance can cause dermatitis, policy changes by other bodies, as when a particular firm of solicitors may start to issue writs if the claim is not settled in a certain period of time, and changes in the perception of methods of work or occupations. British Coal estimate that these will require another 30 changes per year. Some of these changes will be relatively minor, but none the less the cumulative effect of these changes indicates the rapidity with which a knowledge base dealing with this sort of application would go out of date. If the advantages cited for using KBS to support such tasks are to be realised, it is essential that the knowledge be kept up to date, and so a practical system would require continuous updating.

The principal aims of the MAKE project are thus to produce a KBS development environment, MADE (Make Authoring and Development Environment), that encourages the production of maintainable regulation based KBSs and a set of tools to support the maintenance of such systems. The BC application is intended simply to act as a test bed for the methodology and the tools. In this paper the maintenance tools developed, or under development, as part of the MAKE project are described. For further details of the MADE development environment and methodology, interested readers are referred to Coenen and Bench-Capon.[10]

4. Isomorphism and Maintenance

We take as a starting point that maintenance is something which needs to be taken seriously throughout the development of the KBS: it is not an issue that needs attention only when the system is complete and the maintenance phase commenced. For if a system is to be maintainable, this will not occur by chance, but needs to be ensured by the way the system is built. In particular the way the knowledge is represented is critical.

One factor that makes the maintenance of regulation based KBS difficult is that when the Knowledge Engineer encodes the knowledge that he or she has elicited from the expert he or she will often bring together separately presented items in a single rule. We can illustrate the effects of this with the following simple example concerning the increasingly obsolescent Category C Retirement Pension.

Section 39 (1) of the UK Social Security Act states that:

> Subject to the provisions of this Act -
> (a) a person who was over pensionable age on 5th July 1948 and satisfies such other conditions as may be prescribed shall be entitled to a Category C retirement pension at the appropriate weekly rate

To interpret this we need also to bear in mind section 27(1) which provides:

> In this Act 'pensionable age' means -
> (a) in the case of a man, the age of 65 years; and
> (b) in the case of a woman, the age of 60 years.

Now if we consider the kind of knowledge that expert adjudicators might apply to decide claims for this benefit, we might see them allowing claims of men aged 108 and women aged over 103. This would certainly pick out the correct group of people and would be the most convenient expression of the knowledge if the claim form gave the age of claimant. It does, however, 'compile in' both a certain amount of arithmetical expertise and knowledge of the current date, as

---

[10] Coenen, F.P. and Bench-Capon, T.J.M. (1993) *Maintenance of Knowledge Based Systems*, London: Academic Press, Chapter 5.

well as the interaction between 27(1) and 39(1). Moreover, such a rule would need to be amended every 5 July. If the claim form contained not the age of the claimant but the date of birth, however, this would not be the most convenient expression of the knowledge, since a calculation would now be required to get the age from the date of birth, and the expert would be likely instead to operationalise the knowledge as 'men born before 5/7/1883 and women born before 5/7/1888'. This still conflates 27(1) and 39(1). An expert will inevitably operationalise his or her knowledge in a way that is suited to the task he or she is required to perform, but this operationalisation may well remove distinctions which are important when we come to maintain the system.

Suppose for example 27(1) was amended, perhaps to equalise pensionable ages. The impact of this on the interpretation of 39(1) could not be recognised in a conflated representation. This suggests that the representation used for a regulation based KBS should avoid conflating disparate items of knowledge into single structures. This can be achieved if we mirror the structure of the knowledge sources in our representation so as to attain a degree of isomorphism between the representation and what is represented.[11] This can often be achieved by a disciplined use of a representation rather than use of a distinctive representation, although certain extensions are required to Prolog (or any first order formalism) if this is to be possible with regard to legislation.[12] Further we can note that achieving a structural correspondence here will also enable us to record the provenance of all the items of knowledge in our intermediate representation, which is not a simple matter in the absence of such isomorphism, but which is vital if changes are to be followed through from source to knowledge base.

Thus one thing that must be done to ease the problems of maintenance is to use a representation that enables the knowledge base to maintain a close structural correspondence with the original source documents, so that it is possible to identify the parts of the knowledge base which are jeopardised by a given change. Moreover, for this to have its best effect, statements in the representation must be truly declarative. While almost all knowledge representation models have declarativeness as an aspiration, in practice the use of, for example, conflict resolution strategies in production rule systems, means

---

[11] Bench-Capon, T.J.M. and Coenen, F.P. (1992) 'Isomorphism and Legal Knowledge Based Systems' in *Artificial Intelligence and Law* Vol. 1 (1) pp. 65-93; Routen, T.W. and Bench-Capon, T.J.M., 'Hierarchical Formalisations', in *International Journal of Man Machine Studies*, 35, July 1991, pp. 69-93.

[12] Again this is fully discussed in Bench-Capon, T.J.M. and Forder, J.M. (1991) "Knowledge representation for legal applications', in T.J.M. Bench-Capon (ed.), *Knowledge Based Systems for Legal Applications,* London: Academic Press, pp. 245-264 and Routen and Bench - Capon, (1991), *op. cit.*

that it is not possible to detach a piece of a knowledge base from its context and consider its correctness in isolation. If we want to ensure that localised changes to the source material result in correspondingly localised changes to the knowledge base, we must be sure that there are no ramifications of changes resulting from a subtle alteration of the meaning of the statement deriving from its context in the knowledge base.

We therefore conclude that the form of representation used is a crucial factor in the production of maintainable systems. The tools developed on the MAKE project are consequently targeted upon a form of representation which has the properties described above. This formalism is the representation and inference Toolkit developed on the Alvey-DHSS Demonstrator project, particularly for the representation of legislation.[13] In brief, these facilities comprise an inheritance hierarchy, with the classes viewed as logical types, their slots as attributes of these types, and the possible values of these slots specified in the class description. Inheritance is by strict specialisation. This hierarchy represents a vocabulary in which constraints expressing the relations between slots can be expressed. These constraints are expressed in a typed logic extended to include arithmetic.

It is worth briefly noting the objection to this approach to the maintenance problem given in Bratley *et al.*,[14] namely that for a system to be useful the representation must be augmented with the expertise to provide for the interpretation of the law and the resolution of vague concepts. They claim that such an augmentation will necessarily destroy the correspondences which it was argued above would facilitate (or make possible) maintenance. We disagree: in the kinds of domains we are interested in, this expertise is also available in written form, as guidance to the adjudicating clerks. All that we require is that this guidance is also represented in an isomorphic manner, and that a clear separation between the various knowledge sources is observed.

5. Regulation Based KBS Maintenance

It is not the intention of the MAKE project to address major maintenance tasks which may necessitate the entire rebuilding of the system. Of course, if the law changes root and branch, there is little that can be done to accommodate this. The aim is to address minor adaptive maintenance only, i.e. maintenance resulting from the day to day changes in the source material due to changes in regulations and legal texts, the application and operation of the law, etc. In this context, the maintenance required can be considered under a number of

---

[13] Bench-Capon, T.J.M. and Forder, J.M. (1991) *op. cit.*, Chapter 12.
[14] Bratley, *et al,* (1991), *op. cit.*

headings: (a) Rule Base (RB) maintenance, (b) Class Hierarchy (CH) maintenance, (c) changes to the source data, and (d) validation.

In the following subsections each of these headings is discussed in further detail. In each case the nature of the associated maintenance is described and appropriate tools to assist in the maintenance task identified. In the following section the tools are described in further detail. It should be noted that this catalogue of tools expresses some possibilities and areas for work. Within the MAKE project not all of the tools described have been fully developed and implemented. Some are currently in operation, others are in the process of development, and some exist only as a rough specification.

5.1. RB Maintenance

The maintenance of the RB will involve one or more of the following activities:

M1 The introduction of a new Rule.
M2 The modification of an existing Rule.
M3 The removal of an existing Rule

The effect of introducing a new Rule may be unwanted redundancy or subsumption (so that the RB contains a rule which has no effect), or the creation of a missing branch (so that there is no linkage from an intermediate conclusion to an ultimate goal), a hard contradiction or soft inconsistency. A hard contradiction is simply that a logical contradiction, i.e.

$$A \;\&\; \text{not } A$$

is derivable from the KB. What we term a 'soft inconsistency' occurs when some proposition is a consequence of the KB where as it is in fact known that its negation is possible. In the simplest possible case we may have two Rules:

$$P \Rightarrow Q$$
$$P \Rightarrow \text{not } Q$$

There is no logical contraction here, but not P is a logical consequence of the KB. If, however, P represented something which we knew to be sometimes true and sometimes false, this would indicate that our KB was in error.

The introduction of a new Rule will thus involve checking for the following:

C1: Redundancy or subsumption.
C2: Missing Rules or branches.
C3: Hard contradiction.
C4: Soft inconsistency.

Considerable work has been done on the development of suitable ways of addressing these structural defects of a knowledge base. This work has usually been directed towards some constrained representation. In the MAKE project we have produced algorithms to address C1 and C2 for the formalism we use, although some problems remain. Our algorithms cannot currently ensure that all problems of this sort are detected: our view is, however, that the detection of some defects is a help to the maintainer of the system. Algorithms for C3 and

C4 exist in other systems such as Rousset (1988)[15] although these do not address all aspects of inconsistency. Further algorithms to address contradiction or inconsistency have been proposed as part of the MAKE project, but none of these can be shown to be complete. Detecting all such inconsistencies may well be computationally intractable, but defects that are detected can be brought to the attention of the maintainer and so fixed.

The removal of a Rule may also result in the creation of a missing branch or cause a section of the KB to become redundant. Therefore when removing a Rule, checks C1 and C2 should be implemented.

The modification of a Rule has the same effect as removing a Rule and introducing another. Hence the methods outlined above for the introduction and removal of Rules can be used in sequence:

- Remove old Rule;
- Check for C1 and C2;
- Introduce new Rule;
- Check for C1, C2, C3 and C4.

It should be noted that as a result of removing the Rule in this case, some acceptable redundancy and/or missing branches may temporarily be created until the new Rule is added.

It would be rare for a maintenance session to consist of only the removal or introduction of a single Rule. In most cases, a maintenance session will involve all three types of KB maintenance, i.e. M1, M2 and M3. It is therefore proposed that on completion of any KB maintenance, checks for C1 to C4 should always be carried out. Two RB maintenance tools may therefore be identified:

T1   The Rulemap.
T2   Hard Contradiction and Soft Inconsistency Identification.

T1 can be implemented on the RB in its static form and incorporate checks for redundancy and subsumption. It can also be considered to be an RB navigation tool that will allow the user to mover through the RB at the intermediate representation level and the fine grain, executable, level so that missing Rules and branches can be identified and facilitate verification 'by eye'.

T2 is designed to address the dynamic aspects of the RB and will be implemented at both the intermediate and executable representations as appropriate. The existence of redundant and missing branches will only be significant in a task dependent RB.

---

[15] Rousset, M. (1988) 'On the consistency of knowledge bases: The COVADIS system', *Proceedings of ECAI* 1988, Munich: pp. 79 - 84

5.2. CH Maintenance

In the representation used on the MAKE project[16] the CH plays an important role as the means by which the vocabulary to be used in writing the Rules is defined, and as the means of recording the state of an application at any particular time. The discipline that this imposes is important if the representation is to be a faithful reflection of the domain, and hence keep its structure through a period of maintenance, whilst remaining an adequate vocabulary for modelling the domain. The maintenance associated with the CH may involve:

> M4 The modification of an existing Slot by introducing a new Value.
> M5 The modification of an existing Slot by removing an existing Value.
> M6 The modification of an existing Class by introducing a new Slot.
> M7 The modification of an existing Class by removing an existing Slot.
> M8 The introduction of an entire new Class.
> M9 The removal of an existing Class.

5.2.1. *Introducing or Removing a Value*

One of the most basic actions in the maintenance of the CH is the addition of a possible Value to a Slot. In practice a Value will be added to a Slot as a consequence of the introduction or modification of a Rule which necessitates an extension to the vocabulary. The allocation of this addition Value to an existing Slot will not generally effect the operation of any established Rules or the existing CH. The exception to this is if Rules exist that use the possible Values of a Slot to express negation. Thus the Rules that contain the Attribute to which a Value is to be added need to be identified so that the effect of introducing this Value can be determined. For this purpose it will, in some cases, be necessary to go down to the fine grain level of representation.

Removing a Value from a Slot will jeopardise all Rules which make use of that Value either in the Head or the Body of the Rule. These Rules must therefore be identified and presented to the maintenance engineer so that a decision can be made on whether it is appropriate to remove the Rule, remove the atom containing the removed Value, or modify the Rule.

A tool to allow the identification of jeopardised Rules as a result of removing and introducing Values to and from Slots in the CH is therefore desirable. However a more general tool to identify jeopardised Slots and Rules as a result of changes to the Source data or changes to the Rule Base or CH would be more beneficial. Thus:

> T3 Jeopardy Tool.

Because of the inheritance mechanism used, the CH insists on strict specialisation, so that a Value can only be added to an Attribute at the highest

---

[16] For a fuller description see Coenen, F.P. and Bench-Capon, T.J.M., (1993) *op. cit.*

level at which that Attribute appears. If the Rule which motivates the introduction of the new Value refers to a Class which inherits the Attribute from a Super-Class, either the Value must be added to the Super-Class, or some new Attribute must be created in the Class in question. If the Value is added to the Super-Class, of course, the Rules for that Class in which the Attribute appears are jeopardised. Therefore, before a new Value can be added, the user should be confronted with the Class which introduces the Attribute to the CH, which may not be the Class mentioned in the Rule which motivated the introduction of the Value, and the Value added to this Class. If the Class to which the Attribute is added is not a leaf Class, this process would be facilitated by a tool which walks down the CH so that the user is able to determine the correct point, on each path, at which the new Value should cease to apply.

T4 Navigation Tool.

5.2.2. *Introducing or Removing an Attribute*

An Attribute can be added to a Class in two ways. Either it can be added directly to the Class, or it can be added to a Super-Class, and so added to the Class in question indirectly by inheritance. Thus if a Rule needs to mention a new Attribute for some Class, the first step should be to walk up the CH to determine the appropriate point at which the Attribute should be introduced into the hierarchy. Note, however, that adding it to a Super-Class will cause all the Sub-Classes of that Class to take on the Attribute, not only those on the path walked up. Once introduced into the hierarchy Rules may be written using the Attribute. These can then be subject to the usual checks for new Rules already described. The final stage will then be to be walk down the CH specialising the Values of the Attribute as appropriate, until a point range is reached on every downwards path. The process of adding a new Attribute to an existing Class will thus also involve the use of the CH Navigation Tool (T4).

The process of removing an Attribute from an existing Class can be regarded as removing a set of Values. Inheritance, however, means that the Attribute will also be removed from all the Sub-classes up to the point in the hierarchy at which it was introduced. The best approach would therefore be to commence the removal at this point, and then to walk down the CH to determine at which point the Attribute should be reintroduced into the hierarchy if necessary. Class(es) at which it is now introduced and their Sub-Classes will not be affected. Thus the CH Navigation Tool will also be of relevance here.

5.2.3. *Introducing or Removing a Class*

The point at the hierarchy in which the Class should be introduced will be best determined by the Attributes that need to be associated with the Class. If an existing Class contains a subset of the desired Attributes, then it is a potential Super-Class for the new Class. Clearly the Class with the largest such subset (i.e. the lowest such Class in the hierarchy) is the logical Super-Class to choose. Next it must be determined which existing Classes should be Sub-Classes of the new Class. The answer here is that existing Classes with Attributes which are a superset of the new Class should be Sub-Classes of the new Class. A tool to determine the relations between sets of Attributes is clearly suggested. This may be incorporated into the CH Navigation Tool. If a suitable super Class is not identified, the Class can be considered to represent a leaf node, a Sub-Class of the Class with the largest sub-set of desired Attributes.

Removing a Class is, as far as the KB is concerned, effectively like removing a set of Attributes. As far as the Class Hierarchy is concerned, existing Sub-Classes of the Class need to become Sub-Classes of its immediate Super-Class. Problems still arise if any specialisation of Attribute Values, or addition or Attributes, were made in the removed Class. Clearly such Attributes must be re-introduced, or specialisations made, either in the Sub-Classes or the immediate Super-Class, as seems to be most appropriate.

5.3. Changes to the Source Data
At a higher level, Rules will also be jeopardised by changes in the source material, as when legislation is amended. A feature of the MADE development methodology is that a linking facility is provided to link individual sections in the source material through the various analysis stages to the resulting CHs and RBs in the target representation. This provides a useful basis for identifying Rules and Classes that may be affected as a result of changes in the source material and can be automated as part of the Jeopardy Tool (T3).

5.4. Validation
So far only the verification of the KB and CH have been considered. However it is also necessary to validate the KBS after maintenance has taken place. This can be carried out by peopling the Rule Base and determining what conclusions can be arrived at or tracing how inferences are made. Thus:
    T5 Rule Base Animation Tool.

6. The Make Suite of Maintenance Tools
In the previous Section a number of maintenance tools were identified to address different aspects of KBS maintenance. These are summarised below:
    T1 The Rulemap.
    T2 Hard Contradiction and Soft Inconsistency Identification.
    T3 Jeopardy Tool.
    T4 CH Navigation Tool.
    T5 Rules Base Animation Tool.

In the following Sub-Sections each of these tools will be described in greater detail. An indication will also be given expressing the state of development which each tool has reached.

6.1. The Rulemap

The Rulemap, although still undergoing modification, has been in operation for some time now. It consists of a directed (from left to right) bipartite graph which graphically displays the Rule Base either at the Attributes-Rules (intermediate representation) level or the Proposition-Clause (executable representation) level. A number of options are provided to allow the user to walk up and down the Rule Base. By following a path through the Rulemap, it is possible to determine the Leaf Attributes and Propositions into which a Root Attribute ultimately unfolds and vice versa. This gives the user a clear visual view of the rules in the knowledge base, from the various perspectives of source, intermediate representation and executable representation. Utilities are also provided to allow the user to interrogate the Rulemap to display the Rule and Clauses in which Attribute and Propositions appear or to inspect the Values or Entities associated with Attributes and Propositions. It is intended that the facilities to identify redundant or subsumed Rules or sub-sets or Rules will be accessed from this tool.

6.2. Hard Contradiction and Soft Inconsistency Identification

When adding or modifying rules in a KB during a maintenance session a hard contradiction may be introduced. In logical terms this means that there can be no model for the knowledge base, so the knowledge base cannot be correct. Soft inconsistency is a modified phenomenon and occurs when some Proposition is a consequence of the KB when it is in fact known that its negation is possible. This means that the knowledge base excludes some models which are known to occur, and again suggests a defect in the knowledge base. Thus a minimal validation of the knowledge base will involve ensuring that neither of these situations exist. Tools are under development in the MAKE project which will allow such inconsistencies in a knowledge base to be detected. The algorithms used will only serve to detect a proportion of the contradictions and inconsistencies contained in a Rule Base. However it is claimed that some detection is better than none at all.

6.3. Jeopardy Tool

This is a general purpose maintenance tool to identify jeopardised Slots and Rules as a result of changes to the source data or changes to the Rule Base or Class Hierarchy.

The tool will incorporate the following facilities:

    (1) Rules Jeopardised by Slot Changes Identification. Facility to identify Rules jeopardised as a result of changes to Slots in the Class Hierarchy.

(2) Class Definitions Jeopardised by Class Identification. Facility to identify the Sots Jeopardised by the removal of a Class because they are typed to that Class.
(3) Rules Jeopardised by Source Changes Identification. Facility to identify the Rules that are effected by changes in the source material.
(4) Slots Jeopardised by Source Changes Identification. Facility to identify the Slots in the Class Hierarchy that are effected by changes in the source material.
(5) Rules Jeopardised by Rule Changes Identification. In a task dependent Rule Base, Rules above and below an altered Rule may be jeopardised. This facility will identify the sub-set of Rules which have been affected by a KB maintenance session.

The jeopardy tool operates using the links that should be included by the knowledge Engineer during system development. This is an essential part of the MADE methodology. A change in the course can then be linked through to the Rule Base and Class Hierarchy. Some automation has been introduced here resulting in 'warning triangles' being placed at the heads of Rules when changes to the sources are made. Work is still in progress on this tool.

6.4. The Class Hierarchy Navigation Tool

This is a Class-Instance Browser designed to allow the user to navigate through a Class Hierarchy. The tool is intended to give visibility to the author of not just the Class Hierarchy, but also where Slot definitions come from, and will enable the user to determine the best location for new Classes, Sub-Classes and Attributes related to those Classes, and specialisations of attribute values. A version of this tool has also been in operation for some time although some of the facilities have yet to be added.

6.5. The Rule Base Animation Tool

This tool is similar to the Rulemap but addresses the dynamic aspects of the Rule Base. It allows the user to people the Rule Base by creating Instances and asserting Propositions and then to determine what inferences can be made as a result. When the behaviour is unexpected, either because an inference which should not be made is made, or because an inference which was expected fails to be made, this tool will enable the user to locate the precise clause which caused the failure, and from this the rule, analysis and source from which it was derived. Such animation is a necessary adjunct to the 'by eye' validation supported by the static tools, since the practical consequences of a given fragment of the KB may be hard to envisage in the abstract.

7. Conclusion

In this paper we have identified the maintainability of legal KBS as an important factor in their successful exploitation. Unfortunately this issue has attracted too little attention to date. In the MAKE project we are producing a coherent strategy for the maintenance of such systems, embracing a methodology for knowledge analysis, recommendations for representation principles, and a set of tools to support the amendment of the knowledge base. Some useful tools for the maintenance of a KB have been sketched in this paper.

Acknowledgement

The work described above was carried out as part of the MAKE Project, supported by the Information Engineering Directorate of the UK Department of Trade and Industry and the UK Science and Engineering Research Council. The project collaborators are ICL, the University of Liverpool and British Coal. The views expressed in this paper are those of the authors and may not necessarily be shared by the other collaborators.

14
Philip Leith
The Problem With Law in Books and Law in Computers: The Oral Nature of Law[1]

1. Introduction
The history of academic thinking about law and legal analysis in the 20th century has been the history of the textual nature of law. This most solid strand of legal thought has almost completely dominated and blotted out all other views; it is the view that all that lawyers need to know about law sits on the bookshelves in law books. We have evidence of this emphasis from a whole host of places: in 1910, for example, Roscoe Pound was lamenting the difference between law in practice and law in books.[2] And one influential and growing school of legal philosophy has been that which tries to link literature and law. Literature is, of course, a textual discipline.

At its most basic, the textual viewpoint suggests that all answers to what happens or should happen in law can be found in printed sources: that is, in legislation or case report. In another light, the emphasis upon law as logic, which has been a powerful school of thought since the Renaissance, is an instance of seeing law in a print-oriented manner (since today's logic without printed symbolism would be impossible). And the rule-based perspective of law (enunciated by the Oxford philosopher of law, Herbert Hart in the 1960s - but see Leith and Ingram[3] for a critique) carries the implicit baggage that these rules can be 'clear' and easily transmitted (that is, amenable to textual analysis and communication).

This is not to say that non-academic thinking has been totally at one with this perspective, but it too has been affected. For an example of this, I need think only of my own law school when it is visited by television cameras to interview

---

[1] This is a revised version of a paper presented at the annual conference of the Speech Communication Association, Atlanta, October/November 1991.
[2] Pound R. (1910) 'Law in books and law in action', *American Law Review* 44, 12.
[3] Leith P. and Ingram P. (1988) *The Jurisprudence of Orthodoxy: Queen's University Essays on H.L.A. Hart*, London: Routledge.

colleagues on some new legal development, etc. The interviews always take place (at the camera crew's insistence) in our library, in front of rows of law reports and legislation: despite the fact that the interview is being mediated through speech, the background setting is always text - as though the interviewee is a conduit (a priest?) between the books in the background to the viewer in his or her home.

Judith Shklar[4] has described the way that law has been given the seeming foundation of logicality and consistency by abstracting it from its social context. She suggests that this has been done by reifying it as formalistic rules which lawyers believe have actual existence. Of course, in order to have such clear rules, we must believe that they are capable of being clearly expressed and, necessarily, written. If not, then how could formalism provide justice for all, if these formal rules were not open to all who serve the justice system?

And when we wish to change law, we look first of all to the textual nature of it. Jeremy Bentham wanted clarity in legislation with simple language and explanatory text. The US codification movement wanted the same.

The one location which has been relatively free from this concentration upon 'law as text' is that of the advocate - the very role which one might have thought (if the academic view of law is correct) would have substantiated the text-based view. The writings of the barrister in the UK and the court lawyer in the US on what law is, and how advocacy relates to law, is so radically different that one might wonder whether there is any meeting at all of law in action and law in books. The advocate writes of the heights of oratory; the innocent saved from (or lost to) the gallows and electric chair, of the speech to the jury; and of the clever plea-bargain with the prosecution. The academic writes only of rules, principles and dry text.

Why does this difference between the practitioner of law and the legal academic exist? And what does this understanding of the difference tell us about the real nature of law? While some small number of studies of the lawyer in US society have been carried out (for example, Mann (1985)), in the UK there have been almost none - a highly surprising factor. If only one percent of the time spent on analysing appellate-based case reports had been spent on finding out what lawyers actually do, we might more easily have discovered why the gulf between practice and the textbook existed.

However, it was this gulf between advocate and academic which started my (and my co-researcher's) investigation into the barrister, the person who - in the British legal scene - is most involved with court-based advocacy. Our findings,

---

[4] Shklar J. (1986) *Legalism: Law, Morals and Political Trials*, Cambridge, Mass: Harvard University Press.

described in *The Barrister's World and the Nature of Law*,[5] present a radically different picture from that presented either by the advocate's reminiscences or the legal academic's rules. It suggests that there is a highly oral nature to law and legal norms, which is missed by those who emphasise the textual nature of law. In this paper, I wish to provide an overview of our findings and why the law-as-text view has such a strong hold over much thinking.

It is essential for those who wish to use computing techniques in law to discover just exactly why these arguments on the textual nature of law are important to them. The answer is really quite simple: our computers (when used for legal applications) are the text handling instruments par excellence. We strip legal discussion and legal action from our rules when we put them into a computer, and fix them in a manner which is pure, formal and textual.

It can be said, indeed, that there is a tendency for computers to be even more textually emphatic than a law textbook: think of the expert system with, say, 300 rules in it, each rule being a generous 50 words long. That gives us only 15,000 words of text in our expert system. A real legal textbook is frequently 200,000 words or more in length. Yet proponents of expert systems suggest that more 'knowledge' and 'expertise' is contained within an expert system than within a textbook. They can only make these claims because they believe that a concentrate form of text (sometimes logical) is more powerful than a discursive discussion as found in a textbook. That is an example of textual emphasis - better means fewer.

In this paper little will be said about the different kinds of AI techniques,[6] but it is important to realise that all AI approaches are textual - whether they use logic, semantic networks, or pattern-matching - sooner rather than later. By looking to the difference between these approaches and law in real life, we can see why there has been such a difficulty in getting AI systems onto lawyers desks.

2. Changing Perspectives

A word must be said about the substantial problem in any study which tries to look to the nature of 'law', since law (as a concept) seems to sit behind so many facades and barriers that it is impossible to grasp easily. The very idea of law has been argued over in centuries of legal theory, so that it is difficult to get any agreement over what the word 'law' means. However, it is also the case that lawyers themselves have tried to set off their discipline from the world about, and have taken upon themselves the mantle of ideology:

---

[5] Morison J. and Leith P. (1991) *The Barrister's World and the Nature of Law*, Buckingham, England: Open University Press.
[6] See Leith, P. (1991) *The Computerised Lawyer*, New York: Springer-Verlag.

> *'[An] academic lawyer has noted in a similar vein that 'it is possible for the commercial lawyer and the economist, for the family lawyer and the sociologist to regard one area of social activity from standpoints so far apart that contact becomes infrequent and indeed almost fortuitous'. A practising lawyer might not rest with noting the difference between himself and others; he would insist that his was simply the right and true view. That is the meaning of legalism as an ideology.*[7]

Even the public in their cynicism for lawyers are entrapped by the ideology of law. Though they might agree that in law every man has the right to sleep under a bridge, there is still a very developed sense that 'the law's the law'. Both these views tend to exist and contradict each other: cynicism and conservatism. Even sociologists have been declaimed for not being able to see the essential mutability (rather than fixity) of law.[8]

The strength of these views on the nature of law is striking. Yet it is a strength which exists only because of the written nature of law. We could not believe, in the complexity of the modern day world, of the common law or legislative law being so fixed and clear without the written word. This seeming rigidity coupled with the intricacy of law (just think of the sheer size of the Statute Book) could never be perceived in a system of customary law. But, as I argue below, most of what happens in the legal process is not textually 'legal' at all. And where textual law does impinge upon the process, it is most likely to have been reformulated into an oral, customary practice.

In early presentation of our research findings, the aspect which met with most hostility was our argument that substantive, textual law has little to do with the legal process. To legal academics, speech communication is simply a flowery surfacing to the real world of substantive, textual law. We argue - from our empirical findings - that this is an errant perspective. To us, negotiation about and transmission of legal knowledge by speech (that is, rhetoric as communication) is at the very heart of what 'law' is.

3. The Nature of Advocacy

In the following sub-sections, I use some brief extracts from *The Barrister's World*. My intention is to describe some of the aspects of law in action which distinguish it from the academician's textbook view. Much more detailed information can be found in our larger argument, and we also look there to the construction of a sociology of legal knowledge. However, here for space reasons, only an outline of our position is given. In this outline, I emphasise the error of the traditionally conceived dichotomy between 'fact' and 'rule'.

---

[7] Shklar J. (1986) *op.cit.*, pp. 9 and 10.
[8] Riesman D. (1951) 'Toward an anthropological science of law and the legal profession', *American Journal of Sociology* 57, 121.

3.1. Facts

Saying that law is not the simple textual rule-finding that most academic lawyers suggest it is, neither is it what most practising lawyers seem to suggest when they attest that their concern is 'facts' not 'rules'. It is not simply taking some facts and presenting them to the jury in the best light possible:

> *'About ninety-nine percent, I would have thought, of criminal cases really depend upon the facts and the arguments put forward by the prosecution and the defence and the jury having to make up their minds about which they are sure and not sure about ... Subject to an inherent understanding of the law and an appreciation of the evidence, really it's all about facts and the persuasion of advocacy ... the impression that a jury gets.'* [9]

It is not only about this, because there is always - when facts are at dispute between two sides - a considerable amount of confusion about just what the facts are and from where they come. The 'facts' have to be hewn from the mass of information and confusion which is real life. In many of the cases, the barrister - we found - was simply handed a bundle of papers and asked to 'advise':

> *'Solicitors simply hand things over to you because they don't quite know what they are doing or because they panic. They want an outside opinion. Because of that, I find quite often they haven't identified the issues, they don't know what they want you to advice on or what they want for their client in their instructions to you ... even when 'facts' are requested, they frequently don't arrive. You send a direction for proofs and you get to court and you find nothing's been done .. It's usually a plaintiff's case, where you're trying to get the poor sod some money .. and you're going to win but nothing's been prepared properly .. You've done everything but they [solicitors] haven't checked with you before.'* [10]

And, contrary to the advocate's opinion on what the 'facts' are, the case must be run according to the wishes of the client:

> *'Instructions dominate, especially in defence. You've to stick to what your case is ... You cannot run what is called in this country 'The Irish Defence': that is the client is saying one thing but you think it is the better course for him to be arguing another ... For instance, I defended a youngster, fourteen or fifteen years old, on a rape charge about two years ago. His defence was alibi, 'I wasn't there'. It was as plain as plain to me that wasn't true ... His defence should have been 'I did have intercourse with here but she consented'. But that was never my instructions and I couldn't run it on that basis ... I initially cross-*

---

[9] Morison, J. and Leith, P. (1991) *op. cit..*, p. 93.
[10] *Ibid.*, p. 81.

> *examined [the woman] as if his defence was 'He was there but with your consent', and then put it to her, much to everyone's surprise no doubt, that he wasn't there at all ...'* [11]

The barrister here told us that he ran into some trouble with the judge who was hearing the case for his use of the Irish Defence.

The problem of constructing facts is also subject to the problem of presenting them in court. This particularly shows when the facts being presented are presented by witnesses, as the next two quotations demonstrate:

> *'Will he immediately answer questions? Does he answer them directly? Is he comfortable? Would you buy a second hand car from this witness? You will gain an impression if they can tell a story that is important to the case coherently ... You also judge if they seem honest and seem straightforward ... or stupid or intelligent ... or if he is someone who will just exaggerate no matter what you do ... Sometimes you get witnesses who you know are just beyond the pale ... There's not much you can do, it's just one of those things.'*

> *'Chronology is a very important aspect in producing order. There are very few people who think chronologically ... when you meet them, you want to hug them: they do your job for you, they are the very best witnesses.'* [12]

It is important to realise that these short quotations on the problems of fact constructing are only the tip of the iceberg. From our interviews with advocates, we gained the clear impression that much of the process of advocacy is actually to do with trying to marshall (indeed, construct) one's facts both before entering the courtroom and whilst in it. And, of course, the whole process of cross-examination is directed towards controlling what the 'facts' that the opposition bring into the court are. The texts on advocacy even emphasise that the advocate should only ask questions to which he or she already knows the answer.

Even plea-bargaining before entering the court is a process of deciding what the facts are. In an early study of plea-bargaining in the UK,[13] many defendants who had changed their plea from not-guilty to guilty were most upset by the fact that what they saw as a tactical change of plea actually became a 'truth' when they appeared in the court, sometimes only a few minutes later.

If facts are being so constructed, then how - the question must be - is this process being done? It seems clear to us that it is being done by negotiation (that is, speech communication) between all the various parties in the process.

---

[11] *Ibid.*, pp. 84 - 85.

[12] *Ibid.*, p. 110.

[13] Baldwin J. and McConville M. (1977) *Negotiated Justice: Pressures on Defendants to Plead Guilty*, London: Martin Robertson.

Advocates persuade clients, other barristers, judges, solicitors, juries, etc. to place a certain interpretation upon the world which accords with their factual needs.

Traditional legal thinking does not agree with this interpretation of the construction of facts by persuasion. In the traditional view, the facts are seen to be relatively clear and it is the rules which are problematic. However, this is not our finding at all: much the reverse as we will see in the next section.

3.2. Rules

If traditional legal thinking downplays the role of fact, then it most certainly emphasises the role of the rule. Whilst almost every legal philosopher has ignored the problem of facts, almost every one has concentrated upon rules as the central factor of legal thinking. It is here, of course, that we see the emphasis upon the textual nature of law, for rules are seen to be textually oriented. There are those rules which arise from legislation, from precedents, and those which are customary (and appear in textbooks, rather than in the primary sources of law).

In the traditional view, the barrister in the UK (rather than the solicitor) is the one who pores over the legal textbooks, trying to find the one legal point which will save his or her client from conviction or which will save the small family business from the onslaught of a civil case by a multinational. However, we found that legal rules - when discussed at all - are a very different animal from the textual kind. They are much more like customary rules in an oral society: that is they are passed on mainly by word of mouth, and agreed practice, rather than being hotly debated or pored over in the law books.

It is even important to realise that most judges are prone to setting aside rules when they feel that they get in the way of good a decision. As one barrister told us:

> 'I think that merits are very important. When I pick up a set of papers, I try and forget I know any law to start with. I will speed read through all the documents ... I will just ask myself what is the general impression I have - because that is probably what a judge will do ... He will have an impression one way or the other about who has behaved badly and who has not.' [14]

And others told us that it was bad advocacy to present too much law to the judge:

> 'Well, County Court judges, if they see someone with more than a couple of authorities in front of them, they just turn off. High Court judges know the law usually, anyway, and it is a case of teaching your

---

[14] *Ibid.*, p. 111

> grandmother to suck eggs. It is occasionally a bit insulting to High Court judges.' [15]

The judge is, of course, highly important to the advocate and his or her needs must be sought out and satisfied, because:

> 'Obviously there are some cases that are so clear-cut that it doesn't make any difference. You are going to lose the case or win the case no matter who the judge is. But there are very few cases like this ... The success of almost every case is dependent on the judge ... there are certain judges who if you knew in advance were going to hear your case you could virtually determine what is going to happen to it.' [16]

Personal differences between barristers obviously exist: some will be more academically inclined than others. Of this group, one of the non-academically inclined suggested:

> 'There is a completely different sort of barrister to the one I hope I am ... the one who enjoys playing with the law ... Funnily enough we've got one in [our office] ... He loves talking technical points, and all the judges know it ... He's a very bright guy ... he knows ten times as much law as I will ever know but I don't believe he's as practical in his approach, and that I believe causes problems ... Who are you serving? ... At the end of the day, technical problems can usually be overcome. You're only delaying the evil day in most cases.' [17]

In certain cases, where a small group of barristers handle most of the cases in one court, they often can come to agreement over what the relevant law is before they go into court. One of our interviewees who did many cases of child abuse told us:

> 'Because a very small group of advocates do family law, we will be able to talk in very open terms away from the clients, away from the social workers, and away from our solicitors and say 'This is a supervision order... ... We both agree but we are not going to get agreement from the clients to that. But if the judge is telling us that he agrees with that ... then we will deal with this in the most proper manner without delaying it ... And then we are simply giving a proper hearing to all parties and letting the judge see if anything changes his mind.' [18]

This barrister told us that in such a small group, the judges trusted the advocates to handle the cases sensitively. That is, the barristers were being given a relatively free hand to decide legal issues away from the pressures of clients, welfare agencies and, indeed, judges.

---

[15] *Ibid.*, p. 100
[16] *Ibid.*, p. 113.
[17] *Ibid.*, pp. 94 - 95.
[18] *Ibid.*, p. 99.

Perhaps the best summation of the link between technical law and factual issues was put by one barrister as:

> 'You can never ignore substantive law issues ... You have to keep a weather eye on the facts ... but however fancy your arguments on promissory estoppel, if the guy is lying ... You need to keep a firm foot on the ground. You need to know the substantive law ... but it's tailoring your approach to what is happening on the ground ... If you're going to court every day with five or six authorities, the judges are going to get pretty damn sick and pretty soon the solicitors aren't going to want to know you because you are not getting to grips with things as quickly as they want ... When you go down to the Country Court here and you see three days' work listed for one day, the people who are going to get on, and ultimately satisfy their clients, are the people who are going to be brief but to the point.' [19]

Whilst these above factors are mainly to do with pressures from the court process to limit the amount of textual law research, there are also reasons of pressure of solicitor and time:

> 'The solicitor doesn't give a toss if you have read an article in the LQR and incorporate it in your opinion. He is interested to know what you believe basically: what you think the chances are.
>
> Time's short during the week - trying to get time off and time to work - and basically if you have a briefcase full of paperwork you try to turn it round as quickly as you can. You don't have a whole lot of opportunity to go to the library and study the journals as you want to or in a way that is not related to specific cases.' [20]

My argument is not to say that the law has no place in the legal system in the UK, for that is far from true. What it is though, and this is developed further in *The Barrister's World*, is much less important than legal theory actually suggests. Most legal theorists are really only interested in the very highest level of court activity (in the UK, the Appeal Court and the House of Lords) where, perhaps, textual law and analytical study of it is important. But the vast majority of cases (probably over 99%) are not of this kind.

We found that, when it appeared, technical law is discussed and negotiated in the same way that facts are. That is, it is negotiated by the legal actors, rather than argued over in a textual manner. Barristers and judges (if not clients) all want to come to a good and reasonable decision - this is not necessarily a technically correct one. And, of course, this negotiation is carried out through the medium of speech communication - the barristers discuss the law with the

---

[19] *Ibid.*, p. 100
[20] *Ibid.*, pp.93 - 94.

opposition before they go into court; they pick up law from colleagues; and they try to present their law in a manner which will not annoy the judge (especially one who has no interest in technical law).

3.3. Problem Solving

It was put to us that the legal process - especially in civil cases - is best seen as a process of problem solving. Clients of the lawyers have a problem which has not been easily resolved and which then 'goes to law'. Even when solicitors have been found, and barristers instructed, there is still a constant attempt to resolve issues before the clients enter the court. It was clear to us, indeed, that barristers will always prefer not to take a case to court. The reasons for this are that the court process is too indeterminate - one can never be sure how the facts will be constructed in court, and how arguments will be presented. Better, most barristers believe, to settle rather than to fight and lose:

> *'It's a misfortune for the client to go to court - it's expensive, it's time-consuming, it's stressful and nearly always unnecessary.'* [21]

And, of course, having counsel on both sides who take this view can lead to persuasion of the clients:

> *'If you have intelligent counsel on both sides, cases can settle because they depress the expectations on both sides and that leaves a gap in the middle ... where the case can settle.'* [22]

The bargaining and negotiation which occurs outside the court demonstrates one of the main skills of the barrister - that of persuasion of his or her client, or the other barrister. Indeed, it was noted that:

> *'It is an interesting thing that at the bar there are a lot of gamblers ... There is quite serious card playing going on for quite serious money. There are a lot of people who you would regard as really quite grey on the outside ... They get a lot out of throwing big money into the pot and backing their judgement. I think that says something about them.'* [23]

However, it was also noted that the very act of instructing lawyers, and having to think clearly and enunciate the goals which the clients themselves wanted, often aided in the problem solving nature of the pretrial process. To researchers in communication studies, the advantages of such verbal formulations are not a new idea.[24]

---

[21] *Ibid.*, p.122
[22] *Ibid.*, p. 122
[23] *Ibid.*, p.126
[24] See for example: Ong, Walter J. (1989) *Fighting for Life: Contest, Sexuality and Consciousness*, Amherst: University of Massachusetts Press.

4. Conclusions for AI and Law

The academic concentration upon law as text has resulted in an artificial situation where researches into non-textual aspects of law have been treated as non-important. It is almost as though a hierarchy of legal knowledge has been set out, with the dense legal text at the very pinnacle of the hierarchy. But, of course, if my arguments about the nature of law as a communicative system are true, then what we really have is an inversion of the hierarchy. Deep analysis of rules might well be fine for the legal academic, but if we want to develop and encourage gifted lawyers, then at the pinnacle of our hierarchy should go the communication skill of rhetoric - as the essence of advocacy.

The AI attempts to produce legal expert systems are, of course, an attempt to look to the present pinnacle of the hierarchy, and to formalise it even further: rules, rules and more rules. It is obvious why this should be: because we cannot really get our computers to act in communication with lawyers (that is not to say, of course, that lawyers cannot communicate through the medium of computers - see systems such as ABA/Net). We can only use computers to handle text, where handle means store, copy and display. There is no rhetoric in such handling of text.

Importantly, when I discuss rhetoric, I do not mean the flowery speech of the orator, for few lawyers now follow the Victorian ideal of the advocate who is prepared to break down in tears in the court. Most have a work-a-day attitude to persuasion: they simplify complex arguments, present them as clearly as they can to the jury or the judge, and try - whenever possible - to use emotional language within a much stricter framework than, for example, did Marshall Hall.[25] Rhetoric is thus about the wider aspects of communication. Mostly, in the UK legal process, this happens through speech (on the telephone or face-to-face) but there is an element of persuading through written documents which is becoming more important. This latter form of communication, of course, comes after the initial communication by speech (for example: client interviewing, police questioning, etc.).

We should not be surprised by the fact that speech is of central concern in the legal process. For, the trial and the judgement has been a constant factor in history. The fact that our court process is different from previous ages, and that our law exists in printed form and in larger quantity than in previous ages, should not blind us to the fact that there is still a large measure of similarity between the court in ancient Greece, Rome or in tribal settings and in 20th century common law countries. Rather, it should make us look more closely at the nature of the link between law in textbooks and law in action. Only through

---

[25] Cooper, R., (1989) *Shadow of the Noose: Marshall Hall, The Great Defender*, London: Viking Press.

this investigation will we really understand the nature of law in a modern society. For law, in its many forms, is to do with persuasion. Even legislating - the production of new laws - has always, as Ong has stated, had to do with rhetoric and contest:

> *The fact that the term for an assembly in ancient Greece meant also an action at law or a contest calls attention to the terrain we are on. For in the litigious Greek world, as commonly enough in early human cultures generally, an assembly, a getting together to discourse, was rather essentially a mobilization for contest. The assembly came together to debate, to match pros and cons, to struggle, not fatally, but seriously and in dead earnest, man against man. A legislative body was, and still is, an organization for productive struggle.'* [26]

Seeing advocacy and the practice of law as a speech communicative phenomenon is simply extending the understanding all the way from the legislator to the judge. Unfortunately, seeing it in such a way takes us far away from current research strategies in AI and law.

---

[26] Ong, W.J., (1989) *op.cit.*, at pages 43-44.

15
D. Rowland and J.J. Rowland
Competence and Legal Liability in the Development of Software for Safety Related Applications

1. Introduction: Software and Safety

Over the last few years there has been major growth in the use of computer software in applications that are safety critical or safety related. Examples include aircraft control systems, such as in the Airbus A320, process control systems in the petrochemical industry, railway signalling, and the control of medical equipment such as radiotherapy machines and drug infusion pumps. One of the characteristics of almost all software is that exhaustive testing is impossible, so that a fault may remain undetected until a particular and unpredictable combination of circumstances triggers it; thus a system may work perfectly for years and then suddenly fail. In a safety critical or safety related application the consequences of such a failure can be disastrous.

Because of this, the sectors of the software industry that undertake design and development of software for safety-related and safety-critical applications, as well as the relevant regulatory authorities, have become increasingly concerned to establish methods of working that minimise both the number of and the effect of software defects. There is ongoing work towards formulation of standards for the specification, design and implementation of safety related software and systems, under the auspices of the International Electrotechnical Commission (IEC)[1] but there are some difficult problems to overcome and, although drafts have been issued for comment, publication of even the initial IEC standards will be some way in the future. Other bodies such as the Health and Safety Executive have produced guidance on the use of programmable electronic systems for industrial applications and the MoD has produced Draft

---

[1] IEC draft standard, Functional safety of electrical/electronic/programmable electronic systems; generic aspects: Part 1, Generic requirements (IEC reference 65A (Secretariat) 123. IEC draft standard, Software for computers in the application of industrial safety-related systems, (IEC reference 65A (Secretariat) 122.

Interim Defence Standard 00-55 and Draft Standard 00-56[2] which apply to the procurement of safety-critical software and the analysis of safety-critical hazards for software used in defence applications. In addition there are government funded research initiatives and a number of major research projects in progress which are aiming to improve the assurance of high integrity systems, particularly those which have a safety function. Bennett[3] gives an overview of the issues of safety related computer systems.

Not surprisingly the industry has become concerned about the potential legal liability for defects in the design and implementation of such software. In the event of a software failure that leads to physical injury or death, such liability may fall upon systems manufacturers as well as individual designers and software engineers. This has led to discussion about the standard of competence expected of software engineers involved with design and development of safety-critical software and about ways in which such competence can be assessed. Recently two documents have been published that attempt to give guidance to software engineers on their responsibilities and on their presumed legal liability: the Institution of Electrical Engineers (IEE) has produced its 'Professional Brief on Safety-Related Systems'[4] and the Engineering Council has produced a Code of Professional Practice entitled 'Engineers and Risk Issues'[5] which is scheduled to come into force on 1st March 1993[6]. This latter document is centred around a ten point code of professional practice on risk issues that includes matters of professional responsibility, law, management, judgement and so on. However, within each heading, the responsibilities are couched in fairly general terms which may make it difficult to assess whether in any specific case it is being complied with. The IEE document, on the other hand, attempts to provide a much more detailed exposition of the responsibilities incumbent on those involved with the design and development of safety-critical software. It

---

[2] Draft Interim Defence Standard 00-55, *Requirements for the Procurement of Safety Critical Software in Defence Equipment*, U.K. MoD.
Draft Defence Standard 00-56, *Safety Management Requirements for Defence Systems Containing Programmable Electronics* U.K. MoD, 1993.
[3] Bennett, P. (Ed.), (1993), *Safety Aspects of Computer Control,* Butterworth-Heinemann, Oxford, England.
[4] *IEE Professional Brief - Safety Related Systems*, Institution of Electrical Engineers, London, England, 1992.
[5] *Engineers and Risk Issues*, Engineering Council Code of Professional Practice, Engineering Council, London, England, October 1992.
[6] This is in addition, of course, to general standards of professional practice which are dealt with in documents such as the British Computer Society (BCS) Code of Conduct (see *BCS Code of Conduct,* Computer Bulletin, Sept./Oct. 1992, pp 6-7) and the *IEE Professional Brief - Professional Conduct*, Institution of Electrical Engineers, London, England.

culminates in a brief Code of Practice for engineers and managers working on safety-related systems in which one of the key concepts is the 'competence' of those involved. This is so central to the entire document (and reasonably so) that there is a whole section devoted to a discussion of the meaning of competence together with a list of qualities and attributes which a competent person should possess. Attention is also drawn to the fact that although competence necessarily includes appropriate education and training, this cannot on its own be sufficient; competence must be determined by additional reference to other factors including, especially, relevant experience.

The purpose of these publications seems to be to draw to the attention of those planning the development of such systems the factors which they have to consider if they are to avoid both failure and consequent legal liability. In this paper we intend to consider the standard which the courts have developed by which to measure and assess the behaviour of professionals in other fields, and to relate this to the context of the Professional Briefs, Codes of Conduct, and similar publications.

2. Professional Negligence

The area of law with which we shall be concerned is that commonly referred to as professional negligence. This is a sub-species of the more familiar general tort of negligence, which has evolved considerably in the twentieth century and this is particularly true of liability for professional negligence. It used to be the view that a professional person owed a duty only to his or her client, with whom normally he or she would be in a contractual relationship; thus the duties in such a relationship would arise out of the agreement between the parties, rather than a tortious duty imposed by law. In many relationships between professional and client, the agreement is essentially a private one, as doctor/patient or solicitor/client, so that even where there is no contract, the likelihood of foreseeable harm to a third party is small.

However, this idea of professional duty being confined to the client has been eroded and, over a period of time, professionals have been held liable for physical injury to a range of categories of persons with whom there was no contractual nexus. On the other hand, this is not to say that there is automatically a duty to all those who might be adversely affected and the dividing line may not be easy to draw. In the area of safety-critical systems there are policy considerations which can pull both ways:-

(1) The potential for damage may be so vast that it would be unjust to hold the designer liable. For example, the entire safety system of a nuclear reactor is so critical that its specification and design would normally be undertaken by the contractors in close collaboration with the customer and the relevant regulatory authority, and the

> implementation process would be subject to regular audit by the customer.
>
> (2) Where a particular type of expertise is at issue then it may be reasonable to apportion at least some of the liability. In the example given in the previous point, for instance, the customer has some responsibility for the design but the contractor has responsibility for much of the detail. In such a situation the law is likely to apportion liability.

No general principles have been developed which could be applied across the whole range of professional expertise but it seems likely that, because of the nature of the work of engineers, the range of potential plaintiffs will be considerably wider than for doctors or solicitors, for instance.

The standard of care expected of a professional has traditionally been viewed as that of the ordinarily competent member of that profession. The present formulation is usually taken as that of McNair J. in *Bolam v Friern Hospital Management Committee*:-

> *'When you get situations which involve the use of some special skill or competence, then the test as to whether there has been negligence or not, is not the test of the man on the top of the Clapham Omnibus, because he has not got that special skill. The test is the standard of the ordinary skilled man exercising and professing that special skill. A man need not possess the highest expert skill; it is well established law that it is sufficient if he exercises the ordinary skill of an ordinary competent man exercising that particular art.*[7]

This is merely the starting point; since then a great body of specialised case law has developed which attempts to deal with the situations which pertain to particular professions. Unfortunately, this case law has often been decided on a case-by-case basis with the judgement in each case being confined to its own particular facts and circumstances. This means that a careful analysis is required if we are to discern general trends and principles that may be applied to the relatively new profession of software engineer. The process is complicated by the different attributes and characteristics of some professions; furthermore, any analogies made with other professions or even with other branches of the engineering profession must be valid. It is possible though to divide professions loosely into one of two categories:-

> (1) Those professions in which the practitioners cannot guarantee the results of their labour. For example, doctors cannot guarantee to cure the patient, solicitors cannot guarantee to win the case, etc.

---

[7] *Bolam v Friern Hospital Management Committee* [1957] 1 *WLR* 582, 586.

(2) Those professions in which the practitioners can be said to impliedly warrant to produce a particular result.

Professionals such as architects and engineers may fall into the latter category and an implied warranty will arise where, for instance, the professional has a particular knowledge of the end result required. In such cases a higher standard has been accepted by the courts, as demonstrated by cases such as *Greaves & Co v Baynham Meikle*[8]. The problem in this case was that the structural engineers responsible for the design of a warehouse had neglected to take account of the effects of vibration on the first floor of the building even though they knew that heavily laden stacker trucks would be used there. The result was that the floor cracked and affected the walls of the building so that it could not safely be used. There was conflicting expert evidence as to whether the general design was not of the standard expected of the ordinarily competent engineer but in any case, Kilner Brown J., at first instance, could not accept that the knowledge of the result to be achieved should not be a factor in determining whether the design was negligent:-

> 'This means, in my view, that the principle in Bolam's case is not strictly applicable. In the special circumstances of this case......it can be said that there was a higher duty imposed upon him than the law in general imposes on a medical or other professional man.' [9]

3. Professional Negligence and the Software Engineer

There is clear scope for analogy between the above cases and the duties and responsibilities of software engineers commissioned to produce software for safety-related applications. It will frequently, if not invariably, be the case that where software engineers are engaged to design and develop software for use in safety-related systems, they will have been made aware of the need for assurance that the system will not fail to danger, in so far as it is possible to achieve such a result. But on whom does the duty lie to identify that the system is indeed safety-related? Procurers have a duty to engage a competent contractor, which implies that they need to satisfy themselves that the consultant they have chosen is suitable. This could of course be by reference to whether the consultant has been involved in similar projects in the past, but where consultants hold themselves out as being competent and the required product is of a specialist nature it may be very difficult for procurers to completely assure themselves of competence.

---

[8] *Greaves & Co v Baynham Meikle* [1974] 1 *WLR* 1261, aff'd [1975] 1 *WLR* 1095.
[9] [1974] 1 *WLR* 1261, 1269

3.1. Identifying the Level of Competence Required.

That a particular application is safety-critical will often be obvious: if control software is being procured for the chemical industry, it takes no great leap of imagination to recognise the possibility that it may be safety-critical; even the

'man on the Clapham omnibus' is likely to arrive at that conclusion. If, however, it is not immediately apparent that failure of the system may jeopardise safety, on whom is the responsibility to identify this? Following the disastrous consequences of the failure of the Computer Aided Despatch (CAD) system of the London Ambulance Service (LAS) in October and November 1992, Martyn Thomas, an acknowledged authority on safety related computer systems, quoted in New Scientist[10] suggested the possibility that the London Ambulance system was never identified as being safety-critical. The Report of the Inquiry into the incident[11] demonstrates a number of the difficult issues relating to assessment of competence and certainly seems to suggest that the full safety implications of the system were never fully appreciated. It was presumably foreseeable that if the LAS system failed then lives would be put at risk. It appears that this fact was identified but that the LAS ignored or chose not to accept advice relating to both the strict timetable they were requiring for implementation and the high risk of the comprehensive systems requirement[12]. With the benefit of knowledge and hindsight, it is easy to see that precautions should have been taken with to satisfy the safety requirements, but can it be assumed that the LAS Board should have realised that safety-critical applications require design and implementation procedures that are any different from those used for 'normal' computer systems? It may be that this requires the client to have more knowledge and understanding than is reasonable. It has been suggested in *County Personnel Ltd v Pulver & Co*[13], a case involving advice given by a solicitor, that the advice and instructions given should be appropriate to the understanding of the client. The following comments of Bingham LJ are perhaps even more apposite in the case of a technical specialisation:-

> *'It seems obvious that legal advice, like any other communication, should be in terms appropriate to the comprehension and experience of the particular recipient. It is also, I think, clear that in a situation such as this the professional man does not necessarily discharge his duty by spelling out what is obvious. The client is entitled to expect the exercise*

---

[10] Geake, E., 'Did Ambulance Chiefs Specify Safety Software?', *New Scientist*, Vol 136, 7 Nov 1992, p5.
[11] *Report of the Inquiry into the London Ambulance Service*, South West Thames Regional Health Authority, February 1993.
[12] *Ibid* para 1007 (d)
[13] *County Personnel Ltd v Pulver & Co* [1987] 1 *All ER* 289

of a reasonably professional judgement. That is why the client seeks advice from the professional in the first place. If in the exercise of a reasonable professional judgement a solicitor is or should be alerted to risks which might elude even an intelligent layman, then plainly it is his duty to advise the client of these risks or explore the matter further.'[14]

Applying this to the LAS incident, it appears that the Board were not entirely without the requisite knowledge - there had been a previous attempt at implementing CAD which had been abandoned because of its high cost and because of the alleged inability of the contracting software house to understand the complexity of the requirements[15]. This might have been sufficient to suggest to the LAS Board that there were special requirements which were necessary for this system and indeed the Report also concludes that in awarding the contract to a small software house with no experience of this type of system, the LAS were taking a high risk[16]. It also appears though, that they were given a misleading impression of the previous experience of the lead contractor in designing this type of system and neither were they shown independent references which expressed doubts as to the contractor's ability to handle such a project[17]. If there may be difficulties for the client both in identifying that a particular system is safety-critical and in ascertaining that this is taken into account, is there then an automatic supposition that it should be upon the software designers to assess whether there are safety implications associated with the application? This is a much more intractable question. In such situations, the client is likely to rely completely on the expertise of the software designer to produce a system that is appropriate for the purpose intended. Notwithstanding the fact that the client has a responsibility to engage a competent engineer, the standard of care required of the contractor is one of competence which, according to the IEE's Professional Brief includes:-

'an appreciation of their own limitations, whether of knowledge, experience, facilities, resources etc., and a preparedness to declare any such limitation.'[18]

Whilst this point has not been directly considered by a court, a duty to advise clients to seek expert advice where what is required goes beyond the expertise of the contractor has been identified in, for example *Young v Tomlinson*[19] per Quilliam J. This may create difficulties in the case of safety-critical software if it is not identified as such at the procurement stage. In view of the fact that

---

[14] [1987] 1 *All ER* 289, 295.
[15] Report of the Inquiry into the London Ambulance Service, para 3046
[16] *Ibid* para 1007 h.
[17] *Ibid* paras 1007 f, and g.
[18] *IEE Professional Brief - Safety Related Systems*, p19.
[19] *Young v Tomlinson* [1979] 2 *NZLR* 441

apparently 'innocent' software can still have safety implications, perhaps an appropriate form of hazard analysis should be a feature of all specifications. With reference to the LAS incident, the contractor's proposal suggested that they had experience in designing systems for the emergency services although in fact this related to administrative rather than 'mission critical' systems[20].

3.2. Economic Issues.

Design and development of the high integrity systems necessary for safety-related applications is necessarily expensive. What then is the situation when either the budget allowed for the system cannot possibly extend to the provision of an adequate system or the lowest tender is taken for reasons of economy, even though this might prejudice the safety level achieved? The problems of economic constraints are also well-illustrated by the LAS incident. The evidence from the Report of the Inquiry is that the LAS had a proposed budget in mind before the inception of the project and that in any case they were required to conform to the Regional Health Authority Standing Financial Instructions. Basically these required that such contracts had to be put out to open tender and that the lowest tender should be accepted unless there were 'good and sufficient reasons to the contrary'. Little guidance was given on what such reasons might be and the main emphasis seemed to be on obtaining the best, i.e. the cheapest, price[21].

There are a number of issues here: if the client is unwilling to pay for a design of sufficient integrity then there is a duty on the contractor to warn that this is the case; if the designer goes ahead nevertheless, he or she may still attract liability and will not be able to escape merely because he or she has complied with the terms of the contract. This was discussed by Windeyer J. in the Australian case of *Voli v Inglewood Shire Council*[22]:-

> *'...neither the terms of the architect's engagement, nor the terms of the building contract, can operate to discharge the architect from a duty of care to persons who are strangers to those contracts.'*[23]

Windeyer J. went on to explain that this duty is imposed by law not because the contract was entered into, but because of embarking upon the work. The fact that adherence to the contract provides no defence to a charge of negligence was reiterated in *Bowen v Paramount Builders*[24] in the judgement in *Voli* was approved and Woodhouse J. went on to say:-

> *'I do not regard a private contractual arrangement for an inefficient design or for an unworkmanlike or inadequate type of construction as*

---

[20] Report of the Inquiry into the London Ambulance Service, para 3045
[21] Report of the Inquiry into the London Ambulance Service, paras 3030 - 3032.
[22] *Voli v Inglewood Shire Council* (1963) 110 *CLR* 74
[23] (1963) 110 *CLR* 74, 85
[24] *Bowen v Paramount Builders* [1977] 1 *NZLR* 394

*any sort of justification or valid explanation for releasing the builder
from his duty to those who would otherwise look to him for relief.*[25]

The inference from this is that is the competent engineer might refuse a contract altogether if it was clear that insufficient funds were available to ensure the integrity of the system.

3.3. The Role of Standards and Codes of Practice.

It is frequently suggested that if engineers (including software engineers, of course,) adhere to established standards and codes of practice they will have done all that is necessary to escape a charge of negligence. This is firmly in line with the *Bolam* test, being only what would be expected of the ordinarily competent practitioner. There is, not surprisingly, judicial support for this view which was concisely expressed in *Bevan Investments v Blackhall and Struthers*[26]:-

> *'A design which departs substantially from relevant engineering codes is prima facie a faulty design unless it can be demonstrated that it conforms to accepted engineering practice by rational analysis.'*

The effect is to shift the burden of proof onto the defendant, who is thus required to show that what was done was not negligent even though it did not conform to accepted practices. This is all very well in branches of engineering where there are well-defined standards and codes of practice. Although there are a number of European and International standards in the process of formulation, as yet there are no accepted standards which can be used by software engineers developing safety-critical software[27]. Whilst this creates problems in assessing the behaviour of the ordinarily competent safety-critical practitioner, it does seem to be fairly widely accepted that the general practices of software development for non safety-related applications are inadequate for safety-related systems.

To be more precise, the attainment of 'safety' implies reducing the risks to an acceptable level, and the integrity level required of the software is therefore related to the consequences of any failure. Because the number of undetected faults in a piece of software cannot be measured, the attainment of software integrity is primarily achieved through quality assurance during specification, design, and implementation. Such quality assurance is all embracing and has implications for the methods used for specifications (for example, whether written in natural language or in formal mathematical notation), choice of design method, programming language, documentation standards, and so on. For very

---

[25] [1977] 1 *NZLR* 394, 419
[26] *Bevan Investments v Blackhall and Struthers* No 2 [1973] 2 *NZLR* 45
[27] Bell, R., and Reinert, D., *Risk and System Integrity Concepts for Safety-Related Control Systems.* 7th Symposium on Microprocessor Based Protection Systems, Institute of Measurement and Control, London, England, 1992.

high integrity systems there are further steps that can be taken to minimise the effect of any software faults that remain. One such approach involves the use of replicated computer systems, where at least three systems are used each of which should provide the same output; 'voting logic' compares the outputs and, in the event of a discrepancy produced by a fault in one of the systems, takes the majority output as being correct. Such an approach is clearly expensive, but is justified in such applications as nuclear reactor protection systems.

Where the risks are high, the more stringent approaches are desirable and this is reflected in the draft IEC standards. Selection of the integrity level required is necessarily based on a careful risk analysis of the application; this is an essential part of the early stages of a development project. However, although it is reasonable to assume that there is some correspondence between the various levels of integrity required and the methods to be employed, there is not yet a strong consensus amongst safety-critical practitioners and regulatory bodies over this relationship. In principle there should be a similar relationship between the required integrity level and the level of competence required of the engineers involved, and this is where an assessment of competence is most needed. At present, safety-critical practitioners seem to divide into three groups:-

(1) Those who are aware in general of the problems raised by safety-critical software development and are striving to adjust their working practices so as to produce software of what they consider to be an adequate quality.

(2) Those who are attempting to follow, and where possible do better than, the emerging standards.

(3) Those who are developing safety-critical systems and yet are not aware that there are special problems.

The first of these probably most accurately reflects what can be described as the ordinarily competent safety-critical practitioner, whilst a growing number of specialists fall into the second category. It is widely suspected that a significant proportion of companies producing safety-related software belong in the third category, and this is a particular stimulus for the standards activity and for generally raising awareness through, for example, professional codes of conduct.

3.4. The Implications of Novel or Pioneering Designs.

Even when appropriate standards are formulated and accepted, there is still one area which can remain a problem when attempting to define the scope of negligent behaviour, namely the use of novel techniques and/or development of novel designs. This matter fell to be considered in *IBA v EMI and BICC*[28] which concerned the collapse of the Emley Moor television transmitter in 1969, only

---

[28] *IBA v EMI and BICC* (1980) 14 *Build LR* 1

two years after it was erected[29]. To fully appreciate the implications of the judgement in this case it is necessary to consider the facts of the case in some detail:

BICC had already built a number of television masts for IBA of a standard lattice construction in which they had acknowledged expertise. They agreed to build three cylindrical masts following a suggestion from an IBA engineer, who had seen a mast of a similar design in Germany. BICC were confident that they could do this and the masts were erected at Winter Hill in Lancashire, Belmont in Lincolnshire and Emley Moor in Yorkshire. The Emley Moor mast was 1,250 feet high and only 9 feet in diameter at its base; there were no other masts of a similar design and similar height anywhere else in the world (the German mast was only 650 feet in height).

BICC admitted that they had no experience in the design of cylindrical masts, that it was 'both at and beyond the frontier of professional knowledge at that time', that there was 'no available source of empirical knowledge' and that there was no generally agreed practice which could be used as a guide. Counsel for BICC argued very strongly that to find them negligent would be to stifle and inhibit research and development into new designs and techniques, which was essential if technology was to progress.

In view of the potentially catastrophic consequences of collapse of the mast, the House of Lords were agreed that it would have been necessary for BICC to exercise a high degree of care. By applying standard principles of negligence Lord Edmund-Davies deduced:-

> *The graver the foreseeable consequences of failure to take care, the greater the necessity for special circumspection......The project may be alluring. But the risks of injury to those engaged in it, or to others, or to both, may be so manifest and substantial, and their elimination may be so difficult to ensure with reasonable certainty that the only proper course is to abandon the project altogether.....The law requires even pioneers to be prudent.*[30]

It was found that the cause of the collapse was due to a combination of vortex shedding and asymmetric icing on the stays, which would be likely to cause problems at even relatively low wind velocities. The House of Lords unanimously agreed that these factors could reasonably have been foreseen and the fact that the project was at the forefront of knowledge at the time was no excuse. It was foreseeable that large quantities of ice might be deposited on the

---

[29] This case, despite the fact that it went to the House of Lords and is of significance in assessing the scope of professional negligence in respect of novel designs, and therefore has important ramifications for the technological professions, has never found its way into any of the mainstream law reports.

[30] (1980) 14 *Build LR* 1, 28

stays and that this was likely to be asymmetric, but that the resultant stresses would be exacerbated by vortex shedding had never been considered by BICC whose design was therefore held to be negligent.

The behaviour that the law expects of the reasonably competent professional who is operating at the frontiers of knowledge at the time can be inferred from this statement of Lord Edmund-Davies:-

> *'Justice requires that we seek to put ourselves in the position of BICC when first confronted by their daunting task, lacking all empirical knowledge and adequate expert advice in dealing with the many problems awaiting solution. But those very handicaps created a clear duty to identify and to think through such problems, including those of static and dynamic stresses, so that the dimensions of the 'venture into the unknown' could be adequately assessed and the ultimate decision as to its practicality arrived at.'*[31]

The power of software arises principally from the relative ease with which highly complex systems can be created and changed. There is a consequent temptation to undertake development without adherence to appropriate engineering principles and to quite readily undertake a 'venture into the unknown'; after all, software can be changed easily and it is tempting to think that any faults can be corrected easily. However, unless software is designed very carefully a seemingly simple change can have an unexpected side effect that may not become apparent for some considerable time afterwards, so that any departure from strict quality assurance procedures during development almost certainly becomes another 'venture into the unknown'. In the case of software the 'dimensions' of such ventures are not readily assessed, so that departure from established methods can be particularly risky.

3.5. The Status of Special Expertise.

Finally, what is the situation regarding liability where a specific professional has been engaged because he or she is perceived to be a particular expert in the skill that is required? Intuitively it might seem reasonable that a higher standard of care could legitimately be expected, especially as the fee is likely to be commensurate with the degree of experience. A first analysis of the case law suggests though that, at least initially, the Bolam test will be applied. The role of the specialist advisor was an issue in the case of *Wimpey Construction v Poole*[32]. In this case, Counsel for Wimpey attempted to put two 'glosses' on the Bolam test, firstly that the test is not 'the standard of the ordinary skilled man exercising and professing to have that special skill if the client deliberately obtains and pays for someone with specially high skills.'

---

[31] (1980) 14 *Build LR* 1, 31
[32] *Wimpey Construction v Poole* [1984] 2 *Lloyds Rep* 499.

Although this does not seem unreasonable, the court felt constrained by the original Bolam test since this had been expressly approved by both the House of Lords and the Privy Council. However, it seems that this point might more accurately be considered by judging the standard of the expert not by reference to the general class of engineers, say, of which he or she is one, but rather by considering the standard expected of a more limited class of experts in that particular field. This could produce difficulties where the class of experts was small (safety-critical software, for instance) so that it was no longer possible to identify the general standard of such practitioners.

Secondly, Counsel suggested that the duty of a professional person is to exercise reasonable care in the light of his or her *actual* knowledge, and the question whether he or she exercised reasonable care cannot be answered by reference to a lesser degree of knowledge than he or she had on the grounds that the ordinarily competent practitioner would only have had this lesser knowledge.

This second point was accepted by the court but without considering that it in any way changed or qualified the Bolam test, because this result can be obtained by applying more general principles of negligence. If the practitioner has particular knowledge but acts in a way which ignores that fact and would foreseeably cause injury, then he or she is prima facie negligent without the necessity of considering the knowledge of the ordinarily competent practitioner.

4. Indications for the Software Engineer

Although professionals such as doctors and solicitors operate on a 'best endeavours' basis, guided by professional codes, there are clear indications that software engineers have a greater duty when developing safety related systems. They are required to ensure the adequate safety of those systems; they are required to *guarantee* a result. This implies the need for the software contractor to undertake a risk analysis of the application area and to select techniques for specification, design , development, and implementation that will achieve the appropriate level of integrity in the finished product. Whilst in some cases the client may be in a position to undertake the risk analysis, the responsibility for specifying and attaining the required integrity level ultimately falls upon the contractor, who has a duty to advise the client accordingly. Budgetary considerations are no defence; it is the contractor's duty to advise of an inadequate budget rather than to provide a cut-price and inadequately safe product.

Software engineering is a fast moving discipline and software is continually being used in applications to which it has not previously been applied (such as certain critical applications in the nuclear industry[33]). However, in the absence

---

[33] Hughes, G., *Recent Developments in the Use of Computers in Safety and Safety-Related Applications for Nuclear Electric's Power Plant,* 7th Symposium on

of agreed standards, there is a growing body of knowledge that represents established best practice and, on this basis, pioneering work is proceeding safely, in the spirit of Lord Edmund-Davies's comment that 'the law requires even pioneers to be prudent'.

It is clear that if an engineer professes specialist expertise in a particular area then it is reasonable to expect a higher level of skill and responsibility from that person than from the ordinarily competent engineer. Employment, by a customer or his or her contractor, of such an expert, possibly in the form of an independent consultant, would seem, assuming genuine expertise on the part of the consultant, to be of considerable benefit in circumstances analogous to some of the cases outlined in this paper.

Microprocessor Based Protection Systems, Institute of Measurement and Control, London, England, 1992.

Index

Computer Crime 12-9, 145-58
    countering 145-58
        computer forensics 145-50
        courtroom skills 155-57
        forensic methodology 148-9
Computer Generated Evidence 159-93
    common law approach 160-2
        hearsay rule 162-4
        primary evidence rule 173
        computer evidence
        and hearsay 164-66
    admissibility.166-72, 180-4
    Civil Evidence Act ,1968 166-7
    Police and Criminal Evidence
     Act, 1984 169-72
    identification 176-7
    authentication 177-80
    burden of proof 185-87
    security 188-90
    UNCID Rules 187-88, 191-93
    Norwegian law 175-90
        civil procedure 180-4
        criminal procedure 184-5
Data Protection 1-12, 128-41
    EC Draft Directive 6-12, 140-1
    German legislation 132-40
    transborder data flow 129-32
        applicable law 129-32
EDI 29-60, 83-96
    contracts 29-32
        interchange agreements 31
        liabilities 38-41
        network agreements 31-2
        responsibilities 34-8
        SWIFT 34
        TEDIS 39
        TEDIS, Article 8 39-40
        third party agreements 32
        UNCID 34-5
    nature of 29, 44-6, 86-9
    standardisation 46-9
        EC competition 51-2, 55-7,

ETSI 59
intellectual property 52-5,57-9
level 47-9
networks, VAN, PTT 49-50
scope 46-7
type (competitive, co-operative
    and public) 50
Electronic Data Interchange
    - see EDI
EFT 63-82
    electronic payments 63-6
        Article 4A UCC 66-8
        fraud   UCC 72-5
                        UNCITRAL 75
        mistake   UCC 68-72
                        UNCITRAL 72
        negligence UCC 68-75
                        UNCITRAL 68-75
        UNCITRAL Model Law 78-81
Electronic Shipping Documents 83-96
    bills of lading 84-5
        Carriage of Goods by Sea
        Act 1992 91-3
    CMI Rules electronic bills of
        lading 90
    functions 84-5
    Hague Visby Rules 94-5
    Hamburg Rules. 94-5
    delivery orders 86
    sea waybills 85-6
Electronic Transfer of Funds
    - see EFT
Expert Systems 19-26,197-250
    maintenance 209-24
    liability - software 238-50
Intellectual Property 99-127
    Copyright 99-103,
    EC Software Directive 106-11
        idea / expression 102-3
        protection - UK 104-6
        protection - France 104-6
        protection - Germany 104-6

Computer Databases 113-27
   Feist decision 119-21
   field management 122-3
   free format 123-26
   hierarchical 122
   US Law 113-27

Software Development 238-50
   competence 241-50
   liability 239-41
   negligence 239-244
Transborder Data Flow
   - see Data Protection